Parent Burnout

Parent Burnout

By Dr. Joseph Procaccini
and Mark W. Kiefaber

DOUBLEDAY & COMPANY, INC.
GARDEN CITY, NEW YORK
1983

649.1
158
P

Library of Congress Cataloging in Publication Data

Procaccini, Joseph, 1942–
    Parent burnout.

    1. Parenting.   2. Burnout (Psychology).
3. Burnout (Psychology)—Prevention.
I. Kiefaber, Mark, 1949–   . II. Title.
HQ755.83.P76   1983   649'.1
ISBN: 0-385-18041-1
Library of Congress Catalog Card Number 81–43593

To parents everywhere who are all linked together by a common bond: their love for their children.

Contents

Introduction

"Call me anything you want, but don't ever call me a bad mother."
"Believe me, I live for my children." "The kids? Well, they are our
whole life." These are the kinds of comments that are frequently
heard coming from parents who care. They are expressive of the
love, concern, dedication, and sacrifice that go with the role of parent. Every good mother and father has said these things or thought
them many times. However, like every good deed, principle, or vir-
tue, they can be overdone. There can be a loss of perspective and a
lack of recognition of limits. The expectations and demands that
parents place on themselves can surpass the resources available.
When this happens, trouble is on its way.

This book is for and about peak performance in parenting. It is
built on some important premises. First, the most precious resource
a parent has is human energy. Second, human energy is finite, there
is only so much. Third, parents must control their own limited energy supply if they are going to be successful and achieve their
parenting goals. That is, they must be proactive and not reactive.
They must define their own criteria of success and not respond to
the expectations imposed on them by others. Lastly, energy robbers
must be identified and controlled. It is the fundamental assumption
of this book that optimal parenting takes place when the energy
available is in balance with the demands made on it. Energy

supplies can increase and with this expansion comes the capacity to take on more parenting tasks and responsibilities. However, at any given time the amount of energy available will be fixed and when the demand exceeds the supply, burnout begins. Recognizing the need for this balance of energy and demand helps parents recover from burnout or prevent it.

Most contemporary parents have witnessed an increase in the demands made on their energy. More and more women find themselves torn between the obligations of motherhood and the need for a second income or the development of a career. Busy fathers who precariously juggle their job demands and parenting obligations increasingly suffer from the stress of this conflict. Both mothers and fathers find their responsibilities as parents increasing while their control of the factors that affect their children's lives slips further and further out of their grip. All of this is taking place in a quickly changing world, which in itself is full of stress. The cumulative impact of these pressures can be overwhelming. Today's parents are very good candidates for burnout and the caring, idealistic, enthusiastic, in short, "on fire" parent is the prime one.

It is our goal to help parents who have experienced burnout to get back to peak performance once again and to teach those who have not experienced burnout how to prevent it from occurring. The ultimate objective is to develop attitudes, behaviors, and coping skills that will allow parents to rear their children well by taking better care of themselves. This is by no means a book to help parents become self-centered and uncaring. On the contrary, it is our hope that the information presented will expand the love, affection, and dedication of parents by helping them develop the "staying power" for this wonderful, yet awesome, task. However, for improvement to be made and growth in parenting to take place, it is necessary that you recognize and realize that to serve your children well, you have to take good care of yourself. Chronic unselfishness will do neither yourself nor your children any good.

For the past several years we had been providing burnout workshops for nurses, teachers, counselors, policemen, and business professionals. Using a group interaction approach and open discussion, we guided participants to recognize the burnout syndrome and to develop methods for recovery and prevention. During these years we became keenly aware of a pattern of discussion repeated during almost every session. Many participants shared with us that they experienced the symptoms of burnout not as a result of their work, but as the result of their roles as parents. This piqued our interest and triggered our initial research on the subject of parent burnout. After in-depth interviews with these participants we embarked on a systematic investigation of the burnout phenomenon among parents. We concluded that burnout was evident in varying degrees in many parents. As our interest in this topic became known to other professionals as well as the media, many parents contacted us wanting to share their burnout experiences. Many of these wonderful people said that they would not want others to go through what they suffered and this motivated them to come forward. Typical comments were along the following lines: "I thought that I was the only one who felt this way. Your description of burnout and its various stages fits me to a T. I am glad that somebody is studying this and talking about it."

Our investigation of the phenomenon of parent burnout has included a conceptual analysis of the physiological, psychological, and situational causes and consequences of the problem as well as interviews with practitioners who work closely with parents. The practitioners included physicians, psychologists, educators, counselors, social workers, and clergymen. In group and individual settings we interviewed parents who were recommended by practitioners, parents whom we knew, and parents who contacted us after having read or heard about our research through the national or local media. During the past few years we have made numerous presentations on our research to parents' groups. The comments and questions in these sessions have been useful as well. Some were made publicly and some were made in private after the presentations. Whenever possible, we have included these insights and experiences. The case studies used throughout the book are drawn from our interactions with parents in these interviews, workshops, and presentations. The names and some locations have been changed to honor confidentiality.

We would like to emphasize that this book is not a parenting guide. It is not about children. It is about parents. It focuses on the environment in which raising children occurs, the type of work parenting is, and the expectations that mothers and fathers carry with them when they assume the role of parent. This is a self-help manual. It describes the causes, the symptoms, and the stages of parent burnout as well as the methods for burnout recovery and prevention. Special situations that exacerbate burnout or present unique factors are described as well. As a self-help instrument, it provides the basic tools and ingredients for treatment. It is up to the reader to take the ideas and recommended procedures and put them into practice in a systematic and disciplined fashion. The resources recommended in Chapter 10 are presented as supplements that you may wish to draw on during your reading or after you complete the book.

No book can be written without the assistance of many people. We are especially appreciative of the parents who agreed to be interviewed and the professional practitioners who shared their knowledge and experience with us. We would like to acknowledge Janis L. Cromer for her research on the issues of parent expectations and single parents; Dr. Sharyn S. Rhodes for writing the section on the parents of exceptional children; Dr. Lynette Long for her research on "latchkey children"; and Barbara D. Turk for her findings on stepparents and parents of only children. We are grateful to Mulberry Studio for typing much of the manuscript. Special thanks go to Nick Ellison, our agent, and Adrian Zackheim, our editor, for their help and encouragement. We also thank Linda Birney and Ian McNett for their recommendations concerning manuscript revisions; Geraldine Gray and Jean Nyang'ani for their help as reference librarians; and Peggy Nolan for her assistance in typing material.

JOSEPH PROCACCINI, Ph.D.
MARK W. KIEFABER
Baltimore, Maryland

Prologue

BETH: A TRAVELER ON THE ROAD TO BURNOUT

"When I force myself to be totally honest, I have to admit that I decided to have a child in order to fulfill some of my own needs . . . you know . . . for companionship . . . for love. I did expect Billy to be a totally loving and adoring child. . . . I expected that we would spend hours together, playing . . . and me teaching him all sorts of things." Beth paused before continuing, "But it seems that from the minute he was born he was unhappy . . . always fussy. He was terribly hard to keep happy. I was run ragged trying to keep up with the new responsibilities. I thought I'd at least get a break during his naptime, but then there were the diapers and formula . . . and, you know, just everything. I was always working. Here I was, before his birth, thinking I was going to have this lovely child to spend my days with. Instead, I felt betrayed. Billy's crying and constant need for something made me feel enslaved . . . to my own son!

"And worst of all, he didn't make me less lonely. I had to handle him all day long by myself. By the time my husband got home, I was a wreck. It really put a strain on our relationship. And here I'd thought it was going to add to it . . . make it better." Beth finished with an exasperated look on her face.

These comments were about Beth's early days as a parent—during Billy's infancy. As he grew, Beth did not find parenting any less difficult, any less disappointing. "Everything they say about the 'terrible twos' is true . . . it was terrible. He went through a whining stage and I just couldn't take it anymore. I used to turn the stereo on in the living room, lie down on the couch with the earphones on, close my eyes, and totally block him out. He could scream or do anything. But as long as I couldn't hear him or see him he just wasn't there. That's the way I really felt back then. I just wished he wasn't there. That's such a terrible thing to say about your own child, but it just seemed that I was totally unprepared for this. It was so hard to go on. I was totally withdrawn from him."

By the time Billy was four, Beth was exhausted, totally burned out. "I don't remember much about Billy's fourth year . . . it's all a blur. I do remember trying to relate to him. I'd sit there and try to listen to what he was saying . . . try to respond, but so many times I just couldn't . . . I'd just space out. Oh, I also remember the allergies. It seemed that every time I turned around he'd be allergic to something else. There'd be some other food I couldn't feed him. That made life even more complicated than it already was. I really felt angry at him then . . . even though I know it wasn't his fault. A kid can't control whether he'll be sick or not. But back then, dealing with all his problems . . . I thought I'd never be happy again. I resented Billy; I hated my life; and I hated myself for being such a terrible mother."

Beth has traveled the road to burnout. She has experienced all the stages: first enthusiasm and high expectations, then doubts and frustration, next various stages of depression, and finally total resentment and withdrawal. Her story is similar to those of all the other victims of parent burnout we have interviewed. Beth has ended her burnout through counseling. She experiences parenting with a much more positive attitude. She sees herself as more than just a mother now and is happy. The therapeutic techniques that helped Beth are found in the Burnout Recovery Plan described later in this book. All burnout victims can be helped. And many can "heal themselves" if they learn to recognize the burnout feelings and stages, to understand their causes, and to adopt some everyday techniques for arresting the cycle.

1

Burning Out: How It Feels

Parents who can recognize the cacophony of feelings expressed in the passage above are lucky. There are many who do not stop to face the growing tide of emotion that sweeps over them. Accepting the existence of certain feelings toward their children is, perhaps, too difficult for many parents. It is especially difficult for parents who are, or once were, *exceptional* at the role. Burnout is most prevalent in parents who embraced their child-rearing responsibilities not only willingly but enthusiastically. If there has been no fire, there can be no burnout.

The feelings of burnout do not appear overnight. They evolve over time with the feelings most often appearing in stages. These stages are not mutually exclusive. Parents don't leave one set of feelings behind as they approach each successive stage. Rather, the feelings of burnout are cumulative, causing increasing suffering as they proceed. The stages of burnout are shown in Figure 1.

THE STAGES OF PARENT BURNOUT

The beginnings of burnout are so subtle that one might wonder that these early feelings contribute to the syndrome at all. The Gung-ho stage may have begun as soon as a pregnancy was discovered.

Most parents can vividly remember the moment when they both learned that they were about to become parents. Some women probably fixed a special dinner and then slowly hinted at what it was all about. Some others might have waited until their husbands were concentrating very hard on something and then just popped it on them. Whatever the method, that initial moment was probably filled with two powerful feelings: joy and fear. As time went on in the pregnancy, both parents flipped from one emotion to the other and not always in synchronization with each other. The final result of this process was a powerful sense of joy and anticipation coupled with a realization that the responsibilities were huge.

Figure 1

STAGES OF PARENT BURNOUT

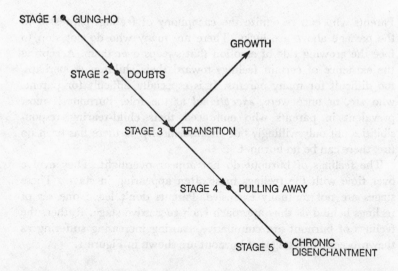

Most of the parents whom we have interviewed and counseled readily admitted that, regardless of the level of effort that they gave to any other duty, they threw themselves completely into the parent role. When they became parents they did not merely take a job, they took on a lifetime responsibility. Many parents want to make this a better world for themselves and their children.

For many the choice to have children sprang from laudable ideals. When asked why they had children, parents often responded with such answers as, "I wanted to leave the world just a little bit better off than when I joined it." Another parent said, "Children are supposed to give you a full life. Without them life would be without meaning." Still another said, "I just knew that I was cut out to be a father and my kids would love me for caring so much for them and supporting them."

For some other people the desire to become parents came from an overwhelming need to "set the record straight." These were parents who had miserable childhoods and told themselves that they would raise their own children differently, and their kids would be happy and love them for it. Regardless of the motivation to become a parent, they almost always held mythical ideas about parenthood. They developed a set of subconscious beliefs about being a parent. Even though they carried these beliefs around, many parents never spoke of them. The following are some of the beliefs that parents in the Gung-ho stage hold:

- Being a parent is the most laudable thing an individual can do.
- Giving 100 percent every day to my children is barely good enough; it is what all good parents do.
- The success or failure of my children depends entirely on me in the end.
- I will never be bored in my role as a parent.
- I will be seen by society as a good and honorable person because of the effort I put into being a good parent.

Needless to say, these beliefs are not uncommon and are often reinforced by society.

We have described the motivation and beliefs of parents at the Gung-ho stage. How do they behave? In general, they are overenthusiastic about their job as parent. They connect too much of their self-worth to the responses of their children. Finally, they establish rigid and unrealistic standards for themselves and their children. Specifically, here are a few examples of stage one behavior:

- Dropping out of all nonparent-related activities in order to focus total attention on their children.

• Refusing to allow anyone else to care for or influence their children in any way.
• Denying their own needs for rest and recreation in order to help their children.
• Doing too much for their children without requiring that they take on the responsibilities that they are old enough to handle.
• Spending every possible moment with their children.
• Taking on additional projects that they feel will benefit their children.
• Feeling guilty if they need a break or want to lavish some time and attention on themselves.

Laura's story is a good example of a parent experiencing the Gung-ho stage.

"Being a mother wasn't supposed to be like this," Laura said as she gazed out the living room window of her four-bedroom home in the Chicago suburbs. "I always believed that home and family would be the next best thing to heaven. I know better now."

Laura, the mother of two children, ages nine and seven, has traveled the road to burnout, and after a good deal of anguish and confusion, is making the return trip to a more fulfilling and satisfying life. But the launch pad was built of high hopes and enthusiasm.

After graduating from a large midwestern university with a degree in art, Laura worked for three years as a graphic designer for an advertising firm. Although she found her work rewarding, she chose to resign from her job six months after she married Jim, a promising young corporate attorney.

Laura took on married life with a passion. She turned her considerable artistic talents toward creating a home that was the showplace of the neighborhood. Friends would tell her that her house was something out of the pages of *Better Homes and Gardens*. "I was tremendously happy in those early years," she recalls now. "Jim was up and coming in his career and I was the elegant hostess. When I learned I was pregnant, I felt nothing could be more perfect. I had it all and I was sure all the fairy tales were true —I was going to live happily ever after."

No mother was ever more prepared to have a baby. Laura read every available child care manual. She plunged into motherhood with the same enthusiasm she had brought to her early years of marriage. "I was determined to be the best mother the world had ever seen. I knew just what I was going to do."

Thinking back to the months before her first child was born, Laura recalls: "I knew my child would be smarter, better-looking, and more precocious than all the rest. I had all the educational toys ready for him. I envisioned spending my days teaching him, holding him, giving him all the chances I missed out on as a child."

Laura's mother had divorced her father when Laura was three. Consequently, her mother had to work to support Laura and her older brother. Laura came home from school to a baby-sitter and rarely got to spend time with her mother, even on weekends, because her job at a department store required Laura's mother to work on Saturdays.

"Sundays were the best day of the week," said Laura. "Mom was home and she and I would spend the better part of the day together. I understood why my mother had to be away from my brother and me so much, but I swore that if I ever became a mother, I would always be there for my kids."

Laura's first child was a boy. He was named Jim, Jr., and no other seven pounds and four ounces ever received more attention or fanfare, Laura said. "Jim and I reveled in parenthood. Our friends told us and we believed we were the epitome of the 'good life.' I kept up with all the former duties of hostess and home decorator that I had before the baby came and my days were filled with sumptuous recipes, new drapery swatches, and most of all, Jim, Jr."

The news of a second baby could not have been more welcome. After all, Laura thought, one child has brought so much contentment. Another one will simply double our happiness. Once again Laura immersed herself in preparing for the baby's arrival. She evaluated the things she would do differently with the new baby. Not that she had done anything "wrong" with Jim, Jr., but she was quite nervous in the early months of his life, afraid that she might make some dreadful parenting *faux pas* that would mar him for life. Furthermore, Laura admitted, "I didn't realize how much time it took to care for a baby and so, when Melissa was born, I vowed to be better organized."

Laura and Jim's children enhanced their lives. They found great pleasure in weekend outings together, making plans for the future, and living out the life of an "All-American family."

As the children grew, Laura always found new challenges to meet. It seemed that each month of development required "Mommy" to master some new child psychology technique. Being the perfect mother was a full-time job and, of course, Laura also had her responsibilities as perfect wife and gracious entertainer.

When both children entered school, Laura maintained her busy schedule by embarking on a complete home redecorating venture, joining the PTA, and taking on some free-lance graphics work. "I found myself working more—at least it seemed like more. I had many exciting projects in the works, just as I always had. However, I seemed to have less time to finish everything. I didn't feel a rush of satisfaction about the things I accomplished any more," Laura said. "I didn't tell anyone about my creeping feelings of lethargy," Laura remembered. "In fact, I went to extra lengths to let my friends and family know how 'wonderful' everything was."

Laura, who once greeted each day with a burst of energy and a long list of activities for herself, found that crawling back beneath the covers of her bed once the children and Jim were out of the house was frequently an appealing prospect. On the few days she indulged her preference for languishing in bed until noon, she spent the rest of the day silently berating herself for being lazy. The following day her list of "things to do" would be twice as long.

Laura admits that much of her early enthusiasm for parenting slowly evaporated as the realities of child rearing warred with her own expectations of fulfilled motherhood. Laura was plunged instead into a reality of constant demands and tedious chores.

Implicit in much of Laura's story is a sentiment indicative of the Gung-ho stage: the belief that only she was capable of raising her children. Many parents share the notion that no other human being could do anything better for their children than they could themselves.

When a parent feels indispensable, two problems related to burnout occur: fatigue due to overwork and guilt feelings when the parent attempts to reduce the load and allows others to help. Parents feel as if they are *shirking* responsibilities. While nothing is inherently wrong with enthusiasm for parenting—it is warranted and desirable—overenthusiasm based on high expectations is a trigger for burnout. When a parent refuses to compromise between expectations and reality, the schism that results heralds the beginning of the second stage of burnout.

Parents moving into the Doubts stage begin to experience a growing sense that something is wrong. Frequently, they internalize this feeling as "I am doing something wrong." Never stopping to realize that high expectations, rather than poor parenting, are to blame, they begin the vicious circle of catch-up. Parents may overextend themselves with child-rearing duties for several days as a result of guilt feelings. Then, when fatigue sets in, they "underdo" for several days, eventually experiencing more guilt. Laura fell into this pattern with her daytime naps followed by resolutions to catch up the next day.

The condition of being *tired all the time* becomes a way of life. Even though such parents may be getting plenty of sleep, they rarely feel rested. There was probably a time in the past when they were high energy people, but now they feel as though they were dragging themselves from one task to another.

Psychosomatic responses often begin during the Doubts stage. It is as if the body is the battleground for the war between expectations and realities. And when doubts or ambivalence go unexpressed, they often gnaw at the body in retaliation. Minor complaints—*Oh, my aching back*—begin to linger on and gradually get worse. Some examples are headaches, general tenseness, indigestion, heartburn, rashes, diarrhea, constipation, and allergies. Some more serious problems are ulcers and colitis. All of these are real physical problems, but are rarely caused by germs. They are stress-related. A tremendous load is placed on the body by distress. Sooner or later, one of the physiological systems will malfunction. Unrelieved, the tensions can produce debilitating heart attacks, strokes, and serious deterioration of the body.

As the Doubts stage continues, resentment toward the children builds and parents experience the *Hey, what about me?* reaction. They feel that all they do is "give, give, give," while all their children do is "take, take, take." Many parents, in their zeal to do more for their families, establish a pattern of constantly putting out more energy than they receive. This is possible for a while, but after a period they tend to suffer "energy bankruptcy." These parents expect that when they get to that point, their families will come to their rescue and "do" for them. They are often disappointed.

Sharon, a mother of two adolescents and a six-year-old, put it this way: "Sometimes I feel like I have nothing left to give. I can't explain it. I feel totally drained, that's all I can say. It never ends. These kids just don't know when to stop. Sometimes I just scream and cry when it reaches the breaking point. Often I hold it in, though. When that happens I feel this 'silent scream' inside me. I am convinced that I could drop dead tomorrow and they could care less. I feel terrible because of these thoughts. I wonder if I created this myself. I don't know. I know one thing: I can't take this much longer."

The emergence of parents' anger toward their children occurs simultaneously with the expression of rage toward themselves. They become overwhelmed by the realization that they are not perfect at their jobs. This feeling is very prevalent during the Doubts stage and may be a reaction to some real event. Maybe the children are bringing home poor report cards. Perhaps one of the teenagers is using drugs. Possibly the children have openly expressed their own dislike of the parents.

But the parents' feeling of failure does not necessarily result from such explicit events. Self-doubts and general feelings of inadequacy may develop almost imperceptibly over time, and often occur in parents who are doing a commendable job of child rearing.

Terry was an example of a parent at this stage. The roadway leading to Terry's mansion was long and winding. The house was nestled on one hundred acres in prime Virginia hunt country. Terry was very much a part of this culture and she had lived in this house with her husband, a former high-ranking member of the military, since their marriage six years ago. Her first marriage ended in divorce after ten years. She and her present husband had two young sons, ages five and three. Terry was an exceptionally attractive woman who looked much younger than her forty-three years. It was clear that her first marriage had taken its toll emotionally. In her conversations she often spoke sadly of her relationship with her first husband and made frequent references to her twenty-year-old daughter, who had been living with her father but was away at a California college now. She felt that she hardly knew her daughter and remembered very little about her growing up.

Terry appeared to have everything to live for now. She had a good caring husband and two handsome children, a lovely home in an idyllic setting. She had plenty of help provided by the household staff, sufficient money for travel, clothing, and other amenities. Her children had strong and secure trust funds. But Terry was an unhappy person. She was tired, bored, depressed—and worried. She was beginning to feel that once again her life was slipping out of her control. She felt herself sliding closer and closer to the point where she couldn't take it anymore. She and her husband, who now spent most of his time farming their property and raising some prime steer, had talked about this situation. He felt that she might be overreacting and might have some unwarranted fears about failing at marriage again. Terry pointed out that her husband would be rather upset if he knew that she was talking about these feelings.

In our conversations with Terry it became clear that she had always been under pressure, sometimes self-imposed but often imposed by her affluent and hard-working parents. Nothing but the best! She recalled her prep school days in Massachusetts and her college days with apparent joy, but when she spoke about her family life, an elusive sadness seemed to come across her face. Her mother was a very busy attorney who demanded much of herself and those around her. From childhood, Terry always felt that anything less than perfect was a shortcoming. She told us that she was in pain because she did not think that she was a very good parent. In fact, she was experiencing quite a bit of mental anguish over this. She loved her children but just could not give them enough time or attention. Paying attention to their requests and questions was difficult for Terry. The disorganization that playing children tend to create was actually unbearable for her. She mentioned that she dreaded the Christmas morning ritual of opening gifts. She just could not stand the mess created by all the wrapping paper being ripped and thrown on the family room floor. It was too much for her to handle and she hated herself for this "selfish" attitude.

More and more her wealthy neighbors got under her skin. She resented their "intrusion" into her life. Being with them demanded too much, more than she could give. She found them boring and resented the fact that they had the time and energy to play tennis and go riding. She was concerned about her sons growing up in this environment and marrying women who would reinforce this same culture, with its heavy emphasis on perfection, "at least on the surface."

Terry spent a lot of time worrying about the future. Would her present husband continue to care for her? Would he always love her? Would her children grow to dislike and resent her? Would her daughter forget her? Were her children happy now and would their unhappiness have a negative impact on their future lives? She had almost a storybook model of what family life should be about. And everything she did was measured against this picture. Down deep she thought that she was truly failing miserably. She was not the always-smiling attentive relaxed mother of the storybooks. What she was she really did not like: a sometimes tired unattentive forty-three-year-old who often got bored listening to the children chattering twelve hours a day, who had difficulty concentrating on the details of the "long version" of what took place at school that day.

Terry was exceptionally sensitive to failure. She felt that she had failed too many times in the past: her first marriage, the rearing of her first child, her difficulty socializing with her neighbors. As she perceived herself failing once again, she worried about it constantly. The more anxious she became the more energy she exerted to counter and cope with this mental and physical pain. Her energy was running out rapidly. She knew this and it made her more anxious. Eventually, Terry would have run out of energy completely.

After going through a half-year period of increased dependence on tranquilizers, Terry, upon the recommendation of her physician, sought counseling. She is progressing well as she works to modify some heavily ingrained attitudes and develop some new behaviors and coping skills.

This dangerous combination of feelings—fatigue, resentment, guilt, and anger—leads parents to the realization that they are suffering. Many parents begin to feel that they are sacrificing their own pleasures and achievement for their children. In return they expect to be eternally appreciated. When the expected appreciation is not forthcoming, the parent feels cheated and abused and often becomes depressed and highly resentful. One can hear these sentiments of martyrdom when Diane speaks:

"Between the demands of my children and those of my boss, there's nothing left for me. I have nothing," she laments. Divorced,

with two children, Diane has worked her way from a secretarial job
to a management position with a successful business. She takes no
credit for her success. "I had no choice. My ex-husband refused to
pay adequate child support and I simply had to provide for my
kids. I didn't work to get where I am because I wanted it. The
realities of paying rent and buying food made me work harder."

Characterizing herself as a survivor, Diane adheres to a rigid list
of rules for motherhood, all of which reflect unending sacrifice. "I
can tell you all the things that mothers don't do: mothers don't run
around on dates, even if they have been divorced for five years;
mothers don't forget their children's birthdays or their favorite kind
of sandwiches for school lunches; mothers aren't tired or out of
sorts with their kids. They save those things for when the children
are asleep. And mothers don't let their children know they are
worried about anything."

The feelings and behaviors that appear during the Doubts stage
result from the parents' questioning of whether or not they are acting in their own best interest. This questioning is not hard to understand, considering where burnout begins: in the Gung-ho stage
when the parents believed that a deep sense of worthiness, happiness, and fulfillment would result from rearing children. The expectations are not met; the beliefs do not turn out to be true.

Burnout is likely when people believe—and act on the belief—
that one role in life can satisfy all their needs, that one focus can
support all their visions. Parents on the road to burnout have built
their identity on sandy soil, subjecting themselves to the winds and
tides of their children's needs and stunting their own growth.

Parents handle this threat to their own identity in one of two
ways: by taking on the challenge and thereby arresting the cycle of
burnout; or by retreating and ensuring that the cycle will continue.
The next stage—Transition—is where these crucial decisions are
made.

Of all the stages of parent burnout, this one is the most critical
because it is likely to determine the happiness and health of the
parent for a long time to come. Parents' experience with burnout
can evolve toward one of two ends: they can either reassess the
condition of their lives and decide to make some changes or they
can continue along the road to burnout until reaching the stage of
Chronic Disenchantment.

The foundation of these choices is actually a question of control. The burning-out parent is experiencing a loss of control in life and by using the Transition stage to take charge again he or she can begin the path to growth. However, there is rarely such a thing as a meteoric rise from the ashes. Parents usually experience several phases of depressive feelings during Transition before making the choices necessary to change.

The first of these feelings of hopelessness might be described as *Stuck in the Swamps*. Feeling smothered by their role of parent and tied down by the endless daily responsibilities, parents feel that every attempt to initiate change is met by interference. The duties of parenthood become drudgery; eventually, they develop the attitude of "Why bother? It isn't worth it."

Ben, a self-employed businessman in his late forties and father of two teenagers, expressed these feelings. "I'm not sure I've gotten that much out of being a father. I'm not sure it's worth all the worrying, all the concern. I keep doing it because I'm supposed to, but sometimes I think, 'Why bother?' "

This attitude has carried over to all aspects of Ben's life. Once a man full of new ideas and seemingly endless energy, Ben now claims most people and activities bore him. "Hobbies!" he exclaims at his wife's suggestion. "Hobbies are for old retired guys. I'm only forty-seven. Besides, I work hard all the time. Why should I get into something that will just be more work in the end?"

Ben's feelings have cut him off from even entertaining the possibility of new ventures: they may bring further disappointments. Ben believes that any new activity risks similar disillusionment. As with many parents in this stage of burnout, Ben has chosen to play it safe and is slowly cutting himself off from opportunities to find happiness.

Implicit in Ben's words and behavior is the expression of another feeling often present during this phase of burnout: depression. Parents reported having an expectation that something was about to happen and though they didn't know what it was, it was not going to be very good. As in Ben's case, when parents' expectations are regularly unmet, they develop a negative view of not only the present but the past and future as well.

Many parents also report feeling that there is too much to do and too little time to do it. There is a general sense of persistent pressure. They feel overwhelmed by the sheer logistics and energy needed for chauffeuring children around, cooking, working, loving, caring, cleaning, and listening. Often there is no energy left to do even routine things like writing thank-you notes, sending greeting cards, or answering telephone calls.

Laura, the "perfect" mother mentioned earlier, reached this phase when the pressures of parenting seemed too much. She couldn't finish things. Six months after the redecorating project had started three rooms of the house were still in the disarray of half-painted walls, floors were covered with drop cloths, and new drapery fabric was bundled and wrapped in the corner of a room. Jim, her husband, asked Laura if she wanted to hire some professionals to finish the redecorating job so that she could have some more time with her other interests. Laura reacted angrily to the suggestion.

"I thought he was implying that I wasn't good enough to complete what I started," she explains. "I thought he was criticizing me, and although I had little interest in the work, I completed those three rooms in two weeks. In fact, I just felt guilty for having let the thing go so long that Jim had to say something. I was disappointed in myself. You know, the perfect wife image had slipped a little, I thought."

Although Laura often rallied to certain activities as she had in finishing the home decorating, she increasingly felt an inexplicable sadness, and she found even the most routine chores difficult to do. She gave up all of her free-lance work, explaining to Jim that she no longer found it stimulating. Besides, she contended, "I want to spend more time with the children."

As with Laura, parents who are burning out often overdo things because of their own very high standards. Such standards may include the expectation that the parents will always have time and energy for their child, or more specific expectations that their sons be Little League stars or their daughters be accomplished pianists by age twelve, etc.

These standards set by parents, which cause the shame and guilt, can also cause a feeling of *I think I'm cracking up.* Some parents establish such high standards for themselves and are so unwilling to modify them that they push themselves to the point of complete

---

28 PARENT BURNOUT

breakdown. Ironically, the breakdown is likely to occur in those people who at one time performed with a high degree of success.

The weaknesses leading to the breakdown are usually "overdone strengths": an orderly and clean home, activity in school affairs, involvement in the children's athletic programs, concern about the safety and health of the children. These virtues, because they are overdone, become sources of distress and detract from high quality performance.

Continued overwork, both emotional and physical, will cause increasing physiological and mental fatigue. The parent who does not use the Transition stage to correct unhealthy imbalances will begin to compensate with increasingly negative feelings and dangerous withdrawal behavior.

2

The Final Stages of Burnout

Parents who take advantage of the warning signs of the Transition stage move toward maintaining or correcting the imbalance which has slowly tilted their feelings and behaviors toward the negative. If a parent has not been willing or able to reestablish a healthy balance, he or she will begin to compensate for the imbalance with more negative and withdrawing actions. This starts the stage of Pulling Away: continued overwork coupled with movement away from the family that will cause the parent to become more fatigued physically and mentally and to drift downward toward illness. Pulling Away leads to alienation from the family.

The withdrawal of this stage is a protective, though destructive, effort. Unlike the previous stage, very few of the factors associated with Pulling Away are positive. The changes that do occur are initially a means to escape the problems of burnout, but often they serve only to further imprison the parent. Those who reach this point usually need counseling.

Laura epitomized the withdrawal of the formerly Gung-ho parent who is plummeting into burnout. Though she claimed she wanted to be with the children more, she really longed for more time away from them. Although she never admitted her desire to distance herself from her kids, she almost always busied herself with some household task every day when the children returned from school. Laura herself did not recognize her increasing withdrawal. However, pangs of guilt would settle in on her after a few afternoons of "being unavailable" to hear her kids' tales about their school adventures. Laura promptly soothed her conscience then by making a surprise batch of baked goodies for the kids or taking them to an after-school movie.

The two most prevalent feelings occurring during the Pulling Away stage often appear simultaneously: *I dislike my children* and *They're out to get me.*

When parents make statements like these, they have usually been driven to the edge of tolerance and finally admit their true feelings with a large mixture of guilt. These parents have not made the distinction between liking the child but disliking the behavior.

The dislike, rarely a result of any personal qualities in the child, results from the growing awareness that the parents have of their own distress and lack of autonomy. They are seeking a target for blame. The child, the recipient of their giving, becomes the focus of their discontent. It often appears that the more tired they become, the more the children demand.

Once blame has been laid, an increasing paranoia sets in. Often, the ordinary mishaps of childhood begin to be viewed as plots devised by the children. Mud on the carpet, noise in the playroom, misplaced scissors, or a dropped glass are blown all out of proportion. One parent said, "They're doing these things because they hate me." Even though the perception is wrong, the formerly giving parent never expected such a return, and it hurts.

An important corollary reaction that develops at this point is the *I can't deal with their feelings right now* response. During the Pulling Away stage, parents are cutting themselves off from their children, and they begin to deal with them on a purely intellectual level. If a child wakes up in the middle of the night afraid of monsters, the parents do not deal with his or her fear but merely explain that there cannot possibly be monsters in the closet. When the child continues the emotional rather than the rational response, the parent becomes angry. Another example is the teenage daughter who mourns day after day because she has not been invited to the dance. The burning-out parent of this girl will shrug off her feelings of hurt and disappointment by telling her not to worry about it and then become angry, believing she is shortsighted and immature.

Parents who are Pulling Away are not just isolating themselves from their children, but are breaking emotional ties with other family members and friends as well. They begin to see less and less of people they are close to. The pressure of "being on" when in the presence of others is increasingly too difficult to bear. They feel they no longer have the energy to play the expected role of the ideal parent.

As Lucy, a mother of three recounts, "I stopped seeing friends, and I declined any hint that we entertain Paul's business associates in our home. I just couldn't put up the facade that everything was just fine. I remember thinking that I should start making arrangements for a surprise birthday party for Paul . . . something that I knew he'd love, especially since we had been seeing so few of our friends at that point. But before I had even completed the guest list, I went upstairs to take a nap. The thought of facing all those people . . . it just took so much energy in those days."

When people very close to burnout are asked what is wrong, they usually don't want to talk about it. Parents feel so helpless and trapped that talking only makes it worse. Their unwillingness to communicate intimately is proof that they have pulled away. Actually, some friends and relatives are of little help to burnout victims. Grandparents, for example, directly or indirectly, often set high expectations for *their* children in the rearing of their grandchildren. After all, this is their second chance to be perfect!

Many parents who are burning out begin to take everything too seriously. They become dispirited and as they become aware that others are avoiding them because they are depressing, their sense of despondency mounts. Marty, a once jovial father of two boys, found himself sulking more and becoming super sensitive about any humor directed toward him. At one time he and his family used to enjoy teasing each other and laughing at each other's foibles. Marty's wife and his children had a lot of fun plotting surprises and tricks on Daddy. Marty always enjoyed these little ploys and felt that they brought the family closer together. However, now he viewed these activities on the part of his family as frivolous, and sometimes thought that his children and wife were making fun of him. He resented this and rejected their playfulness. His kids were puzzled by what they perceived as a sudden shift in attitude. When they tried to break the ice and fool with him, Marty pushed them away, but quickly felt guilty about his own behavior.

Loss of friendships, intimacy, and a growing despondency result in a feeling of *being right on the edge*. Their fuses shortened, burned-out parents feel that they are a powder keg primed to explode at any moment. They often do. With tempers at the point of limited tolerance, parents will often argue in order to hurt someone rather than to solve a problem. As a result, they often drive their children and others away.

Frank typifies the parent who has been pushed to the edge. There he was, standing in the baby's room at four o'clock in the morning with his fist in the air, screaming as loud as he could, "Shut up, shut up, shut up, I've got to get some sleep." Frank had considered himself a pretty good person and well suited to be a father. After all, he was well educated and had a wonderful wife, a good job, hobbies, and a realistic view of the world around him. He and Joan owned their home and they had mutually agreed to wait until they were fairly settled and financially secure to have a child. The first pregnancy resulted in a miscarriage. They vowed to try again, and after a trying second pregnancy a son was born.

On the day that they brought Michael home, the crying began. He would not nurse well. He could not keep any milk down and he seemed so unhappy and helpless. Joan and Frank were good sports. They read more baby books and concluded that this situation could not last forever. Michael was a sweet little thing, but he cried a lot. He could not be comforted. That's what bothered Frank the most. He expected that cuddling and cooing and rocking would soothe Michael. It didn't. He only struggled and pushed away more. When the baby was about two and a half months old, during a particularly violent crying and raging bout, Frank felt the overwhelming urge to smash Michael. He stood over the crib and shook his fist and screamed!

Parents who are surviving solely as a result of the escape measures available to them often have the most difficulty facing the weekends. Realizing that they will have to interact with their children for an extended period of time often causes a comment like, "I get knots in my stomach before a weekend." During the week, parents can postpone or fend off their children's demands with claims that they are too tired because of work. Knowing that they are no longer capable of giving time and emotional support freely or fully, parents find weekends often offer the most opportunities to experience their own failure! Calvin's story is an example of this.

"I didn't realize at first how much I tried to avoid the kids . . . sometimes even my wife . . . on weekends. I'd try to be up first on Saturdays and out doing errands before the boys had a chance to ask me if they could go with me. If I was stuck at home I'd make a point to find work to do around the house that they were too young to help me with. My greatest dread on Saturdays was the fear that my wife would ask me to watch the boys for a few hours while she went shopping. I knew she had a right to some time away, too, but I just couldn't handle it . . . being alone with the boys for an afternoon."

The parents' continued search for a means of escape often results in overeating, heavy drinking, and drug abuse. No doubt, a high percentage of the tranquilizers consumed today is a direct result of this quest for relief on the part of parents. While food and alcohol binges and popping pills may provide temporary relief, they are double-edged swords. They provide temporary comfort, but also tremendous guilt pangs when parents face the consequences of their actions. In the end, parents blame their children for driving them to this point. This resentment fuels the fires of burnout all the more.

"Look at me. I'm hooked on these damn pills. I can't get off them," cries Anita. "I really need them to get me through the day. The kids just demand so much from me." Anita is torn between a concern for her own health and her concern for her children. She finds herself resenting her children for putting her in this dilemma.

As Pulling Away continues, the cumulative negative feelings and actions finally accomplish the task of completely isolating the parent from the potential love and support of the family. This results in the final phase of burnout—Chronic Disenchantment. Parents who have reached this stage objectify their children. In its milder cases, objectification takes the form of abstract labels when referring to children. Instead of Billy or Julie, it's "my two-year-old," "my husband's son," or "my offspring."

Objectification often slips into derogatory or abusive language when parents are addressing or describing children. Terms like "turkey," "meatball," "pinhead," "prima donna," "lazybones," or "the duchess," thinly disguised as terms of endearment, actually convey underlying rage. A passive warfare grows as children respond in kind with their own derogatory terms, such as "the old man," "the old lady," "the warden," or "the grouch." Such passive and disguised hostility indicate that the last stage of burnout is present.

I don't care anymore is another sentiment present during this last stage. At one time enthusiastic, committed, concerned, and heavily involved in the lives of the children, these parents are now passively angry, withdrawn, apathetic, and do not seem to be able to commit energy to anything.

Connie put it this way. "For the past ten years I have been killing myself doing this and doing that, chauffeuring these kids from Little League practice to swimming to Scouts to music lessons. I worried about them continuously. Will they do well in school? Will they get hurt? Will they have success in sports, in music, in friendships? Where did all that running around get me? Nowhere! I see parents who took care of themselves and didn't do half of what I've done. Their kids turned out just as successful as mine—in fact, better. They were the smart ones. . . . Who knows what's right? I don't know and frankly, I don't really care anymore."

Parents in the Chronic Disenchantment stage of burnout report a general feeling of confusion and disorientation. They were accustomed to using their role as parent as a way to structure their behavior and personal identity. Now they are angry, and the vision of themselves that was once perfectly clear has become cloudy and out of focus. Since they have no solid notion of themselves, they have no standard against which they can compare the activities of the day. Often, whole days go by and they can remember very little. They feel unhappy and begin to wonder whether or not they are having a nervous breakdown.

Laura, who started out with such high hopes, confesses her feelings in the end. "I felt like a zombie," she said. "I found the kids' slightest requests to be a burden. I found myself snapping at them for little things—misplaced shoes, rumpled clothes, toys not picked up. No *real* mother would act this way, I told myself. I'm failing at this mothering business, just like I failed at redecorating the house."

The fear of failing as a mother was the most painful for Laura.

"After all," she said, "being a good mother was supposed to come naturally—anybody could do it. Good mothers were not supposed to yell at their children; good mothers weren't supposed to send their kids off to some other mother's house the minute they got home from school; and good mothers certainly weren't supposed to lock themselves in their bedrooms just to get an hour away from their own children. But that's what I was doing."

Another aspect of the final stage of burnout is the boredom. Burned-out people have little energy left to invest in change. Therefore, they often feel trapped in a never-changing routine. This static existence limits their search for new and exciting activities. The malaise often spreads to other areas of the parent's life.

In the early stages of burnout it is possible to limit the burnout symptoms to that area where the parent feels the most stress. As time goes on, however, and the symptoms become stronger and stronger, the burnout problem begins to invade all areas of life. The parent begins to carry the negative feelings of boredom and cynicism to work and into the social and recreational settings as well.

Finally, one of the key factors of burnout is that parents often blame themselves for their negative feelings. Guilt—and it is strongest in the final stage of burnout—is the inevitable result. Self-esteem is at its lowest: when they are feeling bad about feeling bad. Listen to Jill, a victim who has reached the stage of Chronic Disenchantment, express these feelings: "Down deep I knew eventually I would reach this point. Why not? I have failed at everything else I have ever tried. Some people have it and some don't. I guess that I'm just one that can't do anything right. Why shouldn't I fail as a mother as well? For a while I thought that I was going to succeed at this. You can't imagine how badly I wanted to be a good mother. I feel miserable and I can't go on this way much longer."

SIDE EFFECTS OF PARENT BURNOUT

Burnout can have a terrible impact, as a sort of side effect, on four crucial areas of a parent's life: marriage, work, friendships, and leisure.

Successful marriages are built on trust and intimacy. Trust is characterized as giving your best and expecting the best of the other person in return. Intimacy calls for much sharing of information and feelings. Both of these require a high degree of physical, mental, and emotional energy. Often parents who are burning out just do not have the energy to build trust and intimacy. This is usually sensed rather early by the other spouse and quickly resented. Sometimes the offended spouse responds in kind by holding back his or her affection, triggering a vicious circle of mistrust, disaffection, and alienation, usually leading to a state of low communication, thereby cutting the lifeline of the husband-wife relationship. Soon the physical attraction of the other spouse diminishes and sexual relations decrease rapidly. This, coupled with the sheer physical exhaustion of burnout, can lead to a marital situation where physical expressions of intimacy are totally absent. Some couples go on for years in this state.

We have found that when both parents are suffering from burnout to the same degree, there is less likelihood of negative effect on the marriage. They often recognize the problem in each other and work together to alleviate it, serving as a small support group for one another. When only one parent suffers from burnout, the marriage suffers more. Often, the intact parent is insensitive to the emotional and behavioral impact of burnout. Or, if that parent is aware, he or she takes an intellectual or rational approach to dealing with the suffering spouse's debilitation.

Fran, a mother of four teenagers, recounts that when she would get into bed at night and weep because of her mental and physical exhaustion and sense of entrapment, her husband would turn to her and say, "Look, honey, what are you worrying about? There are all kinds of worse problems in the world. You should be happy to have what you have. I can't understand why you are crying so much. Please be quiet. I have to get some sleep so I can be awake at work tomorrow." Often her husband would angrily jump out of bed, take his pillow, and go sleep on the couch in the family room so "I don't have to listen to this whimpering."

If situations like this are allowed to continue for long, irreparable harm can come to the relationship. Eventually the burden becomes so unbearable that one of the spouses, or both, decides that some drastic change is necessary, usually a separation or a divorce. Often the specific cause of the breakup is difficult to articulate. The spouses feel that they "have grown apart, are out of touch with each other, in different worlds."

"Is burnout contagious?" The answer is "Yes." The negative attitude of burned-out parents can be very disheartening and irritating to the people around them. Unless there has been a history of trust and open communication among the members of the family, the introduction of this negative phenomenon will quickly lead to increased conflict in the family. This is often followed by still more conflict as a defense by each of the family members. Soon a vicious circle begins to develop. The best inoculation against the effects of burnout in a family is an atmosphere of respect, tolerance, and communicated affection among the members. If these are missing, parent burnout will do its greatest damage.

A second major side effect of burnout is the impact on work life. Productivity and quality of work performance are very much a function of the amount of human energy available in the worker. If parents are totally preoccupied with their homelife and their children, their performance at work will be affected. After all, there is only so much energy available to the individual.

Many parents who have experienced burnout have discovered themselves torn between family and work, finding it difficult to achieve an appropriate balance. For some their job was a source of renewal and, in fact, helped stave off total burnout or gave them an opportunity to recover. For others their burnout as parents served as a catalyst for burnout in the job. Walter, a manager for a local telephone company, pointed out that he was so irritable when he got to work in the morning after an evening or weekend with the children, that he found himself often flaring up with subordinates and occasionally losing control of himself at meetings. He was passed over several times for promotion because his superiors felt that he was less emotionally stable than they would like. They pointed out that he had a tendency to alienate workers.

Gordon, the financial vice-president for a large manufacturing firm, used to spend most of his workday dwelling on the academic problems of his two sons. He was very concerned about their future, so concerned at times that he would literally become mentally immobilized at work. His headaches and tension clouded his decision-making acumen so severely that he was eventually fired because of serious financial setbacks which he caused for the company.

Some parents who suffer from burnout jump knee-deep into their work, putting more of their time and effort into their careers. They often hope to receive the satisfaction that they are not getting from their family life. Because parent burnout victims are usually super-achievers this behavior often leads to a state of workaholism.

Third, the quantity and quality of friendships can be negatively affected by burnout. There are several common reasons for this. Sometimes parents in this state just do not have enough energy for the give and take of social interaction. Sometimes they have lowered self-concepts because of their tiredness, slovenliness, weight gain, or irritability. Isolation often accompanies burnout as parents sense others conveying the nonverbal message, "You are not much fun to be around." All of these possible reasons for burnout affecting friendships are magnified by the fact that burnout candidates are usually reactive and therefore very sensitive to the approval and acceptance judgments of others. Their mental and emotional systems at this point cannot bear even the thought of disapproval or rejection. So they detach and withdraw.

However, there is one exception to the negative impact of burnout on friendships. Very close friendships are sometimes strengthened by this experience if there is a sharing of feelings. The friends feel honored as a result of the respect and confidence shown them and they reciprocate the feelings, which leads to the development of an even more intimate bond. This can help the burned-out parent tremendously.

Lastly, the leisure of the parent is often affected by burnout. For burned-out parents leisure is usually viewed as either leftover time or wasted time. They have a tendency to leave leisure time out of their priority system because it is not seen as something productive. The whole concept of fun and spontaneity becomes elusive. Or if there is recreation it is considered as just another chore, a process leading to some worthwhile end, such as preventing a heart attack, meeting the right people, or losing weight.

Howard is a case in point. When his physician told him that he had better start taking some time off from his real estate position and relaxing more, he immediately went out and bought a whole jogging outfit—warm-up suit, shoes, shorts, headbands, pedometer, and stopwatch. He mapped out a regime he was going to follow to increase his distance and speed. He felt obliged to jog every day, even though his physician, as well as friends, pointed out that four days a week was sufficient. He kept track of his distances and speed on a daily chart, expressing satisfaction when he "performed" up to par and disappointment when he did not progress at the planned rate. Howard soon found himself telling others, "Too bad I have to jog tomorrow." The burden of going out and exercising became more onerous as the months went on. His secret wish of being able to run in a marathon seemed further from fruition. This bothered him as he saw it as another failure. Howard was not enjoying jogging and he knew it. This potentially beneficial and enjoyable use of leisure time became just another drain on his already low supply of mental, emotional, and physical energy. He was forced to give it up and is now searching feverishly for a replacement.

These side effects of burnout often create debilitating situations and consequences and new sources of distress for the parent. New problems arise in the marriage, with friends, at work, and in leisure time that increase the already heavy physical, mental, and emotional burdens. It is important to recognize that . . . all four areas affected by the side effects can be critical factors in the recovery, alleviation, and prevention of burnout. If these too become weakened by the burnout syndrome, the parents could find themselves trapped in a double bind, losing their key defenses.

DIAGNOSING PARENT BURNOUT

The process of parent burnout is cumulative. People do not move through and out of each successive stage. The feelings collect together, culminating in the near paralysis of the parent. Don't assume, just because you identify with one or more of the feelings described in this chapter, that you are a burned-out parent. Burnout is not comprised of or caused by the experience of a few fleeting feelings of frustration, anger, or even depression. Rather, burnout is characterized by a *drastic* reversal of attitude.

The following index provides a place to record some of your feelings and actions regarding your role as a parent. It is not intended to render a final verdict of emotional health. It provides parents with an objective standard against which to measure their own characteristics. When all fifteen questions have been answered, total the score and interpret it using the key that follows the index.

PARENT BURNOUT INDEX

Instructions: Answer the questions listed below. You need to think about each question before you respond. Use the following rating scale when responding:

1   Absolutely No
2   Probably No
3   Sometimes
4   Probably Yes
5   Absolutely Yes

Points
(1–5)

_____   1.   Do you have feelings that you are irreplaceable as a parent?

_____   2.   Do you dread weekends?

_____   3.   Do you feel powerless to make a difference with your children?

_____   4.   Do you feel persistent pressure—too much to do and too little time?

_____   5.   Do you wish that you could spend more time with your children?

_____   6.   Has your physical appearance changed for the worse?

_____   7.   Are you losing things more?

_____   8.   Are you overextended?

_____   9.   Do you feel like fighting with your children?

_____ 10.   Do you feel that your children really don't appreciate you?

_____ 11.   Are you having more arguments with your spouse, friends, and neighbors?

_____ 12.   Do you get depressed more?

_____ 13.   Do you feel nervous when you try to relax at the end of the day?

_____ 14.   Do you have colds, lower back pain, or insomnia?

_____ 15.   Are you guilty about your lack of success as a parent?

What does your score tell you?

If you had a total score of:

15–30   You are coping well with parenting.
31–39   You are doing fine, but pay attention to any changes in attitudes, feelings, or behavior.
40–49   You are on the edge of burnout; take preventative action.
50–60   You are slipping into warning stages.
61–69   You are sliding into alarming burnout reaction; take action immediately.
70–75   You are burned out; seek help at once.

Some additional explanation of the scoring key is required. The score of 15–30 is perfectly normal. This would indicate that you are not experiencing much distress in parenting and you do not feel trapped. Good for you. The score of 31–39 is still fine. The pattern is essentially positive. The next category of scores, 40–49, indicates that you are moving into the burnout syndrome. You are probably worried about the negative feelings that you are beginning to notice. The next group of scores, 50–60, indicates that you have progressed to the point where something needs to be done. You are at stage three, Transition, and could be on the brink of entering stage four, Pulling Away. Scores from 61–69 place you in serious trouble as a parent and indicate that you are at stage four. The action to take immediately is prescribed in Chapter 7. A score between 70 and 75 would indicate a massive amount of negative charge and the distress would be overwhelming. Parents scoring this high are usually living lives of quiet desperation. They are in stage five, Chronic Disenchantment, and they ought to seek counseling at once.

BURNOUT: A DEFINITION

What is saddest about burnout is that it happens to the highly motivated and most enthusiastic parents. Burned-out parents are those who were the most prepared for, and most willing to assume, child-rearing responsibilities. Their stories and feelings bear a remarkable similarity to each other, as they do to the stories of burned-out professionals. Actually, studies of burnout began in the work environment.

One of the earliest burnout researchers was Dr. Herbert J. Freudenberger, a psychologist in New York City.[1] In his work with drug clinics, he noticed that many of his volunteers would work feverishly for about a year and then quit suddenly, saying that they "couldn't handle it anymore." After tremendous effort, time, and resources were invested in their training, the volunteers would leave just as they became useful and effective.

Many of these volunteers used the street term "burned out" to describe the composite feelings they experienced: frustration, cynicism, and depression. Some even felt abused. These volunteers had been dedicated, and although they had helped many people, they now felt useless and impotent. Dr. Freudenberger was the first to adopt the term "burnout" and defined it as "exhaustion resulting from excessive demands on energy, strength, or resources."

While Dr. Freudenberger was writing on burnout, another researcher at the University of California, Christina Maslach, also was investigating the phenomenon. Dr. Maslach expanded the burnout definition, seeing the problem as part of a larger issue—depersonalization. Depersonalization occurs when people become detached from others. This process is what causes workers—particularly those in the helping professions—to treat their clients as if they were not human. The detachment, disassociation, and denial of clients' needs become so severe at times that they can lead to physical and emotional abuse.[2]

Based on her studies of the helping professions, Maslach defined burnout as "a syndrome of emotional exhaustion in which the helping professional has very little concern, sympathy, or respect for his clients. The worker often loses his enthusiasm, his creativity, and his commitment. Over time there is a psychological detachment from clients and a shift in the helping professional's attitudes toward the cynical or negative. . . . Many professions were studied and what was common to all of these people is that hour after hour, day after day, they are intimately involved with the psychological, social and physical problems of troubled human beings. This close continuous contact with clients involves a chronic level of emotional stress, and it is the inability to cope successfully with

[1] *Burn-Out* (Garden City, N.Y.: Anchor Press/Doubleday, 1980).
[2] "Burned-Out," *Human Behavior* 5 (September 1976), pp. 16–22.

this stress that is manifested in the emotional exhaustion and cynicism of burnout."

This definition is very comprehensive. Although it takes into account only the problems of helping professionals, it reflects many of the experiences described by burned-out parents. Particularly, parenting and the helping professions are similar in their constant high level of involvement in the intimate psychological, physical, emotional, and social problems and needs of other human beings. Indeed, their role as intercessor causes the intense demands and emotional stress. Helping professionals and parents assume similar roles and exist in similar situations, which are highly conducive to the evolution of burnout.

This striking similarity led to our research and to the following definition of parent burnout:

Parent burnout is a downward drift toward physical, emotional, and spiritual exhaustion resulting from the combination of chronic high stress and perceived low personal growth and autonomy. The stress usually comes from continuously having to meet the needs of the family. Efforts to satisfy these requests, which often seem endless and overwhelming, drain away the parent's energy and enthusiasm. Burned-out parents feel angry and guilty about their loss of enthusiasm, and blame either themselves or their families for this change in their outlook.

In essence, burnout-prone individuals are those who assume a new role, be it parenting or professional, with boundless enthusiasm. They are charged up, ambitious, motivated, and eager. When high expectations combine with chronic high stress, constant responsibilities, and the low autonomy of child rearing, the kindling of burnout has been lighted.

3

Foundations of Burnout I: Parent Expectations

Monday will bring a special treat your way
As you sit back and watch baby coo and play.

Tuesday will bring lots of fun too
As baby sings his first song to you.

On Wednesday life will seem so right
For baby sleeps his first full night.

On Thursday you'll be in the clouds
For baby says "Momma" out loud.

Thank goodness for Friday, the best of the week,
As baby plants his first kiss on your cheek.

Saturday you'll wonder once more
That this lovely child whom you adore

Could make your life so happy, so sweet—
A wondrous miracle that can't be beat.

And as Sunday comes and you're in deep thought
Your heart will be filled with the joy that
this baby has brought.

We came across this poem on the wall of a nursery in the home of a new parent. It had been hand-sewn by one of the parent's closest friends and given to her as a baby shower gift. Any parent will recognize that this poem is a sentimental and idealized image of raising children. The friend chose to ignore the aspects of parenting that do not lend themselves to soft words, happiness, and caring. What about the dirty diapers, temper tantrums, sleepless nights, and unending demands for "just one more cookie"?

If parents experienced the kind of week described in the poem, not only would the phenomenon of parent burnout be nonexistent, but the world would witness a tremendous population boom. The earth would be overrun with enchanted fulfilled parents and hordes of charming cooing children.

The reality of being a parent, of course, is far different from the classic depiction of fathers as benevolent saints and mothers as doting madonnas. Just as marriages are not "made in heaven" and career success is rarely achieved "overnight," children are not simply "bundles of joy."

Despite some recognition that the job of "parent" probably offers disappointments in equal measure with rewards, parents and nonparents alike continue to hold extremely unrealistic notions of what being a parent is all about.

Virtually everyone has an opinion on the characteristics of a good parent. There are shared visions of how mothers and fathers *should* act; about what parents *should* and *should not* do; about what they *should* say and even how they *should* look. One parent recently told us that her son did not want her coming to his school to meet his teacher and be seen by the other children because he thought that she was too fat and did not dress well enough. He was a third-grader!

"American society has the collective need to idealize mothering. If we didn't sell motherhood, no one would apply for the job." This quote from *Parents' Magazine* may be uncomfortably close to the truth. Many of the exaggerated expectations about parenting, that it will provide limitless fulfillment, that an absolute set of parenting ideals exist, or that children are predictable creatures easily added to any lifestyle, seem to be derived from some kind of national media blitz. The collective hype of parenting in books, magazines, television, and even greeting cards is overwhelming. As with all good advertising, the benefits are stretched to the borders of credibility and the drawbacks are minimized to microscopic proportions. The effect is all the more insidious because it works below the level of consciousness. Everyone approaches parenting with a set of hidden, ingrained expectations. These expectations are formed by subtle forces: basic personality traits, innate life values, and years of expectation tracklaying by one's own parents.

Although parents can consciously see the touch-ups in the glossy reproductions, unconsciously they have been overexposed. Their dreams, hopes, and wishes of how grand parenting can be have been laid bare, an easy prey to media exploitation. In spite of themselves, parents wind up believing in dangerous myths: "We will be as *parents* what we are not as persons—all-knowing, all-patient, all-caring. Indeed, if we fall short of these ideals, we are not worthy of having children. And our children will be as we were not: all-brilliant, all-praised, and all-satisfied. We will give them everything we never had when young."

Why are these myths so dangerous? The obvious answer is because they are untrue—impossible. Not all parents recover from the devastating realization that they do yell and scream when they are angry, that they are not endlessly patient or infinitely wise, that they are not able, as they had hoped, to meet each and every need of their children. Nor are those children miniature Einsteins, Thoreaus, or Roosevelts.

Although practical reasoning shows us that the parent ideal cannot be reality, the expectations placed upon the roles of father and mother are lofty. More importantly, these expectations, regardless of how utopian, are readily adopted as the standards by which parents often measure their success or failure. It is these expectations of themselves and of their children that lie at the root of the burnout phenomenon.

HOW EXPECTATIONS SET THE STAGE FOR BURNOUT

Consider Gloria: In many people's view, Gloria had it made—a very comfortable income, a promising career in accounting, a husband dedicated to his family life as well as his own banking profession, and three children, each progressing well in school with a cadre of well-behaved friends. Yet, Gloria (and her husband) grew listless, depressed, and increasingly viewed her life as meaningless.

How could someone seemingly so successful come to view herself and her pursuits as valueless? Of course, myriad circumstances, prior events, and predispositions may account for parts, or all, of Gloria's dissatisfaction. However, her perceptions of "success" in her career, in her marriage, and with her children illustrate how expectations can trigger the disillusionment associated with burnout.

When asked to describe her expectations of herself, Gloria wrote the following: "In my career, I should be the best. I should be the sharpest accountant in the office so that one day I can launch my own firm. My work should never interfere with my responsibility to my family, however. I must spend a lot of time with my children and husband. I should always be there when they need me and I should provide a home setting complete with cookies made from scratch and regular family outings on Sundays. To my husband, I should be a partner, confidante, seductress and keen bridge player."

Taken all together, Gloria's expectations tell her that to be successful, she must be "all things to all people at all times." The standards she has set for herself are exceedingly high. She does not merely *want* to be the best mother, wife, and career person, she *expects* nothing less than the best from herself.

While high standards of self-performance often motivate a person to strive for improvement, those same high standards can backfire, causing a great deal of guilt and feelings of failure. Those standards must allow for a generous measure of self-forgiveness and an ever-present recognition that standards for oneself are goals to be achieved, not rules that always must apply.

Gloria's expectations for her life are most commendable. But her expectations are too high, they leave no room for her to be anything less than perfect. When asked, "What happens when you don't live up to these expectations of yourself?" Gloria said, "I get angry, depressed, tense, anxious. When I have to stay at the office a little late or have to do some work on Saturdays, I feel that I'm not a good mother. When I spend my time with my children being the epitome of Betty Crocker, I am guilty about not aggressively pursuing my career goals and I become convinced that I don't really have what it takes to be successful in the professional working world. The end result is that I can't think of one thing that I truly am good at doing. Eventually, I start to back away from trying to do anything because I convince myself I won't do it well enough."

Holding to excessively high expectations often leads to repeated disappointments if no room is left for human frailty and fallibility. Disappointments not only can impede a person's progress, but can also launch a retreat from new goals. Self-anger for not living up to those expectations, and the accompanying guilt, can provoke adoption of the attitude: "I don't do anything right, so why try?"

What does "doing it right" mean? The standards by which parental success are measured may be largely at fault. Many parents are led to believe that a world exists that is populated with obedient children and contented adults. This image belies the truth of their own more mediocre existence.

CHILD CARE MANUALS AND PARENTING GUIDES

The sources for this misconception of what parenting—and children—are all about are multitudinous. Sadly, some of the major perpetrators of the myth are the "experts" themselves. Though many parenting guides contain valuable advice, they mislead readers through the conspicuous absence of other information. One often finds in these guides only parents who explain but never yell, forgive readily, never tire of entertaining a toddler, and who, in short, reap their greatest rewards in life from being a parent.

Many books focus solely on the needs of children. Parents' worries, ambivalent feelings, and problems are rarely explored. This leaves readers with the impression that "normal" or "good" parents must not have any doubts or negative attitudes toward their role of mothers and fathers. Even where ambivalent feelings are acknowledged, they often are analyzed minimally and dismissed blithely. For example, the following passage from *How to Parent*, by Fitzhugh Dodson, published in 1970, is still believed by many parents:

"Remember that for thousands of years mothers have tried to overcome these twin ogres of Inadequacy and Resentment. You can do it too . . . You will have unpleasant times and you will probably cry a little. . . . Sooner or later, like millions of mothers before you, you will work your way through the psychological swamps of inadequacy and resentment and find yourself on dry land. When that happens, mother and child will assume their proper roles in a new type of 'we relationship.' "[1]

A few guides do acknowledge that parents will be away from their children at times, but they do not stress the *need* for private time or the corollary feelings of guilt accompanying recognition of that need. For instance, Dr. Lee Salk in his book *Preparing for Parenthood* entitled one chapter "Organizing a Life of Your Own Away from Your Baby." However, he concentrates his advice only on how to handle baby-sitters and the pros and cons of taking "baby" with you to restaurants. This manual makes no mention of the value of pursuing interests outside the home or the need for parents to seek emotional support from friends or other parents.

Worse, after extolling the virtues of parenthood, most guides go to great lengths to impress their readers with the importance of correct parenting and the dire consequences of not performing. "Taking parenthood for granted can have disastrous effects," warns one guide. Says another, "Parents completely shape their children's personalities during the first five years of life and what is done during that time is irreversible." The message to parents is clear: Being a parent is a joyful, satisfying experience, but make no mistakes because the fate of your children's lives is at stake.

Many child-rearing experts have promoted similar notions over the years. They periodically claim that children, given proper guidance, can be "toilet-trained in a day" or "reading before the age of three." Of course, children are not as malleable as many child care books would have us believe. As any parent can testify, children are not so much putty to be molded by their parents. Rather, each child has his or her own agenda, and often it is the parents who are shaped by the child's needs and not vice versa.

TELEVISION AND ADVERTISING

Child care books are not solely responsible for establishing the "good parent" criteria and the consequently high expectations parents hold for themselves. Just as the mass media has touched every part of our lives, television has helped form the public's concept of what makes a good parent.

[1] *How to Parent* (New York: New American Library/Signet, 1970), p. 34.

"Ozzie and Harriet" live on as standards by which to measure real-life parents. In this situation comedy, despite the minor trials of family life, the television parents always projected an image of total understanding, clear-cut leadership, and perfect harmony. Regardless of what dilemma the children presented, the mother and father could always come up with a resolution and a tidy moral by the time the closing credits ran. No matter how difficult the problem, the *good* TV parents could bring peace and happiness back to their living rooms within the allotted thirty minutes.

Skipping ahead to more contemporary programming, family shows such as "The Waltons" and "Eight Is Enough" dealt with more realistic family matters, but the themes and the end results were similar: The model of what a *good* parent is prevails in an idealistic form. Today, television can deal with more complex problems—death, divorce, and premarital sex—but throughout the family struggles, the parents still reign as the voices of reason, complete caring, and ultimate devotion. Standard weekly programming rarely depicts parents who are slowly withdrawing from their children, living with the day-to-day frustrations of balancing economic needs, or coping with a chronically belligerent and delinquent teenager.

On a conscious level, viewers know that all family crises are not resolved so easily. But television reaches people on a more subtle, less than conscious level as well, establishing and reinforcing expectations of what parental traits are necessary to a successful homelife. The Ingalls parents of "Little House on the Prairie" could become the subconscious ideal that is never reached!

And then there are the commercials. Consider, for example, the advertisement for a fabric softener with "added whitening power." The mother in the commercial exclaims, "How would it look if my son went to school with a gray, dingy T-shirt on? What kind of mother would I be?" The implicit message is that she would be a bad mother; good mothers make sure that their sons have sparkling T-shirts.

Some commercials pay lip service to the reality that mothers often have to work as well as parent. One commerical opens with a young boy in the kitchen reading a note posted on the refrigerator door and then lifting the advertised product to an automatic can opener. The voice of the boy's mother is heard, saying, "I can't always be there when they get home, but at least I can make sure my children have something wholesome for a snack." Although the commercial recognizes that many mothers do have full-time jobs, it still implies that good mothers must provide this or that homey touch, even when at work.

In addition to the ads directed to adults, the Saturday morning television hours are packed with specific appeals to children. The ads for toys and cereals, which dominate the time, are based on the assumption that if the kids are convinced that they "need" the products, then they will exert pressure on their parents to buy a continuous stream of new dolls, candy, and bubble gum.

Most parents can testify that their children can mount quite a campaign to buy *Star Wars* paraphernalia, video games, or Count Chocula cereal. For the burning-out parent particularly, simply putting up the money for these products may seem the easiest way to stop their children's nagging. If they don't have the money, parents may keep themselves aloof from the children to avoid the demands.

Parents who are burning out often turn to television as part of their withdrawal from life. As burnout begins, their cognitive abilities begin to wane and the parents become more subject to the emotional, expectation-laden messages of television programs and commercials. As they imbibe larger and larger doses of these messages, their feelings of inadequacy become exaggerated. What is supposed to be relaxation becomes, in fact, another source of distress.

THE CONSUMING SOCIETY

Television plays a large role in perpetuating the trend of measuring success by material acquisitions. Americans particularly have "bought into" the idea of keeping up with the Joneses. Many expectations revolve around the power to amass "things." The attainment of these things—big houses, luxury cars, foreign vacations, designer jeans, microwave ovens—is not only viewed as necessary evidence of success, but the things are also seen as *solutions* to problems.

Television reinforces the consuming standard by encouraging in viewers conscious or unconscious thoughts such as: "My life feels lousy. TV implies that my life is lousy. TV tells me that a new car would make my life less lousy. But I can't afford a new car, so I feel even lousier." For those who believe that material wealth is the key to resolving life's issues, inability to participate in the madly consuming world is a further frustration and further evidence that they are not living up to their expectations.

Most parents probably would deny that providing material wealth is an essential part of good parenting. But the sales records of the nation's child-oriented businesses tell another story. The tragedy is that buying many things for their children may supplant parental focus on imparting other qualities such as honesty and self-reliance to their children. Most parents try to meet both expectations.

MOM AND SUPERMOM

In the last twenty years, the roles that women have undertaken have changed dramatically. Economic pressures and raised consciousness have motivated women to more active places in the work force. Over time, the standards for mothers have altered. In addition to carrying on as loving, domestic homemakers, mothers now must be tough, business-minded professionals.

Alice, the young mother of two preschoolers, explained: "I'm lucky, I guess. My husband makes a great salary, so I don't have to work. But I feel guilty that I don't have a job. I even find myself avoiding telling people that I'm only a housewife. All my life I was told that when I grew up I'd be a mother and a wife. I never expected or wanted anything more. I enjoy raising my kids on a full-time basis, but when I look around and see all the women who are lawyers, doctors, or whatever, and parents, too, I ask myself, 'Why are you so dumb?' If other women can do both the career and home scenes well, what's wrong with me?'"

The myth of "supermom" has come into being. The original intention of the women's movement was to expand the options available to women, to convey the message: Being a tax accountant is a legitimate role for women. Likewise, being a mother is okay, as is being a pilot, a nurse, an engineer, a housewife, or any combination of the above. Unfortunately, the optional emphasis of this message seems to have gotten lost. Instead, society's message to women seems to be: "You should be all things to all people. You should be a loving wife, tender, compassionate mother, *and* a successful career woman." The supermom expectation doesn't give new options to women—it simply adds more duties to the original job description. A supermom is supposed to wake at 6 A.M., jog two miles, fix a hot breakfast, bundle herself and family off to jobs and school, close several business deals, and when the children are asleep, turn into an alluring sex object for her husband.

Working Mother magazine and other publications epitomize these heightened expectations of the modern woman. The magazines are an amalgam of job-interviewing tips, recipes, articles on day care, promising career opportunities, beauty advice, and office politics. The publications, through their dual emphasis on home and work, reinforce the growing belief that not only is being a supermom an achievable goal, but it is the desirable life goal for women today.

Needless to say, attempting to live up to the supermom myth is a quest full of pressures and conflicting values. Yet, many women have adopted this goal as their own individual pursuit.

However, just as the perfect-parent stereotype was unrealistic, so is the supermom ideal. Many women have their feet planted in very contradictory cultures. One culture says: Concentrate on your nurturing; be there for your children; your satisfaction is to be found giving to others. The other culture tells women: Be autonomous; make your achievements solely your own; satisfaction will come by making an individual statement to the world. Standing with each foot in a different world is okay as long as those worlds stay relatively close to one another. Unfortunately, in the case of the supermom, the expectations of mother-at-home and mother-on-the-job frequently are very far apart from one another. Thus, the woman may find herself pulled in two opposite directions—a human wishbone, split by the demands she may place on herself as a "traditional" mother and those she adopts as a contemporary careerist.

When expectations collide in this way, the effect can be damaging. And women—or mothers—are not alone in their susceptibility to conflicting expectations. Fathers can experience the phenomenon of wanting to be too many things to their children, of having goals that are mutually exclusive, of straining to be in two places at the same time. David, a lawyer in his mid-thirties, and father of three,

experiences this dilemma sharply. He works hard to provide the
financial comfort for his children that he never had, but he also
tries to be present as often as possible to provide the emotional support his children need. These expectations conflict, causing David
constant self-examination and self-recrimination.

"I work as hard as I do mainly because I want my children to
have all the advantages I didn't have as a kid . . . you know, private schools, Ivy League colleges, the works," says David. His work
frequently requires twelve-hour days and overnight travel, causing
guilt feelings that he is not meeting their other needs. "I sometimes
wonder if my kids will grow up to feel that they never really knew
me because I wasn't there enough. I wonder if they will resent me.
Even now, I feel extremely guilty when I'm with them and they
automatically turn to their mother for help or attention because
they aren't accustomed to me being there to fulfill their day-to-day
needs. And I feel guilty when one of them says, 'Oh, Daddy, do you
have to go away again?' Or when one of them asks me to do something and I can't because I have to work. The disappointment on
their faces cuts me to the quick. At those times I ask myself: 'Is the
money I'm making worth all of this?' "

Don't be mistaken—maintaining a career and a family is not impossible. Countless men and women are successful at both en-
deavors. The key, as with all expectations, is that the demands you
place on yourself are not so unreasonably high that achieving some
success in both areas is possible.

MEASURING PARENTAL STRESS

The parents' ability to assess how well they are doing in any
given area is the key to their sense of satisfaction and well-being.
Furthermore, being able to determine, with some degree of relia-
bility, successes and shortcomings prevents parents from falling
prey to self-imposed or externally imposed expectations that may be
unrealistically high or unattainable.

For example, if Gloria—described earlier in this chapter—could
assess her efforts as an accountant realistically and know that she
was doing an admirable job, her self-expectation that she be the
best accountant would become a goal, not the yardstick by which
she measured all her current deficiencies. Instead of saying, "I'm

not the best so I must not be very good," she needs to be able to say, "I'm doing fairly well. Eventually, I hope to be the best." The lack of clear ways to determine individual success in parenting allows parents to perpetuate the lofty societal expectations reinforced by the sentimental, idealistic depiction of mothers and fathers on television, in advertising, and in many child care books.

THE PARENTS OF PARENTS

Michael's father was a yeller, a screamer, and a hitter. His hair-trigger temper often was directed at his children. Michael, now a father himself, bitterly resented his father's behavior and now contends a good father does not have such outbursts at his children. As a result, Michael feels very guilty when he is the least bit angry with his children. While he certainly never replicates his father's stormy behavior, Michael finds that even momentary episodes of raising his voice or speaking angry words to his children make him feel as if he's not measuring up to his own view of good fathering.

Sarah, on the other hand, idolized her mother, a woman who spent virtually every spare moment doing something for her children—knitting sweaters, chauffeuring the children and their friends, cooking special meals with fancy desserts. Sarah, with three children of her own, must now work full time as a bookkeeper to supplement her husband's salary. This leaves her little time for preparing elaborate meals, making doll clothes, or doing any of the "extras" her mother had done for her. Despite the fact that Sarah's mother never held paid employment, Sarah often feels that she is not the mother she envisioned she should be because she does not do all the things her own mother did. "I feel that I'm letting my children down," Sarah says. "I just am not as good a mother as my own mother was."

In these, as in many cases, parents behave toward their own children as they wanted to be treated as children; to succeed for their own children, where their parents failed them. Often, this expectation is reflected in the statement: "My children will have all the opportunities I did not have as a child." One might, however, replace "opportunities" with words like "love," "independence," or "closeness."

Marlene, for instance, says that one of her expectations as a parent is "to allow and encourage my children to meet life head on, experience everything, without me intruding on their freedom." Marlene's mother, she says, was the classic "doting, overprotective" parent. "She made me fear life and made me very dependent on everyone around me," Marlene claims. "I'll never do that to my kids," she vows.

Parents try to be the perfection for their children that they wanted for themselves. But an unrelenting quest for perfection, more often than not, leads to disappointment.

PARENTS' EXPECTATIONS OF THEIR CHILDREN

"I'm not sure it's worth it anymore," Eric declares. When asked what's not worth it, he exclaims, "Everything, just everything." Eric is forty-two years old, a self-made businessman in retail sales. When questioned further, his frustration seems to center around his three teenage children. "I've tried everything. I've given them cars, trips, telephones in their rooms, anything they ever asked for, somehow I managed to get it for them," Eric complains. "They just don't appreciate anything. They take everything I do for granted. Don't get me wrong," he continues. "I don't mean that I just bought them things. I spent time with them, too—you know, Little League, Father-Daughter dinners, camping trips, the whole bit. But I still don't think they know or care about me."

Like most self-employed businessmen, Eric spends long hours at his store. And recently, the long hours have gotten longer. "I don't see any point in coming home. My kids are never there. They have their own friends, parties, and whatever. My wife has her friends, her clubs, her job, and her shopping sprees. So what's the point?" asks Eric.

In the early days of his marriage, Eric had to work the twelve-hour days. The business was just getting off the ground, and feeding three small children took a good chunk of the small profits. Now, however, with the business a proven success, with employees to manage the day-to-day affairs, Eric doesn't really have to work as hard as he used to. Furthermore, he doesn't really enjoy the business as he did in previous years.

Why does he continue the breakneck pace? "I can get lost in it," he claims. "I'm really not accomplishing a lot but at least I know that I'm successful here. Sales go up so I figure I've done a good job. I thought I was doing a good job at home with the kids, too, but how can you tell?"

Eric did not go to college. He launched his business with a small loan from his parents and married his high school girl friend. "I loved her then and I love her now, but I expected things to be different for us," Eric explains. "I thought the business would flourish into still other businesses. Independently wealthy, that was my goal. I've done all right, I suppose." Eric paused. "But the kids . . . it's just not what I thought it would be like. I imagined that I would be my children's adviser, friend—that they would come to me with their problems. I was going to be trusted, old reliable Dad, but it seems like I'm not even missed except at bill-paying time."

Eric's resentment, disappointment, and withdrawal are typical of the burned-out parent whose expectations for his children, as well as for himself as a parent, have not been met.

DISAPPOINTED EXPECTATIONS

Eric's anticipations of gratitude and respect for all of his giving are among the many expectations parents may have for their children from the cradle into adulthood. For example, they may expect that their children be healthy, well adjusted, smart, friendly, or any one of a thousand other qualities. But what happens when these expectations are not met? What if the child is frail or contracts a serious illness? What if the child is hyperactive? Or what if the child does not learn as quickly as other children? What if the child gets into repeated trouble at school or in later years? Or has a problem with drugs or alcohol abuse?

When parents' expectations of their children are not met, the immediate, most common reaction is, "What did I do wrong?" Frequently, parents readily accept the blame for any and all of their children's problems. The net effect is that parents believe and expect that they are the sole guardians of their children's behavior and lives. And when something goes awry, the parents assume "it must be my fault." And even if they don't think it is their fault, parents often believe they must rectify the problem.

Feelings of disillusionment and disappointment are greatly exacerbated when parents have children who are having special difficulties intellectually, emotionally, physically, or socially. It is estimated that in the United States today, approximately 40 percent of all school-age children are not capable of performing up to par because of some physical or psychological problem, learning disability, or difficulty in socialization. Parenting a child with one of these problems, however "mild," can add a significant amount of stress to the parents' life.

Often, parents' expectations for themselves are so much a part of the fabric of their lives that they don't know they hold them. It may take a little help to uncover one's expectations. The two checklists will help you gauge the number and types of expectations you hold.

EXPECTATION CHECKLIST #1

Put a check next to the statements that generally describe the expectations that you hold for yourself as a parent:

_____ 1. I should listen to my children more.

_____ 2. I should provide my kids with a better standard of living than I had when growing up.

_____ 3. I should know my children's friends well.

_____ 4. I should not raise my voice in anger with my children.

_____ 5. I should spend more time with my children.

_____ 6. I should inspire my children to lead productive, healthy lives.

_____ 7. I should be an available shoulder for my kids to cry on.

_____ 8. I should be a friend as well as a parent to my children.

_____ 9. I should be firm, but understanding with my children.

_____ 10. I should be able to give my children the things and opportunities I did not have as a child.

_____ 11. I should be a role model of success for my children.

_____ 12. I should take more of an active part in my children's interests.

_____ 13. I should appear strong and dependable to my children.

_____ 14. I should be viewed by my children as someone in whom they can always confide.

EXPECTATION CHECKLIST #2

In your mind, turn back the clock. Before you had children, what were your visions of them? What were your hopes, expectations? Place a check beside the statements that describe your expectations of your children before you became a parent.

_____ 1. My children will be smart.

_____ 2. My children will be hard-working.

_____ 3. My children will be attractive.

_____ 4. My children will share my outlook on life.

_____ 5. My children will respect me.

_____ 6. My children will be loving.

_____ 7. My children will be healthy.

_____ 8. My children will follow in my footsteps.

_____ 9. My children will rely on me for advice.

_____ 10. My children will be creative.

_____ 11. My children will be a source of comfort to me in my old age.

_____ 12. My children will have a better life than I did as a child.

_____ 13. My children will be friendly.

_____ 14. My children will be more successful than I am.

Scoring: Add up the number of statements that you checked on both lists (a total of twenty-eight statements). If you checked more than fourteen statements, you most likely hold a set of expectations that inevitably, through no fault of your own, will never be met. By identifying more than half of these statements as standards to which you hold yourself accountable, you may be setting yourself up to be terribly disappointed.

The key, of course, is the degree to which parents believe these expectations must be fulfilled. Frustration is bound to set in if you feel that you must always adhere to these standards. Parents often hold expectations of themselves that may be mutually exclusive. For instance, perhaps they believe that their children should experience a better standard of living than they did as children. Fulfilling this expectation, particularly in times of high inflation, may require working longer hours or taking on a second job. This naturally means less time with the children. If they also believe that being good parents requires spending a considerable amount of time with the family, expectations are on a collision course.

This duality leads to a great deal of conflict. The parents' reasoning may go like this: "I can't be a good parent if I don't provide for my child's material needs, college costs, and other necessities. It is my responsibility to do this for my child so I'll just work more. On the other hand, I can't be a good parent unless I have the time to spend with my kids."

Realistically, it is impossible to enter parenthood with no expectations. But the task at hand is to restructure those expectations so that they better reflect reality. Parenting—like all aspects of life—has its negatives and positives; its fulfillments and disappointments. The parent who learns to see the muted tones between will best be able to thrive during any hard times and prevent the onset of burnout.

4

Foundations of Burnout II: The Stress Response

Stress. You hear your four-year-old daughter suddenly shrieking in the backyard. You rush outside, blood pumping, mind totally alert and ready to deal with a potential crisis.

Stress. Your boss rushes into your office five minutes before quitting time, asking you to stay late to finish a report. With stomach churning and pulse racing, you quickly decide how to handle the problem of finding a sitter for the kids, who are expecting you at home.

Stress. You have just brought a newborn infant home. His cries for food at 2 A.M. initially startle you awake. But instantly alert, you can soothe the baby, mix the formula, heat bottles, and feed your son, smoothly, efficiently, almost effortlessly.

In all these instances of stress, the human body and mind reacted as intended: They responded to a sudden change and took action to adapt to or to alleviate the stressor. A child was comforted after a fall from a swing. A sitter was found after a few phone calls. An infant was fed; his needs, though new to the family, were met and accommodated.

These are all very simple, common examples of what stress is and how it affects people. Unfortunately, stress is capable of producing much more complex and damaging reactions and symptoms, usually because of its *duration*, not necessarily its *intensity*.

Amy is a prime example of chronic high stress. A twenty-seven-year-old mother who works as a bank teller, she is torn apart by the conflicting demands of parenting in today's world—being a mother and working to help support the family. Speaking of her "no-win" situation, she says: "I went to work when my two sons were ages four and one. I hate my job but my income is essential to support my family. I would prefer to be at home with the kids, but I can't. My husband also dislikes his job, but he can't quit working either because both paychecks are needed. I face each day with the same feelings: I dread going to work, and feel I'm cheating my children by being away so much."

Amy summarizes her Monday-through-Friday life in two words: guilt and dissatisfaction. "I go to the bank feeling guilty about leaving the kids. I come home promising myself that I will make up for my daytime absence by being particularly loving and attentive to them, but usually either there are a hundred house chores for me to do or I'm so aggravated from the job that I am irritable and impatient with the kids."

When asked if she sees any way out of the guilt and dissatisfaction, Amy replies, "I always hold out the hope for improvement or, at least, acceptance of the situation. But hope is all I have. What can I do to change things? I don't have any control over the amount of rent we pay or the price of milk, and it's those things that got me to go to work in the first place."

THE NATURE OF STRESS

Amy cannot escape from the conflicting requirements of family and work. She feels constant pressure as she adapts to the new demands that are placed on her. Chronic stress of this kind is an age-old problem and studies about it abound in recent medical and psychological literature. However, in spite of all of this interest, there are still some common misunderstandings. We would like to clarify some of these in this chapter and demonstrate how stress is a major foundation for parent burnout.

The most succinct and applicable definition of stress was made by Dr. Hans Selye, an endocrinologist.[1] He defined it as "the nonspecific response of the body to any demand made on it." Selye

[1] *The Stress of Life* (New York: McGraw-Hill, 1956, revised edition, 1976) and *Stress Without Distress* (Philadelphia: Lippincott, 1974).

saw stress as critical for life and growth. In fact, the failure to react to a stressor is an indication of death.

Stress, then, occurs whenever the body or mind or both have to respond to something that takes place outside of themselves. However, when the body and mind seek to adjust to the new situation, the stress involved demands an expenditure of human energy. And each human being has a finite amount of energy. Unless the energy can be replenished, the well can go dry under the continuing demand of numerous and increasing stressors. In the case of parents, family life often does not allow sufficient time to restore lost energy supplies.

Sometimes the causes or triggers of these stressors are sharp, as when the child shrieks in the backyard. Other stressors are less acute and permit adjustment to take place over time. A new baby, a change in residence, vacation, or the Christmas season always cost some adjustment energy. Many stressors are not recognized. Some lie beneath the surface in such situations as report card time, an in-law's visit, or evening meals. Though individuals are not consciously aware of the impact, the body and mind do respond.

Stress, then, is due to change; the more *continual* the change, the greater the stress and, eventually, the less one is able to deal with it as energy runs out. The following rating scale will help you assess the amount of stress in your life. This scale is the result of some pioneering research on stress by Dr. Thomas H. Holmes and Dr. Richard H. Rahe. It is widely used.

SOCIAL READJUSTMENT RATING SCALE[2]

Instructions: Look over the events listed below. Place a check in the space provided if it has happened to you within the last twelve months.

			Points
1.	Death of a spouse	1._____	100
2.	Divorce	2._____	73
3.	Marital separation	3._____	65
4.	Jail term	4._____	63

[2] Reprinted with permission from the *Journal of Psychosomatic Research*, Vol. 11, 213–18, Thomas H. Holmes and Richard H. Rahe, "The Holmes and Rahe Social Readjustment Rating Scale," copyright © 1967, Pergamon Press, Ltd.

5.	Death of a close family member	5._____	63
6.	Personal injury or illness	6._____	53
7.	Marriage	7._____	50
8.	Fired at work	8._____	47
9.	Marital reconciliation	9._____	45
10.	Retirement from work	10._____	45
11.	Change in health of family member	11._____	44
12.	Pregnancy	12._____	40
13.	Sex difficulties	13._____	39
14.	Gain of new family member	14._____	39
15.	Business readjustment	15._____	38
16.	Change in financial state	16._____	37
17.	Death of a close friend	17._____	36
18.	Change to different line of work	18._____	36
19.	Change in number of arguments with spouse	19._____	35
20.	Mortgage or loan for major purchase (home, etc.)	20._____	31
21.	Foreclosure of mortgage or loan	21._____	30
22.	Change in responsibilities at work	22._____	29
23.	Son or daughter leaving home	23._____	29
24.	Trouble with in-laws	24._____	29
25.	Outstanding personal achievement	25._____	28
26.	Spouse begins or stops work outside the home	26._____	26
27.	Begin or end school	27._____	26
28.	Change in living conditions	28._____	25
29.	Revision of personal habits	29._____	24
30.	Trouble with boss	30._____	23
31.	Change in work hours or conditions	31._____	20
32.	Change in residence	32._____	20
33.	Change in schools	33._____	20
34.	Change in recreation	34._____	19
35.	Change in church activities	35._____	19
36.	Change in social activities	36._____	18
37.	Mortgage or loan for lesser purchase (car, TV, etc.)	37._____	17
38.	Change in sleeping habits	38._____	16
39.	Change in the number of family get-togethers	39._____	15

40.	Change in eating habits	40._____	15
41.	Vacation	41._____	13
42.	Christmas	42._____	12
43.	Minor violations of the law	43._____	11

Scoring: . Add up the number of points next to each of your check marks. Place the total in the space below.

My score: _____

Interpretation: Drs. Holmes and Rahe have shown the relationship between recent life changes (exposure to stressors) and future illness. Listed below are the score categories and the related probability of illness during the next two years for a person scoring in that range.

0–149	No significant problem
150–199	Mild stress with a 35 percent chance of illness
200–299	Moderate stress with a 50 percent chance of illness
300 or over	Major stress with an 80 percent chance of illness

A fundamental assumption of the researchers is that it will take approximately one year to replenish the energy expended in adjusting to any of the changes described in the scale. The potential debilitating effect that exposure to too many stressors has on the health of the individual should be clear.

EUSTRESS AND DISTRESS

Few people regard any stress as positive. However, stressors are neither inherently positive nor negative. All require the expenditure of energy to adapt to the changing situation. All can lead to exhaustion. But some stressors are endured because the results are seen as beneficial: like having a baby. The stress is very high, but the consequences are seen as worth the cost.

When the level of stress allows significant time for adaptation and replenishment of energy, an individual can perform at optimum levels. This is called *eustress.* When stress is continuous and the loss of energy prevents adaptation, exhaustion occurs. This is called *distress,* a far more familiar concept and term to most people than *eustress.* Figure 2 illustrates the positive and negative results of stress.

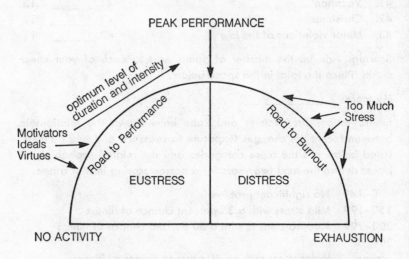

THE RELATIONSHIP BETWEEN EUSTRESS AND DISTRESS

Figure 2

The diagram clearly shows that the absence of stress leads to no action—a state of lethargy and lack of performance. Motivators are stressors that cause people to react and change. They can be concrete, such as income, prestige, or career advancement; or abstract, such as personal or moral ideals. The motivators get people going and keep them moving until they are doing their best. Once that stage is reached, the trick is to stay there. At this level of peak performance, energy replenishment must balance energy use. Once the person passes the peak, the demand on energy is exceeding the supply.

It is important to recognize the symptoms of distress. Early signals are a feeling of tiredness and physical ailments such as lower back pain, increased pulse rate, higher blood pressure, increased tension, and gastrointestinal disorders. If the intensity and duration of the stressors are not reduced, or if they are increased or new ones are added, the individual probably will continue down the road of distress to burnout with the accompanying lower levels of performance. Laura's situation illustrates this. She tried to be the perfect mother, wife, entertainer, and even career woman. She found herself only wanting to go to bed after a time. Her performance declined in all the areas. She could not complete projects she started and did not have any desire to take on new challenges.

Signals that one is on the road to complete exhaustion are irritability, "short fuses," and avoidance of socializing. As the stressors accumulate and intensify, one feels overloaded and finds it very difficult and burdensome to concentrate. At this point—a crucial stage—a strong desire to be alone sets in. A general feeling of always having to meet someone else's needs occurs. A sense of boredom and entrapment is common as well.

People often turn to popping pills, usually tranquilizers, or drinking alcohol heavily to relieve their internal pain. Just before complete exhaustion and chronic high distress, individuals experience a spreading distrust of others, bordering on paranoia. They question basic and sometimes lifelong values and beliefs. "Is all of this really worth it?" "I have been a good person all my life and where did it get me?" It is very common for people at this point to conclude that a major change in their lives is necessary.

The stages of distress parallel those of burnout. As stress persists without relief, a person proceeds through the burnout stages.

THE SOURCES OF STRESS

Stressors come in three main varieties: physical, mental, and situational. The stresses of parenting are largely situational. However, they are compounded by any physical or mental stressors that affect the parent.

Physiological Causes

The physiological causes of stress include heredity, biological rhythms and cycles, diet, exercise, and rest. Some people are more prone to stress due to congenital or genetic reasons. It is not clear whether this proclivity for stress is inherited or results from early conditioning, or both. Likewise, some factors that develop during pregnancy may have an impact on the development of stress. For instance, the use of certain drugs or medications could result in a chemical imbalance in the system that affects the occurrence or intensity of the stress response.

Biological rhythms and cycles also have long been associated with stress. Some of these cycles are brief, and affect only a small part of the body. Others can last years and affect the entire body. The menstrual cycle of women is one of the more widely recognized. Many others include such functions as pulse rate, body temperature, body weight, stamina, and mental capability. These rhythms and cycles are interrelated and interdependent in a complex fashion. Their synchronization ensures that the body will maintain an internal and external balance. During critical periods of adjustment—such as the beginning of a cycle—stress is likely to be pronounced. The stress often causes the disconnection of the rhythms, which threatens the balance of the body.

Diet is a third physical source of stress. The mind as well as the body needs nutrition to function well. The need is more essential in stressful situations. The body under stress requires more energy to help it adapt. Nutrients feed this energy-producing process. A person can deplete his or her energy supply, and with no further resources available, become exhausted in an attempt to continue functioning. The need for a healthy and balanced diet to cope with stress is obvious.

The amount and intensity of exercise are additional major physiological factors in stress. Physical exercise clearly affects psychological well-being. Muscles that are not exercised enough become shortened, flabby, and inelastic. They lose their ability to release tension. This results in back pains, stiff necks, and headaches. Poor posture, as a result of little exercise and weak muscles, makes the problem worse. It reflects lack of self-confidence and often leads to a lower self-image.

The amount of rest is the last physiological factor in stress. Fatigue is symptomatic of a temporary loss of or an inadequate supply of energy. Usually fatigue results from too many stressors that were too intense within a given period of time. Fatigue may be due to simple things such as overexertion or more complex situations like heavy cigarette smoking, excessive drinking, heart disease, or anemia. It often predisposes a person to stress-related illnesses.

Stress, then, may result both from phenomena that can be controlled and from those that are beyond the control of individuals.

Parents need to learn to distinguish between the two—biological cycles and diet or rest, for example. They must accommodate to the conditions that they cannot control, and recognize those conditions over which they do have power.

Psychological Causes

Personality: A super-cause. One of the most important bases of stress is personality. A famous study[3] by two cardiologists, Meyer Friedman and Ray H. Rosenman, pointed out that there are two basic personality types, which they labeled Type A and Type B. The types relate to the kind of behavior demonstrated rather than any locked-in personality traits. Type A personalities are very competitive, impatient, always trying to beat the clock, short-fused, irritable, driving, and rather hostile. They have difficulty tolerating ambiguity and resent words like "perhaps" and "uncertain." They have a lot of trouble dealing with "loose ends." They demand much of those around them and have a low degree of tolerance for errors or shortcomings. A Type A father generally will be dissatisfied with his child's report card if it shows even one or two B's or B+'s as opposed to all A's.

Type B personalities are basically low-keyed, relaxed, deliberative, and friendly. They are able to understand and accept change and are more tolerant of complex and ambivalent situations. The researchers found that Type A personalities were much more prone to suffer stress-related illnesses, especially heart disease.

Perfectionism is critical to burnout. It motivates parents to keep increasing the intensity and duration of the stressors. Perfectionist parents are generally highly rational, logical, systematic, and organized. Their minds usually supersede their feelings and passions. They are "by the book" parents. They are fact-oriented and not overly sympathetic to the emotional difficulties of their children. They have a tendency to "reason" things out.

There are several causes of perfectionism. First, how perfectionist parents were parented themselves and how feelings and authority were handled in their childhood are important.

A second critical factor in perfectionism is idealism. Idealistic parents believe that everything that is going to take place in family life should and could be positive.

[3] *Type A Behavior and Your Heart* (New York: Knopf, 1974).

Albert Ellis, a leading psychologist, points out that some individuals have a tendency to create several major "musts" for themselves.[4] For idealists these "musts" are even more magnified and they live their lives, as Karen Horney once noted, by the "tyranny of the shoulds."[5] These are some of the more common "shoulds" of mothers and fathers who burn out:

1. *The strong need for success and approval:* Parents feel that their efforts at child rearing and guidance should achieve nothing short of complete success. Furthermore, this complete success should be fully rewarded and publicly acclaimed. It is important to keep in mind that the need a person is trying to fulfill dominates his or her consciousness. Parents who have this need are very sensitive to what they consider to be anything less than total achievement and approval. They are supersensitive to any lack of appreciation or any form of rejection, no matter how slight.

2. *The strong need for consideration:* Often, idealistic parents feel that they should *always* receive kindness and consideration. When they do not receive the levels of consideration they think they deserve, they overreact in their blame, anger, and resentment. What often are the results of simple forgetfulness or adolescent indifference or teenage selfishness are blown all out of proportion and viewed as "ego bruises."

3. *The strong need for appreciation:* Idealistic parents need immediate reinforcement for their behaviors, particularly their "giving" behaviors. They are often compulsive in their yearning for constant rewards. The need for appreciation becomes intensified when the parents feel that they have undergone some form of pain or deprivation, in short, when they have paid some price. They often express amazement at the lack of gratification extended to them by their children. When the rewards are not returned on the initiative of the children, the parents frequently demand it either indirectly, by letting everyone know how much they have done or suffered for their children, or directly and explicitly: "Keep in mind, Dave, if it wasn't for me, you would not be where you are today." In either case, this behavior on the part of the parents is resented by the children.

[4] *Reason and Emotion in Psychotherapy* (New York: Lyle Stuart, 1962).
[5] *Collected Works* (New York: W. W. Norton, 1942).

Individuals who have these kinds of absolute ideals are sure to create distress for themselves. They will be striving to meet goals that are really unattainable. And they will eventually burn out in the attempt.

The causes of idealism in parenting are many and diverse. Some are explicit and are transmitted through ethnic, religious, or cultural models of parenthood. Other sources are less obvious, but just as strong. These are usually transmitted by implication and are in the form of adages, maxims, even poetry. They appear in many forms: wall posters, books, decorative plates and flower pots, and greeting cards. Here are a few:

> *Men are what their mothers made them.*
> *—Ralph Waldo Emerson*[6]

> *The hand that rocks the cradle*
> *Is the hand that rules the world.*
> *—William Ross Wallace*[7]

> *All that I am or hope to be, I owe to my angel mother.*
> *—Attributed to Abraham Lincoln*[8]

> *God could not be everywhere, so He created mothers.*
> *—A popular proverb*

Idealistic parents take these and similar messages seriously. They believe them and respond to them, often subconsciously, hoping that they can live up to them.

Emotional Causes. In addition to personality, several other psychological factors cause stress. Fear, worry, guilt, and other emotions can serve the useful purpose of self-protection. However, they become distressful and detract from high quality performance when they are intensified out of proportion. In fact, they can literally immobilize a parent.

Because parent burnout victims are not focused on the present, they become prime candidates for being overwhelmed by any or all

[6] *Emerson* p. 1350 *The Home Book of Quotations.* New York: Dodd, Mead, 1967.

[7] *Wallace* p. 562 *Oxford Dictionary of Quotations.* Oxford University Press, 1979.

[8] *Lincoln* p. 1350 *The Home Book of Quotations.* New York: Dodd, Mead, 1967.

of these emotions. For instance, fear occurs when people think about the future. They become prone to burnout when they dwell on potential future disasters. Several parents of young children we interviewed expressed fear that they would not be able to provide for the future of their children. Parents said things like, "With the economy the way it is, how will I get my children through college?"

While parents who worry about the future fall prey to fear and anxiety because of potential undisclosed threats, parents who worry about the past usually are plagued by guilt. They have a strong drive to make up for some imagined or magnified real wrong. They remain angry at themselves and other people or situations that caused some dreadful past event. While the future-oriented parent spends much time saying, "I will be happy when" or "I can't wait until . . ." the past-oriented parent wearily ponders, "If I had only . . ."

Barbara and Jenny live in the same Maryland neighborhood and are good friends. Each in her own way induces distress by her respective time orientation. Barbara has "disaster fantasies" that her son, age ten, will, through no fault of her own, let her down someday. "Watch, here I am killing myself to give my son everything and provide him with the best values and he will probably go off and marry some college sweetheart who will change him so that he will ridicule all that I have taught him. Besides he'll probably end up living in California and I'll only see him once every three years!"

Jenny, on the other hand, spends most of her time reconstructing past parenting decisions. "If we had only sent Matthew to St. Jane's School for the elementary grades, he wouldn't be having this difficulty in high school now."

Situational Causes

There are several situational factors that are closely linked with high distress and burnout among parents: responsibility without control; pace of change; new technology; sex and drugs; and economic conditions. Parents, particularly those who care, are prime candidates for the potential devastation of each of these.

If stress is the response of the body to a demand put on it, then there can be few greater stressors then the *situation* of parenting itself. Parents have brought change into their lives that is more or less permanent. Although a child's demands change, their *demanding* remains constant. Child rearing is a situational stressor, causing the parent to adapt and expend vital energy constantly. The challenge to the parent—as with all people under stress—is to find a way to replenish the energy. Unfortunately, the circumstances of parenting do not lend themselves to usual coping strategies. There are stressors *within* the stressor that increase the chances of exhaustion and burnout even in parents with the most temperate dispositions and moderate expectations.

Responsibility Without Control. One of the most severe circumstantial stressors is what many parents call having responsibility without control. Unquestionably, today, more than twenty years ago, many issues of child rearing are beyond family control. The world has crept into our living rooms and eroded the ability of many parents to raise their children the way they want.

Once the average American family consisted of a father who worked and a mother who didn't. Today, the "typical" family more likely consists of a divorced working mother with two or more children in school or a day care center. One out of every five families with children under eighteen years of age is headed by a single parent. In fact, fewer people are "staying together for the children." "Divorce is such an accepted way of life these days," says Myra, "I can't say with any certainty that it won't happen to me as a parent. I feel that erodes my ability to ensure my children's security."

The awareness of having responsibility without control is evident in Carla's statement: "Having two incomes in our family is absolutely necessary. I don't have the luxury of choosing not to work and neither do most people I know. Putting clothes on my children's backs and food on the table depends on two paychecks." Today's economy is definitely out of parents' control, yet they still have the responsibility to provide for their children.

Many parents report an increased amount of peer pressure, especially among adolescents, compared with a generation ago. By the time children enter high school, parents also report, peer pressure supersedes parental influence, particularly in the areas of premarital sex and drug use. "She's sixteen," complained Lois, "and she listens to her boyfriend more than me. I know that she has had sex with him, but what can I do? If I ban her from seeing him, she'll just sneak out behind my back. I can't stop it."

Said Arthur, "I have tried to teach my children about the dangers of using drugs, but I can't watch over a fourteen-year-old every minute of the day. Who knows how far a teenager will go just to be accepted by his friends?"

In all these instances, parents expressed the feeling that they were still responsible for the outcome of their children's development, but at the same time they also knew that their influence over their children's lives was increasingly limited. This low autonomy with high responsibility is a stressor. It affects almost every parent. The parent who consistently reacts to every instance of low control with the stress response is a candidate for burnout. The following exercise will help determine how you feel about the amount of responsibility and control you have over your children's lives.

1. Review the list of "parent issues" below and place an "x" to the left of each issue that you believe is one of your responsibilities as a parent.

Responsibility Column	Parent Issue	No Control	Complete Control	Limited Control
_____	1. Present family income	_____	_____	_____
_____	2. Family income in five years	_____	_____	_____
_____	3. Amount and nature of television programs your children watch	_____	_____	_____
_____	4. Your children's health	_____	_____	_____
_____	5. Friends with whom your children associate	_____	_____	_____
_____	6. Providing a safe, crime-free	_____	_____	_____

environment for
your children

_____ 7. Quality of your   _____ _____ _____
children's education

_____ 8. Values your children   _____ _____ _____
adopt

_____ 9. Your children's   _____ _____ _____
happiness

_____10. Amount of   _____ _____ _____
expenditures for
living expenses
(food, shelter,
clothing)

_____11. Preventing your   _____ _____ _____
children's use of
drugs

2. Read through the issues again, this time marking an "x" in one of the Control Columns, according to the degree of control you feel you have over each issue.

3. Tally the number of "x's" in each Control Column and in the Responsibility Column.

Explanation: You probably identified at least eight of the issues as parental responsibilities. Most of your Control Columns' x's will be found under the Limited Control heading.

Each parental issue listed is an area where, for the most part, parents' actions can influence but not definitively determine outcomes that affect their children. For parents, it is often most frustrating to realize that in matters as important as family finances, their children's safety, moral development, and education they have only a limited degree of control.

This frustration is compounded when these areas of limited control are also areas that the parents view as personal responsibilities.

Compare your Responsibility Column to the Control Columns. Issues that received marks in both the Responsibility Column and the Complete Control column are less likely to be a source of worry or concern for you. After all, if you feel responsible for the "quality of education your children receive" and also believe you can alter or control that quality, you can take actions to fulfill that responsibility. (Granted, you may feel guilty if you do not exercise your control over the issue, but at least the option for "doing something" exists.)

On the other hand, you may feel responsible for the "values your children adopt," but you checked Limited Control because you recognize that your children are adopting values from the baby-sitter who cares for them while you are at work. In this case, you may very well feel frustrated about your inability to alter the outcome of an issue that you consider a parental duty. You feel that you are meeting your responsibility to maintain the family income by working outside the home, but in doing so, you feel you fall short of meeting your responsibility of guiding the moral development of your children because they are adopting someone else's values.

The frustration is apparent. You cannot fulfill one parental responsibility without forsaking another. Consequently, you cannot feel in control because regardless of your path of action, you are unable to discharge satisfactorily both of your parental obligations.

The pace of change. The number and magnitude of societal changes over the last twenty to thirty years contributes greatly to parents' growing loss of control. In fact, change itself is the second situational stressor causing problems in most parents' lives. Few people would disagree that raising a family today is different from child rearing a generation ago. But is the job of being a parent actually more difficult now? The answer is Yes.

What once could be depended on no longer is entirely reliable. Institutions once strong in support of traditional family life—schools, churches, communities, relatives—play less of a role in guiding people's lives, particularly children's lives. Here is how Dora, a forty-five-year-old mother of two teenagers, describes the instability she sees in her children's world as compared with her own upbringing. "I grew up in the kind of neighborhood where if I did something wrong a block away from home, my parents knew about it before my hand touched the front doorknob," she recalled while sitting on the steps of her modest duplex house in Philadelphia. "I live in the exact same neighborhood now and my kids don't have that sense of community, the feeling that your home extended to the streets and houses all around you. I know if there were still communities like that today, a lot of parents would rest easier at night."

Dora says that as a teenager she often resented all the relatives and neighbors who seemed to "always be hanging around, looking after me, and getting into my business." However, in retrospect, she credits her solid, predictable environment with developing in her an immutable standard for "what's right and what's wrong."

Children today do not have those standards, she says. "How can the kids know the difference between right and wrong? No one tells them. They don't hear it in church because they don't go. The schools don't tell them because it's not part of reading, writing, and arithmetic and many teachers would prefer to look the other way. And parents don't have the time to tell them because mothers and fathers are so busy working to make ends meet. No one is talking to the kids. Their world must look awfully scary to them."

Technology: Competing with Pac-Man, Space Invaders, and Hard Rock. A well-known satirist once said that punishing children by sending them to their rooms was like throwing Brer Rabbit into the Brier Patch: "Their rooms are full of enough stereos, televisions, video games and other electronic gadgets to keep any normal adult entertained for a month."

While every American child may not have a room wired to the world, the impact of technology on kids is irrefutable. The widely published and inexhaustible debates about the influences of television pique a great deal of parental concern. Television brings murder, mayhem, and a ton of sugar-laden cereal into the living rooms of most children before they can walk. Countering the television messages and enforcing selected viewing among children are difficult jobs for parents. "Television is the universal pacifier," said one parent. "I don't think it's good that my son watches so much TV, but after working all week, the chores are piled up for Saturday, and the only way that I can get some peace to do them is by saying: 'Go watch the cartoons.'"

"I have little control over television watching," said one mother. "I don't want my kids to reach the twelfth grade having spent more hours in front of the tube than they have in school, like all the studies predict they will, but if I limit the television use too strictly, they complain that they have nothing to talk about with their friends and that they are becoming social outcasts. I know that's ridiculous," she added, "but that all-my-friends-are-doing-it line is a powerful argument."

The technological impact on children extends far beyond television. "My teenage son literally is plugged into a rock station on the radio twenty hours a day. Between the car radio, the stereo in his room, and the portable one he carries with him, I often consider calling the radio station just so the disc jockey will let him know when dinner's ready," joked one mother, and then added, "Seriously, his obsession with rock music interferes with my attempts to hold any meaningful conversations with him. How can I compete with Rod Stewart?"

The results of recent education studies indicate that today's students, having grown up with television in their homes and rock music in their ears, are more attuned to audio-visual teaching techniques than traditional paper and pencil lessons. While some experts fear that these findings will signal a further decline in reading and writing abilities, other educators claim that education has not kept pace with technological society and that effective teaching today requires the increased use of computers and other electronic instructional tools.

What does this mean for parents? Some fear that increased reliance on technology in the classroom will further limit parental control and involvement in their children's at-home education. "I was never trained in using computers. How will I be able to help with homework assignments?" asked one father. Other parents are apprehensive because they believe more affluent families will be able to purchase equipment to replicate classroom settings at home, placing the children of parents who cannot afford such equipment at a disadvantage.

Sex and drugs: The fearsome twosome. Parents' frustration about having little control over areas that they nevertheless view as their responsibility is most dramatically evident in any discussion of adolescent drug use or sexual activities. Approximately 1 million teenage girls get pregnant each year and newspapers and the broadcast media continually convey to the American people the ravages of drug and alcohol abuse among young people. In many instances, parents, despite their efforts to instill a strong value system in their children, view their offspring as merely "a pill or a drink away" from serious drug use problems. Societal changes in this area have been rather dramatic and quick-paced during the past few years.

Sex and drugs are among the most terrifying issues for parents. In today's society, if a parent's fondest mental image is his or her son or daughter graduating with honors from Harvard Medical School, then the opposite extreme surely is one of the most horrifying images a parent could envision—a son sitting in a dazed stupor with a needle in his arm. For their daughters, many parents still view teenage pregnancy as the ultimate misfortune.

Economics: Parents' Perpetual Nightmare. Money, "the root of all evil," is also the root of many changes that have completely altered American families and, consequently, posed problems and difficult choices for parents. Children were once considered financial assets. They were expected to work on the family farm or provide supplemental income to the family through employment in city factories. Furthermore, children were parents' Social Security. They were the financial providers in the parents' old age.

Today children remain primarily dependent on their parents' finances throughout their teen years and, in many cases, until a college education is completed. The children are expenses for the family, not additional sources of income or a guaranteed investment for the parents' later years. And they are very high-priced expenses at that. Parents, living in an urban area, with a child born in 1958, spent about $30,000 to raise that child through high school graduation. A child born in 1976 is estimated to cost his or her parents approximately $85,000 by the time that child is eighteen years old. If the child needs braces or wants piano lessons, the expenses climb. If the parents support their child through college, an average of $25,000 is tacked on to the price tag. A private education, of course, adds a substantial sum to the cost.

These increasing costs of raising children have fostered profound changes for parents and children alike. Most notable among those changes is the number of women who now work in jobs outside their homes. Economic need, not simply a desire for self-fulfillment through paid employment, accounts for the tremendous increase in women joining the labor sector.

Some parents examine the rising cost of living and conclude that the only way to provide their children with college educations, special training such as dance or music lessons, and all the other "extras," is to work very diligently at jobs that require their almost exclusive attention. These parents believe their concentration on work is an investment that ultimately will pay off for their children in the years ahead.

However, this investment for the future does exact an immediate price on parents and children alike. For the children the price might be diminished contact with their mother or father or contact with a parent who doesn't have the energy to listen, to express any real interest. For the parents the cost is often a megadose of guilt.

PARENTAL STRESS IN THE 1980s

Today's grandmothers might look about the contemporary home, complete with dishwasher, color television, and central air conditioning, and proclaim how easy life is for the family in the 1980s. There are labor-saving devices that keep housewives from bending over too much, from standing too long, and from thinking too hard. And for those who have entered the home computer era, there are even devices to keep track of all the other devices.

However, there are other "innovations," such as rising crime statistics, increased divorce rates, and unrelenting financial pressures. These are the "products" of the same rapidly changing society that brought us video games, fast-food restaurant chains, and frost-free refrigerators.

The breakneck pace of change that our nation and our world have undergone in the last twenty years has not killed the American family, as some sociologists had predicted, but the tumultuous nature of those changes is leaving some gaping wounds and fostering some dramatic mutations in traditional family life.

A key difference between the impact external factors have on parents today and that exerted on the parents of earlier generations is the instability that, over the past twenty years, has eroded even the most formidable of our social institutions and traditions.

The foundering of these institutions has left parents feeling that perhaps they could not trust the schools to be totally responsible for the education of their children; that the churches alone could not imbue a strong moral code in young people; and that the streets of the community were more often a source of danger for the kids than a network of protection.

Modern society has brought us many time-saving and energy-saving devices to make our lives easier and less taxing. These same devices bring with them monumental changes and increasingly less control of our children's lives—and ultimately in our parental roles. The changes increase the amount of stress. Parents who do not find ways to face these changes and adjust to this lower amount of control are prime candidates for burnout.

But there is hope. The very conditions that lead to burnout are the ones that indicate the nature and direction of the change. The stages of burnout are road signs that a change in life is needed. The first change must be in attitudes. Perfectionism must be abandoned. Parents need to learn to forgive themselves more for situations over which they really do not have control. And they need to find ways in which to reduce the stress, to replenish their energy resources, to find time away from the constant demands and pressure of parenting in the modern age.

5

Parenting Styles and Burnout

During the past two decades there has been a flood of books and guides focusing on the "oughts" and "ought nots" of parenting. Many parents have seen the pendulum swing from periods of permissiveness to rigidity and back again. Others have witnessed the rise and fall of parenting "gurus," each spelling out his or her formula for effective parenting. Many mothers and fathers have even been involved in disagreements (sometimes battles!) with their own parents concerning the appropriateness of one parenting style or another. One Rhode Island mother whom we interviewed recalled furiously the day that her own mother literally burned her dog-eared copy of *Dr. Spock* in the family backyard incinerator while baby-sitting. This proud grandmother was totally convinced that she knew "a heck of a lot more than this modern-day fellow who is messing up all the kids." Her daughter remembers the "impossibility" of communicating with her mother on this issue.

Most likely, many readers have experienced similar kinds of clashes with relatives, close friends, or professionals who might be servicing them. Almost every elementary school teacher has experienced several conflicts with parents concerning what each considers to be appropriate expectations of children. Pediatricians, likewise, often encounter individuals with parenting views quite different from what they would recommend.

Many psychologists, physicians, and other professionals point out that one of their most difficult and most energy-consuming tasks is the attempt to modify the parenting styles of their clients. There is a fundamental dilemma in parenting: on the one hand parents must control their children's behavior if certain goals are to be achieved. On the other hand, children must be allowed to develop self-direction and autonomy. Many parenting style problems originate from either a lack of appreciation of or a simplistic approach to this dilemma.

In our research we have found that there are two basic styles of parenting. We call these Style C (Controller) and Style D (Developer). However, there are very few pure C's or D's. Most parents fall somewhere along a continuum, but lean toward one side or the other. Before you proceed to an examination of the difference between C's and D's, complete the following *Parenting Style Index* to determine your own style.

PARENTING STYLE INDEX

Directions: Indicate your level of agreement or disagreement with the following statements. Think about each for a few moments before answering. Use the following rating scale when responding.

1	2	3	4	5
I Disagree Fully				I Agree Fully

_____ 1. Family customs should keep up with the times.

_____ 2. Children naturally try to do what is right.

_____ 3. Parents should try to explain reasons behind their decisions.

_____ 4. Children should gradually be allowed to make their own decisions.

_____ 5. Peer pressure often is beneficial for children.

_____ 6. Venturing out into the world is an opportunity children need.

_____ 7. Once your children are on their own your role as a parent changes in many rewarding ways.

1	2	3	4	5

I Disagree Fully   I Agree Fully

_____ 8. Worrying about your children won't do them any good.

_____ 9. Children should develop their own values.

_____ 10. It's enjoyable to include children in adult conversation.

_____ 11. There are better ways of disciplining children than spanking.

_____ 12. Most children will naturally use their potential.

Scoring Key: Add up your total points and determine your parenting style by using the key below:

Points

12–18   Super C and Minimal D

19–30   High C and Low D

31–41   Moderate C and Moderate D

42–53   Low C and High D

54–60   Minimal C and Super D

It is a fundamental premise of this book that Style C parenting is more conducive to burnout than Style D. Style C parents are much more susceptible to burnout unless they make some modifications in beliefs, attitudes, and behaviors. On the other hand, Style D parents are more growth-oriented and proactive and suffer from burnout to a lesser degree. However, there are some traps that affect D's more than C's and we will point them out. The following list of characteristics will further distinguish Style C from Style D parenting.

STYLE C	**STYLE D**
Protective	Democratic
Dogmatic	Nontraditional
Structured	Sees children as individuals
Directive	Values children's curiosity
Traditional	Likes change

Sees children as extension of self	Good listener
Change-resistant	Expressive of feelings
Resents children's curiosity	Relationship-oriented
	Sees diversity as a chance to grow

The differences between a Style C and a Style D parent are crystallized when one looks at parenting behavior at the various age levels of children:

INFANCY (0–1 YEAR)

This is a period of total dependency, when the child is developing his or her basic view of the world or outlook on life. It is a time of major demands from the baby and of service on the part of parents. The parents are almost entirely the doers and controllers and the children are the receivers and the controlled. It is a time of high worry and low communication between parent and child. Style C parents expect this from parenting: they are to be the caretakers, protectors, fence builders. They generally like this period of parenting.

Style D parents, on the other hand, often find this to be a difficult period. This is their most vulnerable point. Because they thrive on reciprocal communication, mutual respect, and feedback, their needs are not met.

The major trap for the Style C parent is that he or she will continue to maintain a relationship of control with the child. While the dependency period may justify the need for control during these first months, that need will soon dissipate. Two dangers are possible: the parent may continue to build fences, attempting to control the child's environment more and more; or the parent may force (consciously or subconsciously) the child to develop a sense of dependence on the parent that could reach inordinate and even unhealthy levels later in life.

Randy and Kara are good examples of Style C parenting. They have mapped out a whole plan of achievement and success for their infant son, Teddy, who is a month old. It reads like a script. They have put together an entire repertoire of expected behaviors: he will start to smile at two months of age; roll over on his own at four months; begin to sit up at six months; creep around at eight months; and begin to make sounds at eleven months. They have rigid plans for his educational, social, and physical development. Kara has already set up a pecking order of local nursery schools that would be best for Teddy. Randy speculates about the sport to which he should have his son direct his attention.

Randy and Kara are "checklist parents." They have developed a mental scenario describing how life should be for their child and they will spend most of their parenting time seeing to it that the script is followed like directors of a play. They will judge their own success or failure as parents against these criteria.

Brian and Vera, both Type D parents, were in their late twenties when their daughter, Claire, was born last year in the Detroit suburbs. Brian, a social worker with a public agency, and Vera, a nurse, had been looking forward to having a child since their marriage a few years before. They both felt that parenthood was serious business and they prepared themselves by doing a lot of reading. They also attended a seminar series for expectant parents at the hospital where Vera worked. They looked forward to the new addition to their household and felt that the arrival would make their family "complete." Vera busily furnished and decorated the nursery for the baby as Brian helped his wife with other household chores. They often speculated about the sex of the child and fantasized with each other about how their life was going to be so much better when that wonderful day came. Neither one could imagine anything that would have made them happier. They saw it as the capstone to their marriage—something that would bring them even closer—and as the beginning of a whole new phase of their life together.

Needless to say, the birth of Claire turned out to be the magnificent event that had been anticipated. Brian was pleased that both mother and baby were in excellent health after the delivery. Vera was ecstatic to be a mother. The first days back home after the hospital stay were filled with the normal stresses and confusion of having a new baby. There were many new chores and responsibilities that were not even anticipated by Brian and Vera in spite of all their planning. Of course, Vera was tired and suffered the normal postpartum blues. Like most babies, little Claire did her share of crying and her screams for her 2 A.M. feeding were like clockwork! Because Vera was breast-feeding, Brian was not able to participate except for some attempts at soothing the baby, who was colicky at times. After a few months of this routine, Brian began to feel somewhat detached from the situation. He felt that he was putting a lot of energy in, but getting very little "psychic charge" in return, as he put it. Brian told us, "It seems like I could walk out of there and not ever be missed. Of course, I pay the bills but the baby doesn't even know that. Here I am up half the night and she doesn't even smile at me. Maybe I'm just tired. I don't know. But, something is wrong. And Vera, well, she spends all her time with the baby. This is to be expected I suppose. But what about me? I need attention too you know."

Brian's experience is typical for Style D parents. Because these parents are basically relationship-oriented, they thrive on and get their energy from being connected to others, especially their loved ones. They only have so much energy and their source of replenishment is others. This places demands upon those around them to supply the energy. When the energy is not supplied, Style D parents become very vulnerable and can be hurt easily. They often turn away from those who they think are "rejecting them." They sometimes seek the reciprocal return of interest and energy from others outside the family. It is not uncommon for Style D parents, especially fathers, to spend a lot of time relating to close friends or to even be attracted to the opposite sex during this period. For months they have been under stress and burning off energy anticipating the birth of the child. The first months after birth are equally stressful, causing a further drain of energy. There is little opportunity to rebuild the energy supply. And for someone who thrives on getting energy from others by being connected, this is often a devastating period.

Brian was able to recognize his strong desire for mutual involvement with his infant daughter. He realized that his expectations of how Claire's presence would satisfy some of his needs were unrealistic and that this was causing him considerable anger in the form of frustration. He was willing to wait for his child's development to reach the point where she could recognize him and overtly return his affection.

PRETODDLER (1–2 YEARS)

During these years the development of the child begins to speed up. While this period begins to please the Style D parent, it can pose a potential threat to the Style C parent. While the D's focus on the interaction that is now possible as the child starts to talk and respond, the C's see this as the time to "shape the tree," to begin the serious programming, and to lay the foundation. C's often see this as the first challenge to their control, as the first threat to their power. They feel the need to begin to build the fences and do this by developing some external controls such as slaps on the wrists when the baby touches something he or she is not supposed to or through the use of verbal admonitions. In addition, they begin to build part of the internal "should system" through exhortation as well as punishments, shaming, and rejection.

While C's focus on control, D's become thrilled by the emergence of the child's personality. They can't run to the toy store fast enough to buy items that will expand the child's personality. They may even tend to overemphasize social development. They seek out every opportunity to expose their children to other children. They place a heavy focus on educational television and books. They try to improve themselves (e.g., their language, smoking habits, etc.), realizing that children learn by modeling and not by preaching. D's do not see their control challenged but instead see their growing ability challenged.

Mike and Carol were Super C parents. They felt that the first two years of the child's life were a "make or break" period. If they lost control, then it would be all over for them as well as their child. From the time Karen was able to touch anything, both parents began rewarding and punishing. They bordered on the hysterical as they got into shoving matches with their one-year-old over the most insignificant issue. Either she was going to "win" or they were! As Karen began to develop speed and agility and curiosity, it became clear to both Mike and Carol that their little girl had more energy than they did. Carol, in particular, became more physically exhausted as the days went on. Karen actually thought that the whole "control-me-if-you-can" game was a lot of fun. Her parents did not, and as their inability to maintain *total* control became obvious, they became more irritable. They began to resent Karen's "tactics" and literally devised ways of "getting her." They became embarrassed by what they thought others surely perceived as a lack of control and parenting ability. As a result, they slowly withdrew from visiting friends and relatives. Being rather sociable people, they felt all the more deprived. One day, in a tirade, Carol became so enraged that she locked herself in her bedroom and sobbed profusely while her daughter cried and banged on the door, "Mommy, Mommy, what is wrong? Please let me in!" Carol stayed in her room for about an hour while Karen became more frantic. For the first time, Carol realized how detrimental and dangerous her current mental and physical state was to her success as a parent. "I said to myself, 'Something has to give,'" Carol recalls. She and Mike discussed their painful feelings at length for several days after this incident. Both are in counseling now and they are shedding some of the assumptions of the C Style and moving closer to D. They are enjoying Karen more and growing with her.

Ned and Dale, the Super Style D father and mother of a two-year-old son, are what one would call "new age" parents. They are contemporary in every way—home, clothing, values. Both are in their early thirties and have successful management careers with Fortune 500 firms in Southern California. Both are achievement-oriented and career-minded. They take their parenting role equally seriously and want nothing but the best for their son, Jeremy—not only material gain, but also personal and social development as well. They want him to be a "high quality child," as Dale put it. "There are just too many factors militating against quality these days. We don't want this to rub off on our most precious asset—our little boy. He has everything going for him and we want to do all that we can to allow him to develop his potential. The sky is the limit—really," Ned chimed in. "And, let's face it, parents are the key to the whole thing. They make all the difference. Children learn almost all their attitudes, values, ambitions, you name it, from their parents," Dale added, and Ned agreed.

Both are very sensitive to how they come across to their son. They feel that they are always "on" whether they like it or not. When Jeremy's behavior is not what it "should be," they immediately and keenly examine the possible flaws in their behavior. Is their son picking up some bad habits from them? Some unpleasant attitudes? Could they be doing something that they are not now doing? Is there room for improvement?

If Ned and Dale continue on their current action path, they are sure to experience burnout. And they will do so because they are making one fundamental, but critical, error: they are holding themselves totally responsible for something that is not totally in their control. While the impact of parental behavior on children's development is certainly important, there are many other factors that are outside the full range of control of the parents. To attempt to be at the "cutting edge" of all of the latest developments that improve the quality of life of young pretoddlers is very likely an insurmountable task. While the contemporary challenge to parental growth is stimulating and ultimately good for both parents and children, there *are* limits. It is essential that Ned and Dale learn those limits and accept only a reasonable amount of responsibility for the development of Jeremy at this point in his life. Otherwise, there is no doubt that they will begin to resent the unnecessary burdens and accountability that they have placed upon themselves.

TODDLER (2–3 YEARS)

During this period Style D parents find themselves hurt and overwhelmed. What they have been trying to do is build up a trusting and warm relationship. But all of a sudden, the level of antagonisms dramatically increases. Many D's respond by feeling rejected; they can't believe how sour the parenting experience has become. It may be the first time they feel resentment, which they express in such statements as "After all I've done for them."

While Style C parents don't like this period, they have their expectations met. This is exactly what they anticipated: children challenging authority, being disruptive, and disobeying. They feel happy that they have prepared themselves for this. The major trap for C's is that they have a tendency to initiate lifelong hostilities between their children and themselves.

It has been our experience that parents of children of this age are at one of the more susceptible and vulnerable points for burnout. Likewise, it is important to point out that this is one of the few ages where Style D parents are just as subject to burnout as are Style C parents.

Fred and Debbie are Style C parents. They planned to have a rather large family when they were married five years ago in a small town in Massachusetts. High school sweethearts, they had spent a lot of time before their marriage sharing their mutual desire for parenthood. They saw their role as probably the most important one either of them would ever perform. Sometimes they would wonder out loud whether they would be able to take on such an "awesome responsibility," as Debbie would say. "Raising kids today is no easy job," Fred would add.

The first two years after their daughter Lisa's birth were enjoyable for both Fred and Debbie. Like all new parents, they reveled in the baby's presence and bragged about her accomplishments to family and friends. However, beneath this enjoyment lurked the ever-conscious obligations of parenthood—the sense of responsibility for Lisa's development. They "knew" sooner or later this "honeymoon period" between parents and child would have to dissipate and the "reality" of raising their child would come about. In some ways they wanted to prolong her infancy. Fred used to say jokingly, "Sometimes I wish that I could freeze Lisa just where she is right now."

Both Fred and Debbie had heard a lot about the "terrible twos" from their friends and relatives. "Wait until next year. Enjoy her now," was a common remark. So, when Lisa became a toddler, Fred and Debbie got exactly what they expected; everything broke loose. Lisa's favorite word became "No!" And her most cherished activity was to throw her toys as far as she could. Standing in front of the television screen while Fred was trying to watch baseball games was another of her pastimes. The angrier her parents became, the more she misbehaved, giggling with glee at their exasperation. In spite of their mental and emotional preparation for this period of their daughter's development, both Fred and Debbie felt that they were "losing the battle." They were absolutely convinced that their daughter was behaving in a way that was even more terrible than the *normal* "terrible twos." How did they let it get this far? Were they losing control? Was there something "wrong" with Lisa? These mental gyrations, coupled with the sheer physical exhaustion generated by their attempts at controlling Lisa, sent both Fred and Debbie into moods characterized by hostility and irritability. They frequently pushed the responsibility and task of dealing with Lisa's antics on each other. "Well, you control her, damn you. I've worked all day and didn't want to come home to this," Fred would yell as he sat down to read the newspaper after dinner, a meal that was often spent in silence. Debbie would yell back, "I've been in this house all day. What do you think I am made of?"

Both parents were getting angrier and more frustrated by the day. Their feelings were fueled by a deep sense of guilt about the existence of a situation over which they had lost control. Were they good parents? Were they even cut out to be parents? Maybe not. Many doubts set in. They began to resent their daughter for putting them in this arena of failure. The ambivalence of this resentment, coupled with their ever-strong love for their daughter, created an internal anguish that was becoming unbearable. Debbie especially found herself more erratic in her relations with her daughter. She would literally shift from behaviors of affection to those of hostility inside of a half hour. Lisa became more and more sensitive to these mood swings, causing her to become more hyperactive as she responded to this anxiety. A vicious circle was developing and eventually it would begin to feed on itself. If left uncontrolled, it could become a destructive force between parent and child.

Fortunately for Fred and Debbie, their pediatrician was able and willing to discuss their difficulties with them. He explained the normal behavior patterns of toddlers. Their behavior may not be what many parents would have asked for if they had designed human nature! Nonetheless, it is what they, in fact, have to deal with. He also explained that parents can control only so much. There is much that takes place that is beyond their control, but is nonetheless normal and healthy. The real issue may be the *parents'* need to control, whether that be out of a sense of responsibility or the perception of the obligation to protect one's children. Fred and Debbie have come to understand that healthy children at this age follow a growth pattern that is neither "good" nor "bad." They now see their role as a monitor and not a controller of this natural process. The seeds for growth are there if they will only let them flower. And, furthermore, they are not as much "on the line" for their child's behavior as they might have thought. To hold themselves accountable for something beyond their full control is not good for them or for Lisa.

When Byron was born, Brad and Penny were both in graduate school pursuing their degrees. They lived in a small apartment near the campus of their large urban university. While the arrival of the baby was stressful at first, they soon redesigned their hectic routine and adjusted to the responsibility well. Brad had to take a part-time job at a local convenience store because of the new expenses. Their fellowship stipends just were not enough. This job commitment robbed Brad of valued study and research time, but he felt that the joys of fatherhood far outweighed the added constraints. He continued this frenetic pace for two years until he completed his studies. "There were days when I couldn't find time to even think about what I was doing. . . . Go, go, go. . . . That is all I remember," Brad recalls. Penny is currently working on her thesis and will complete her degree in about a year. She, too, has been on the go, juggling her motherly and academic responsibilities.

Brad and Penny pride themselves on being "enlightened parents." They want their son, now three, to be as independent as possible. Above all, they do not want to be doting parents. They feel that they will be effective if they let little Byron learn how to make his own decisions as soon as possible. They look forward to seeing him develop and having him experience life fully. "We want him to grow beyond us and we want to grow with him. We want him to have his own identity," Brad pointed out. "In fact, we didn't even name him after Brad, but chose 'Byron' so that he wouldn't become just a 'junior.' This upset some of the family because he would have been Bradley III. We hated to disappoint everybody, but we feel quite strong about his freedom and independence."

While Style D parenting worked well for the first months of Byron's life, it began to create some strains as the youngster entered the toddler stage. When Byron went into the normal states of "rampage" for a three-year-old, both Brad and Penny would attempt to communicate with him to determine "why" he was on this "destructive binge." Byron usually responded by throwing one more toy across the room, giggling wildly, and dashing off into another part of the apartment. On several occasions when Brad and Penny were entertaining guests, Byron would decide to invade the social gathering and display his temper. While some of the guests expressed acceptance, or at least indifference, to the intrusion on their adult conversation, several were obviously disturbed by it. Both parents usually tried to "reason" with Byron at these times, much to the consternation of visiting family and friends. One Sunday afternoon at a restaurant outing with some close friends and their children, Brad and Penny recommended that they leave after sitting down and getting comfortable because Byron wanted a hot dog and the restaurant did not have them on the menu. Brad's closest friend, who was halfway through a cocktail when this was suggested, became furious and recommended that he not try to reason with a three-year-old. Brad responded quite assertively, "Look, I respect his right to make a decision. If the restaurant doesn't have what he wants, why should he stay? I don't blame him. He is not going to be a sheep." The rest of the day was a disaster and no one really had a good time. The friendship of these families has been on the decline ever since.

Brad and Penny, in their desire to let little Byron develop freely, found themselves becoming more and more isolated from others. This caused them considerable pain because they were rather sociable and enjoyed family and friends. They also were more cognizant of their own mental and physical exhaustion as they attempted to respond to the consequences of Byron's decisions and often erratic behavior patterns. Their quest for developing "meaningful" communication with him often went unsatisfied. Brad began to think about and then to articulate to Penny that he was putting an awful lot into his role as a father and was getting very little back from Byron. "After all, let's face it, he's caused us to lose almost all of our friends. Both of our families think that he is out of control and have lost respect for us. We really haven't had a good time with him around since he was a baby," he pointed out to his wife. These thoughts and comments seriously frightened both Brad and Penny. What was happening? Why were they having these terrible feelings? Why were they really so disappointed?

Both were wise enough to know that these doubts were serious ones and that they ought to discuss them with someone who could be a little more objective about their parenting style. After several sessions with a counselor skilled in parenting techniques, both Brad and Penny came to realize that while their intentions of wanting their child to develop his individuality were admirable, their need for helping to bring this about was in conflict with some other basic needs that they both had: the need to be connected to friends and family; the need to continue to develop their own individuality; the need to live well-rounded, balanced lives; and the need to take control of their child's behavior and make it more compatible with the family's *common* goals. The counselor pointed out that Byron was quickly becoming the dominant factor in their lives to the exclusion of all other facets. Ironically, Brad and Penny had unknowingly given up their own freedom and development for the sake of their son's. In the long run, this was sure to make them bitter (especially in the years when Byron would leave the "nest") and would do neither Byron nor them any good. The counselor further explained that parents serve their children well when they allow them to grow and be free, but they serve them better when they themselves are free as well. The sooner this relationship of "unity and support through individual strength" is developed, the better for all members of the family. Two or three years old is not too early to begin this relationship.

PRESCHOOL (3–5 YEARS)

The major activity of children this age is learning. There are two basic approaches to learning: didactic and experiential. Style C parents are going to be more comfortable using the didactic (or telling) direct approach. The D Style parents focus on letting the children experience reality. These two differing approaches are used not only for teaching facts but also values. The trap for the Style C parent is the expectation that exhorting and lecturing and telling will have payoff. However, everything that we have discovered through recent research on how children learn tells us exactly the opposite. The fact is that children learn by doing, by experiencing, and by modeling the behavior of adults. Parents cannot command their children to know certain facts or accept certain principles or beliefs. The learning process is gradual and it takes time. Children have to think about and *feel* the benefits themselves. Style C parents have a tendency to deal with children at the intellectual level as opposed to the feeling level.

This was the case with Lynette and Barry, parents of Kevin, a five-year-old who was "destined for greatness" because of his "unusual" and "natural" premature interest in reading and math. Barry, an engineer with a large defense contractor in Virginia, bought his son only "educational type" toys. Lynette planned to enroll little Kevin in the best nursery school in the area and went out of her way to have him participate in the local library's enrichment programs. Both parents expressed some concerns about the inadequacy of the local public schools and were beginning to panic because Kevin was late getting on the first-grade waiting list of a prestigious independent school in nearby Washington, D.C. While Kevin was allowed to play for a certain amount of time each day with the children of a working colleague of Barry's and the child of one of Lynette's friends, he pretty much followed a rigid schedule of planned learning activities and was not allowed to "waste or squander time." Music lessons in a local "top-notch" program were planned as well.

One evening Kevin began screaming in the middle of the night. Both Lynette and Barry jumped out of bed and rushed to his room to find him hiding his head under the covers. When they asked him what the problem was, he told them that he had seen a ghost hiding in the closet. Barry, using his rational approach, tried to explain that ghosts did not exist. "Go back to sleep, Kev, everything will be fine!" The same thing happened the next night and Barry took a similar approach: "Don't worry about it, Kev, go back to sleep!" A week passed, and just when Barry had forgotten about the incident, lo and behold, the same thing happened. Little Kevin began screaming and claiming that he had seen a ghost. Kevin was obviously afraid and what he really wanted was his mom and dad to deal with his feelings. As is typical of Style C parents, Barry approached the problem from an intellectual perspective. A Style D parent would have been more empathic. (An interesting discovery in our study has been the near obsession on the part of Style C parents with selecting the "right" school for their elementary and even nursery school children. They visit every possible option. They ask their friends and associates incessantly about the advantages and disadvantages of the various schools.)

MIDDLE CHILDHOOD (5–10 YEARS)

From the perspective of most children in this age bracket, there is nothing that parents can do wrong. Parents are idealized by the children. Fathers are viewed as more powerful than the President of the United States, more capable than the star quarterback for the Super Bowl championship team, more courageous than the astronauts, and smarter than Einstein. Mothers are more beautiful than any movie or television star, the kindest person alive, and the best cooks in town. Superlatives are used rampantly by the children. "My dad and mom are the best!" Some parents jokingly see this period as their belated reward for having suffered through the "terrible twos." While parents are busy during this period of rearing, the occurrence of burnout, particularly at the higher stages, is diminished. The major reason for this is that parents are generally getting rewards in the form of outward expressions of love, praise, and appreciation commensurate with the energy they are expending in their parenting. There is one potential problem, however: The parents could begin to believe that they do actually have all of these qualities and then come to expect this level of worship to continue. They become set up for disappointment when it is pulled away or at least diminished in its intensity, as indeed it will be.

Both Style C and Style D parents can become victims of this phenomenon. However, the pitfalls differ. While C parents feel obliged to live up to the idealization, D parents thrive on the emotional feeding they are receiving from their children's adoration. Roy, a Style C father, and Don, a Style D, are cases in point. "For a long time I felt compelled to live up to my eight-year-old son's perception that I was a better ballplayer than Reggie Jackson. I believed that he really needed to believe this as a motivator. I wanted to be a model that he could look up to. Of course, it used to get embarrassing when my boy would tell people who knew me well and for a long time that I had been a great star," Roy, a father from Long Island, New York, told us somewhat sheepishly. "I remember my older kid going through this same thing a few years ago. Only he was into football and then it was Roger Staubach. I always feel depressed when the kids start this because I know someday they are going to find out the truth about me and be terribly let down. The day of reckoning will come! I know that I am going to feel kind of ashamed then and a little awkward and embarrassed. But, what can I do? It's too late for me to go back and become something that I wish I was. I guess that I will have to suffer through it as painful as it is."

Don is the father of two sons, ages twelve and eight. He has been very close to his boys and has spent much time with them. However, he has witnessed a marked change in his oldest son's attitude toward him during the past year or two. It was hard to put his finger on it at first, but then it became clearer. He first became aware of this shift one Saturday morning during the summer when the family was driving off for a long weekend in West Virginia. As they drove along, Don noticed his son checking the map to see if his father was going the right way. Don asked his son why he was checking the map and his son responded: "Because you usually go the wrong way, Dad." Don was shocked and somewhat hurt by that comment, but held it in and did not say too much about it. A few days later, the family was watching and commenting on a Baltimore Orioles baseball game, and the older son shouted out, "What do you know, Dad? What you said about that batter makes no sense!" Don was totally jolted. This time he confronted his son, "Dad doesn't know anything, hah? I thought that you said that I was the best baseball player you knew. What happened?" His son replied, "Yeah, that was before I knew better. You're okay, but you're not the greatest. You know that."

Don admitted to us that it took him a while to adjust to this knock off the pedestal. It became crystal clear to him that his son had discovered the reality of his father's strengths and weaknesses. This depressed Don. The myth was shattered. He found himself spending more time with his youngest son, who still "worshiped me without reservation." While the pain that Don experienced was not severe, he nonetheless remembers it very well. Fortunately, he had some discussions with his knowledgeable minister, who told him that this was a normal stage for children. As enlightened as Don is, he too almost became a victim of temporary idealization.

ADOLESCENCE (10–15 YEARS)

"Rearing teenagers is like trying to hit a moving target. Just when you think that you understand them, they shift on you," pointed out one father of three in St. Louis. Many parents would agree that adolescence can be a monstrous period for children and a nightmarish era for dads and moms. This is the case for several major reasons: 1) children look at their parents more objectively; 2) there is a struggle for identity; 3) peer pressure is strong; and 4) change is constant and rapid.

Children in this age group discover the weaknesses of parents. They are able to look at their parents more objectively and, as such, they have a tendency to magnify the shortcomings. Low tolerance for what they consider to be too cautious, too slow, or fumbling behavior on the part of their parents manifests itself. Hostile glances, disagreements, and verbal challenges begin to appear. Many parents are aggravated by this. How ungrateful!

Second, the struggle for identity usually triggers a negative reaction on the part of the parent. Style C parents respond angrily. They see it as a challenge to their control. They look at the children as objects and try to increase their power over them by increasing or withdrawing money privileges and positive reinforcements. Style D parents tend to respond with shock and sadness. They identify more with the anguish of the adolescent struggle. "I feel so bad for him, for what he is going through." They are able to empathize more with their children and let them know that they understand what they are feeling. They do more listening than talking and try to assure the children that they are with them and not against them.

Third, children's peer pressure affects all parents. In adolescence the peer acceptance and pressure can literally take over the control of children, even children whose rational and moral foundations seem to be solid. They may violate standards that their parents have established. Style C parents usually respond with vigorous and almost desperate attempts at discipline. Usually, there is only one-way communication. In many cases this discipline backfires and drives the children deeper into the influences of friends and other peers. Often this is accompanied by a drastic drop in school grades, an increase in the consumption of alcohol, drug use, or sexual promiscuity. At this point Style C parents may realize for the first time that from here on in these attempts to *control* their children will be fruitless.

The Style D parents' pitfall in his or her response to peer pressure is often to compete with their children's peers. It is usually a losing battle. They misinterpret the attempts of their children to break away and establish their own identity. What they should be doing is supporting their children rather than interpreting the adolescent phase as a personal rejection of them.

Marc, a Style D parent, felt very close to his eleven-year-old son.

Finally, they were really starting to relate to one another. They could actually sit and carry on a conversation. Marc had been waiting for this for a long time. He had a good number of friends, but he felt that his best friend could be his son. This is the kind of relationship he wanted—one that he did not have with his own father. Whenever he could, he managed to drive his son to school or pick him up so they could chat. A salesman for an office equipment company, Marc would take his son with him occasionally as he made his rounds during the summer months. Often during their outings, Marc would do a lot of talking and questioning: "Are you happy?" "What do you want to do when you get older?" "Do you want to go to college?" "Is there anything bothering you?" If he received any response at all, it was usually a one-word answer. Sometimes it was, "I don't know, Dad," accompanied by a wincing expression of mental pain. This would annoy Marc and sometimes he would press his son further, "What do you mean by you don't know? Daddy is only trying to help. I'm interested."

Within a short period of time, Marc's son began to opt out of taking long rides or of having long conversations with his father. This became noticeable to Marc and he worried about it. Was his dream of true friendship with his son in jeopardy? Did his son not enjoy his company? Find him interesting? Boring? Would they end up having a formal controlled relationship such as he had with his father? Never be friends?

Marc discussed these innermost feelings and concerns with his wife, who was a little less of a Style D parent. She pointed out, quite accurately, that it is difficult for parents and children to develop a relationship based on friendship. First of all, adults and children have a different time orientation. While parents, because of their experience, often know the importance of planning and investing for the future, children are more present-time directed. They do not enjoy relating to individuals who push them into an uncomfortable mental framework. Instead, they find people with similar time orientations more interesting and they have a tendency to want to associate with them. Therefore, children will be attracted to other children more than to adults. This discrepancy in time frameworks makes it difficult to develop a high level of mutual interests, which is the cement of friendships. Marc is becoming more appreciative of the basic, but real, differences between his son and himself. While he should continue to develop a closeness with his son, it is also important that he be sensitive to where the youngster is in his chronological, mental, and social development. His son will be happier and so will Marc.

Adolescents change in three specific ways, but only the physical changes are obvious. The second change is in the area of thinking. Adolescents are able to use abstract thought and they begin to focus on themselves as special and unique, to focus on their idiosyncratic characteristics as opposed to their commonalities. When a parent preaches about the danger of drugs or reckless driving or the risk of pregnancy, a common response is, "It could never happen to me!" Teenagers are heavily focused on their individuality and for the first time see themselves as controlling their own destiny. It is a new realization. They generally like it and they magnify its value.

The third major way adolescents change is in their feelings. They are "up" one hour and "down" the next. One day they are intrigued by sexual issues and the next day they are afraid of them. One week they are independent and aloof and the next week they are dependent and childlike. In short, because they are dealing with ambivalent impulses, adolescents are difficult to predict. They are upset internally. With boys it is often expressed as hostility and anger. With girls it often takes the form of tears, indifference, or boredom.

This period of the child's life requires a high degree of understanding as well as tolerance on the part of parents. A major recognition is that there is no guarantee that all of these changes— physical, thinking, feeling—will occur at the same time. Often parents infer one kind of change when they observe another area of growth. Very often the inferences are erroneous and parental expectations are not met. This situation often leads to the development of an adversarial relationship between parents and teenagers. Parents are assuming changes that really have not taken place yet. These premature expectations often lead to confusion and hostility between parent and child.

Style C parents have difficulty with the ambiguity surrounding the discrepancy of these various stages of change. It often reaches the point of "adolescence phobia," where the parent assumes that once one change starts taking place, all the others have as well. As soon as they see the first hair on the lip of the son, or the first maturing of the daughter's breasts, they assume drinking, crazy driving, sex, and drugs cannot be too far behind. When parents convey these expectations to their children they often get what they expect. Parents create a self-fulfilling prophecy that leads to a vicious circle of control and the defiant avoidance of that control by their children.

Pete was a hard-working construction foreman for a large building firm in Rhode Island. He died last year of a massive heart attack at a rather young age. Everyone says that Pete's health problems started several years ago when his fifteen-year-old daughter started giving him "a lot of problems." It was Leslie's first year in a public school, the local town high school. Pete never really wanted her to go to the public school because of what he had heard went on there. He would have preferred that she continue on with parochial school education. But after many family arguments and the intercession of his wife, Pete agreed to have his only daughter attend the public high school. Pete, expecting problems from the onset, was suspicious from the first day of school. He developed a list of rather rigid rules for Leslie to follow. On rainy days when he wasn't working, he would take a ride by the school or bus stop to "spot check" on his daughter. The rigidity of his rules and the intensity of his surveillance increased steadily. "The best defense is a strong offense," he would say. "Those monkeys aren't going to ruin my daughter. Not after all I've put into raising her." He wanted to know everything that went on and would interrogate his daughter continuously. Within a short period of time the communication became almost entirely one-way. His daughter would walk out of the room when he walked in. The intensity of the hostility increased to the point where it began to become an obsession for Pete. He felt that he was losing control of the situation and he didn't like it. He felt that "they" were winning and he was losing the battle. In a last-ditch effort to recoup control, Pete confronted Leslie with a whole new set of rules that she was to follow. In essence, he wanted to know everything that she did and he was going to be boss as long as she lived under his roof. Leslie's mom, in what she considered dutiful support of her husband, went along with these rules although she had some reservations.

Leslie tried to conform for a few weeks, but found herself attracted more and more to her friends and turning to them for support and understanding. One June afternoon, about a week after school was over, Leslie left her house to go see a nineteen-year-old boy whom she had met a few months before at a local fast-food restaurant. They drank some beer, smoked some pot, and drove off to Cape Cod, where they stayed for the weekend until the police located them. Pete was totally beside himself and had literally considered killing both the boy and his daughter. Leslie wouldn't even talk to her father when she returned to her home. She threatened to run off again if "you start pressing me." Their stormy relationship continued until Pete's death.

YOUNG ADULTHOOD (15–20 YEARS)

During this age period the major issues of parenting relate to the exercise of moral judgment and the degree of success in life. Parents begin to see the results of all their hard work. Will he get into college? Will he get a job? Will her marriage be successful? Basically, are the children becoming productive happy adults? At this stage many parents' burnout symptoms revolve around the "Where did I go wrong?" syndrome.

Jodi, the seventeen-year-old daughter of a Super Style C father, left home last year and decided to live with some understanding neighbors in her small Maine factory town. Jodi said that she just couldn't take it anymore. Feeling totally oppressed most of her life, she finally decided to leave the day that her father accused her of wanting to be sexually promiscuous because she expressed a strong interest in going off to a state university where she would have to board. A teacher and a local priest who tried to intercede for Jodi with her father were almost literally thrown out of the house. Today Jodi attends the university and her father miserably complains and believes that he has been defied and has wasted many years and a lot of money raising an ungrateful daughter: "Where did I go wrong?" He has recently begun to suffer from migraine headaches as well as high blood pressure. He has become increasingly hostile to his wife, other children, and friends. His wife says that this is "killing him." She couldn't be more accurate.

Another major concern in this age range has been called the "empty nest" phenomenon. Many parents have used their role as parent to structure their lives. Their lives literally revolved around their children. Once the children begin to leave home and focus their love and attention toward spouses, their own children, and careers, these parents who have not structured their lives around their own personal values and goals lose their feeling of purpose.

ADULTHOOD (20–30 YEARS AND BEYOND)

Style C parents see this as an end and Style D parents see it as a beginning. Because C's see themselves as protectors, defenders, and controllers, they reach the conclusion that their role is essentially over. Style D parents' philosophy is one of continual growth and, therefore, they look forward to participation in the modified relationship with their children that naturally develops as they get older. For example, if their children are married, they look forward to the opportunity for new intimacy with in-laws. Style C parents, on the other hand, see in-laws as an intrusion on their power and therefore are not that trusting. They, in fact, often feel threatened and their in-laws respond accordingly, generating a network of negative relationships that eventually puts sons and daughters in a difficult position.

Nick, a wealthy New Jersey businessman, felt that he had a major burden when he contacted us recently because of his "problems" with his children, ages twenty-six, twenty-eight, and thirty-two. His opening remark was, "I have been successful all my life. I have been able to accomplish anything I set out to accomplish. However, I feel that I have failed in one area—my kids, especially the oldest one. He married a girl that is impossible for me to deal with. You know, my son listens to her more than he listens to me. Sometimes I think that I lost him the day he married her." Nick was also rather upset because his youngest child, a daughter, had recently moved to Chicago to pursue a master's degree and he really didn't know "what the hell she was doing." His second oldest son was close to home, but Nick was concerned that his daughter-in-law was too much of a career person and didn't spend enough time cooking and cleaning. He truly wanted us to tell him what "he had done to deserve these problems!"

Craig is a good example of the results of Style C parenting. The only child of a rather affluent upper middle class family, he had a high quality prep school education in Maryland before going on to college and law school. He realized at the age of thirty that he really couldn't make a serious personal, professional, or financial decision without getting approval from his parents. Mom and Dad had so entwined themselves in his psyche that he literally could not function without them. He became so despondent and depressed when they would not approve of the girl that he wished to marry that he came close to a nervous breakdown. After several years of psychotherapy, he finally was able to break loose of these parental bonds, but only by moving away to the West Coast, where he is now married to another woman and has his own children. To this day his parents have not forgiven him for his move away from them. Having only occasional communication with him, they are terribly unhappy and spend endless hours blaming each other for this "tragedy."

6

Parent Traps: Accelerating Burnout

In our research we have discovered several factors that are critical to the incidence of burnout or accelerate the course of burnout in mothers and fathers. We call them "parent traps" because they are often either concealed or appear attractive to the point of not being recognized as dangerous. Like many traps they lure the victim in; getting out, while possible, is much more difficult. Several parent traps that can have an impact on burnout are time use; "crucializing"; money; grandparents; guilt; and what we call the "seven deadly sins of parenting" (pride, lust, sloth, anger, envy, gluttony, and greed). Keep in mind that these are *potential* factors in burnout for some parents. However, if a parent is entrapped by any one or more of them the likelihood of burnout is increased and its development exacerbated. It is important that you become aware of the traps to which you may be vulnerable. At the end of the chapter we will ask you to identify your own areas of vulnerability.

TIME TRAPS

Time is one of the most precious resources a parent has. However, there is a fundamental dilemma relating to time: most parents do not feel that they have enough time, but every parent has all the time there is (twenty-four hours a day). Isn't it interesting that some parents have several children, loads of community responsibilities, hold down full-time jobs, and yet manage to have time to play tennis twice a week, while others may have one child and much less responsibility but never seem to catch up? The key differential is not the amount of time available (because that is the same for all), but the *management* of time.

Before you go on, complete the *Parent Time Use Index* below. It will help you determine your susceptibility to the time-management traps.

PARENT TIME USE INDEX

Directions: Check whether your attitudes and behavior correspond with the statement. Mark YES if you almost always feel or act consistently with the statement. Mark NO if your actions and feelings are generally not consistent.

YES	NO		
_____	_____	1.	I know what I value in my role as parent.
_____	_____	2.	I have identified *my* most effective and productive time (e.g., mornings, evenings, etc.).
_____	_____	3.	I have a list of long-term parenting goals and review them periodically.
_____	_____	4.	I have a daily list of things *to do.*
_____	_____	5.	I prioritize my daily activities.
_____	_____	6.	I eliminate low priority activities as quickly as possible.
_____	_____	7.	I delegate to others whatever I can.
_____	_____	8.	I ask myself often, "Is this the best use of my time?"
_____	_____	9.	I regularly examine old habits and routines for possible modification.
_____	_____	10.	I keep things well organized to avoid spending time looking for them.
_____	_____	11.	I try to enjoy what I am doing as a parent.
_____	_____	12.	I give myself time off to relax.

Scoring: Add up the number of items that you have answered "YES." Interpret your score using the following table:

Number of Yesses

10–12	Excellent Time-management Skills
7–9	Good Time-management Skills
4–6	Fair Time-management Skills
1–3	Poor Time-management Skills

There are several dangerous traps relating to time use and management: time orientation; time control; and inability to delegate and say "No." First, time orientation is an integral part of personality. Some parents are future-time oriented. Others are past-oriented. And there are those who are focused on the present. Questions such as "What will happen if . . . ?" "Suppose I get sick?" "What if we don't have enough money?" "I wonder whom she will marry?" dominate the thinking of future-time oriented individuals. Past-time oriented parents spend most of their time reconstructing past decisions. "If I had only," "I am glad that we did," "Too bad we didn't know about it," "We shouldn't have moved," dominate their consciousness. While concern about the future is certainly prudent and essential for planning and while it is wise to review our past so that we can learn from it, future- and past-time orientations can cause a high degree of anxiety and exhaustion that leads all the way to immobilization. Many parents consume tremendous amounts of energy worrying about the future. They are plagued by "disaster fantasies," especially in relation to their children. Whether it be crib death, straight teeth, correct manners, sex, drugs, safety, or what kind of girl the son will end up marrying, they worry continuously.

Other parents express their future orientation in a more optimistic way. Their motto is "I can't wait until . . ." They dwell on a future more rewarding and pleasant than the present, even though they may be happy in the present. When the children are babies, they focus on the time when they will be able to walk and talk. When these feats are being accomplished, they fantasize about the children's schooldays or Little League days or ballet days. When the children are in high school, the parents focus on college and beyond. It never ends . . . marriage . . . the grandchildren . . . on and on.

They postpone immediate rewards for some future payoff, which often never comes. Joe is a good example of this kind of future-oriented parent. A high achiever, Joe is working his way up the corporate ladder at a rather fast pace and at a young age. The father of three young children, ages nine, seven, and four, Joe travels out of town at least two days a week and often works one day on the weekend. There are several days during the week when Joe literally does not talk to his children, even when he is in town. He leaves before they wake up and he returns home after they are in bed. Joe told us that he is working as hard as he is and sacrificing now so that he can relax someday and really enjoy his family in the style that he would like. He wants his children to go to the best schools and he wants to be able to pave the way for them with his corporate connections.

Like so many of his corporate colleagues, Joe is in for a rude awakening. It is quite likely that he will never really enjoy his children as he fantasizes. He makes one fundamental error: he thinks that they are going to wait for him. They will not. They need his attention and time now. When he is ready for them, they will not be ready for him. They will have their own responsibilities and interests outside the home. Also, they will have probably grown accustomed to living without his involvement. Parents who think and act like Joe usually undergo serious depression. The stark realization that their delayed gratification is not coming and most probably will never come in the fashion that they had imagined devastates them.

Likewise, some parents have become entrapped by the past. They relive past decisions and feel that they now must live as victims of past mistakes. They blame themselves internally, but usually are externally defensive because they believe that others see their "errors" as they see them. The past issue that haunts most parents who suffer from burnout is financial status. Many feel that if they had only been shrewder, more hard-working, more intelligent, luckier, or better-connected, they would have been able to provide a higher standard of living for their children. It seems that everything that they have today (even though it may be substantial) is second-best to "what could have been."

Luke is a biology teacher in a large suburban high school. An excellent educator with fifteen years of experience, he spends most of his time dwelling on the fact that he was "almost admitted" to dental school. He feels that if he had just achieved a little higher score on his dental-school admissions tests, he would have been in. So he fantasizes about how life would be if he could have been a dentist today, how much more he could have provided for his children. It is the first thing that he talks about after initially meeting somebody, especially socially: "I should have been a dentist. If I had to do it all over again, that is what I would do. I would kill myself studying. What a fool I was!" One day in a discussion with one of the authors, Luke literally cried as he related what he thinks life would have been like for his children financially, if he had gone to dental school. He feels that he "really owes them" and has to make it up to his three sons somehow. Most people who know Luke say that a general sadness pervades him most of the time. As one of his colleagues put it, "He always seems to be in deep thought."

When it comes to relationships, time orientation can be a double-edged sword. Having a different time orientation can be an asset or a liability. It can cement relationships in a complementary fashion or it can destroy them. For example, a husband who is future-time oriented coupled with a wife who is present-time oriented might make a productive team. The husband will see to it that their long-range needs are attended to and the wife will remind her husband to stop and smell the flowers occasionally. On the other hand, such a situation could be fraught with tension as each individual frowns on and devalues the importance of the other's orientation. How can he spend so much time worrying about our retirement income? Why can't she see beyond tomorrow?

In parent-child relationships, the congruence of time orientations is equally important. Children, by nature, are very much present-time oriented. Many parents, particularly burnout victims, are future- or past-oriented. Parents often forget this and appeal to future rewards or lack of rewards when attempting to motivate children. "If you don't study hard, you won't be able to go to college," to an eight-year-old is almost a meaningless statement.

Parents often get exasperated because their children act "irresponsibly"—they do not look at all of the ramifications or consequences of an action; they don't plan or think ahead. What they fail to recognize is that the future for a youngster is tomorrow and long-range planning may be the weekend at best! Likewise, parents often pull their hair out when they see children making the same mistakes over and over again, not learning from the past. What they forget, however, is that for most children the past is not really very long. It may be only a few years or more depending on the child's age. In addition, what past there is is probably not in focus. There is little order or structure, not to mention implications, stemming from their experiences.

Time control is another area presenting several traps. Many parents who burn out have never really sat down and looked at how they use their time. They often plunge into the tasks of child rearing without a careful plan. As a result, they make several critical errors: 1) they take on more than they can accomplish; 2) they pursue low level priorities and never get to what they consider most important; and 3) they procrastinate.

Parents who burn out are often overachievers. Some frantically try to chauffeur children from home to school to ball field and back again; volunteer for the PTA; work full time or part time so that the children can have more clothes; serve as a den mother; and cook sumptuous meals. If they were to sit down someday and look at all they were trying to accomplish in the allotted time, they would most likely realize that they are setting themselves up for the kill.

This is the case with Mary Ann, whose third child has just graduated from high school. She recalls being involved in so many activities with her family that her kitchen at one point looked like "Grand Central Station, with kids and parents coming and going all hours of the day." She recalls several major emotional crises stemming from the times that she forgot to pick up one or another of the children or when she and her husband got their wires crossed. "In some ways those years are out of focus. I don't really remember too many of the details, but I do remember being tired all the time. I dreaded that alarm clock every morning at 6:30 A.M. It started with my son, Phil, going out to do his morning paper route before school and then it continued on and on. I usually felt like a zombie and, thinking back, had really superficial relationships with my kids and husband because I was so tired. I always felt kind of guilty and resentful about that." Mary Ann has mixed emotions about her last child finishing high school. She will miss her involvement in the school, but looks forward to a rest. Mary Ann says that she feels bad about this desire for rest, but becomes less sad when she realizes that a lot of her friends have the same feelings. Nonetheless, she says that she still often senses that she has very little left to give, that she is spent.

This feeling of taking on more than one can accomplish can lead to a sense of failure. Parents often forget the lack of balance between goals and time available and focus more on their lack of accomplishment. Because most burnout victims are idealists and perfectionists, they have difficulty accepting this situation. They blame themselves for not having reached these goals, even though it is an impossible task.

Parents who have poor time-management skills have difficulty sorting out high priorities from low priorities. They have not analyzed what is critical in their child-rearing activities and what is not critical. As a result, they often spend their time pursuing low priority objectives to the detriment of the higher level ones. Often these parents are shocked to find out that the things they are pursuing are really not the most important priorities. When they discover this, they feel quite tense and stressed; they feel that they have lost control of their destiny and that their life as a parent is quickly slipping away.

A third trap relating to time use is the inability to delegate. Parents who burn out inevitably are poor delegators. They truly believe that only they can do what is needed for their children. They believe that they are indispensable. They take on more and more tasks and fail to utilize effectively the people and resources available to them. Generally they are perfectionists, wanting total control. Sometimes they fear not being needed or being disliked by their children or being viewed as an ungiving mother or father. Often one spouse, usually the burnout victim, totally dominates the parenting effort in terms of time. There is little covering for one another and very seldom a true sharing of feelings. This parent generally has few time-outs or emotional breathers. This situation usually develops when families initially have a rigid division of responsibilities. For example, Mom may do all the cooking and Dad all the shopping. Duties get parceled out on an equal basis at first, but the balance is often not maintained. Sooner or later one spouse takes on a totally disproportionate amount of duties. Mom may become the only chauffeur in the family and as the children get older and more involved, this task becomes quite burdensome. Dad may become the sole disciplinarian and as family life becomes more complex, this task could add a rather serious new stress on him.

Parents, likewise, must be aware of a kind of "delegation in reverse," whereby children, spouses, and others delegate their duties and tasks to them. The burned-out parent often has been the victim of this phenomenon. There are several causes for this on the part of others: fear of doing something and failing; avoidance of responsibility; laziness; overdependence; lack of experience; or fear of risk. Parents must learn to distinguish between legitimate requests for help and these kinds of behaviors. Not making that distinction could be costly. Remember, an almost universal characteristic of parents who burn out is their inability to say "No." Rate yourself as a delegator in the checklist below:

1. **Do you work longer hours than anyone in the family?**
   _____ Yes _____ No
2. **Do you spend time doing for others what they could be doing for themselves?**
   _____ Yes _____ No
3. **Do you spend time on routine details that others could handle?**
   _____ Yes _____ No
4. **Do you always have to rush to meet deadlines?**
   _____ Yes _____ No
5. **Are you unable to keep on top of priorities?**
   _____ Yes _____ No
6. **Do you have much difficulty asking your spouse or children to do things for you?**
   _____ Yes _____ No

Score: *Number of Yesses*

0–2	Effective Delegator
3–4	Average Delegator
5–6	Ineffective Delegator

THE "CRUCIALIZING" TRAP

Parents who burn out have a tendency to see all things as major issues. It starts at birth and even before. Will the baby be healthy? Am I taking care of myself well enough during pregnancy? Will the baby bond to the nurse if I do not hold him within ten minutes of birth? Should it be cloth or disposable diapers? Should I breast-feed or use formula? What kind of formula is best? What kind of rubber nipples? Which kind of mobile is best for the crib? Then, there is the draining concern over crib death. Parents constantly check their sleeping infants to make sure that they are still alive. When it comes to car seats, which are the safest? Nursery, elementary, and secondary school decisions are often "crucialized" as well. There are stories bordering on the hilarious about parents in some areas putting their yet-to-be-born children on waiting lists at prestigious local elementary schools. Many of these parents truly feel that children who don't get into these schools are "finished." They will not have performed as effective parents. They will have "missed the boat." Not only are educational decisions, understandably important, crucialized, but so are dress decisions. They, in effect, develop "designer children" who must wear the "right" shoes, shirts, slacks, and socks with all the appropriate symbols, whether they be foxes, alligators, or dragons.

Parents who crucialize often burn out. They magnify the importance of decision points beyond recognition. They truly believe that their child will suffer irreparable harm if he or she does not get the right kind of feeding, clothing, or schooling. While all of these are, no doubt, important, it is the *magnitude* of their importance that is intensified beyond what is reasonable. This intense concern literally consumes the energy of the parents. What is routine becomes crucial.

Crucializing certainly takes its toll. Parents who suffer from this find their days becoming increasingly taxing. The cumulative impact of the high state of anxiety begins to feed upon itself, causing the mind to exaggerate problems and issues beyond any reasonable semblance of their importance.

Kathy was a "grade A crucializer." She was a well-educated young mother, who had worked as an accountant for four years before having her son, Jeff. Kathy admits that she never really enjoyed her pregnancy because she spent most of her time worrying about the development and health of the baby, even though her physician routinely advised her that she and the baby seemed to be doing well. Her husband, Bill, tried to support Kathy with assurances that everything would be fine. After Jeff was born Kathy followed every child care book available. When the baby had the slightest problem, Kathy quickly paged through her manuals, checking and double-checking to relieve her own anxiety. Often Kathy would sit down, cry, and have a glass of wine after these "ordeals." "I remember spending many nights not sleeping a wink worrying about the health and safety of Jeff." No matter what the task—buying toys, selecting reading materials, television shows—it was approached as a crucial decision. By the time Jeff was ready to enter nursery school, he had become a pampered and overprotected little boy. Kathy and Bill both recognized this and worried about it, each often blaming the other for what they had "produced." Jeff would hear them arguing and become totally distraught, adding to the tension in the house. Kathy's state of "continuous exhaustion," stemming from her constant concern, could not bear this additional stress brought on by the arguments with her husband. During this period of discord she began to drink more heavily, often having several glasses of wine during the day and two or three cocktails before dinner. She did this so that she could "numb the pain of this terrible situation." After about a year, Kathy decided that she just couldn't take it anymore. "I thought that I was going to die."

One rainy evening in March, following an argument with her husband and an accompanying tantrum by her son, Kathy sat down and drank so heavily that she literally passed out and had to be carried to bed by Bill. She woke up the next morning physically and emotionally immobilized. She couldn't do a thing. She stayed in bed for nearly two days while Bill took time from work to help care for Jeff. This episode made it clear to Kathy that she needed some professional help. She is still in counseling and is convinced that if she had only been more realistic about the importance of the issues and events affecting her child, she would have been a more effective parent.

Some would say that worrying is part of parenthood. It goes with the job. We agree. However, overworry and crucializing do take

116   PARENT BURNOUT

their toll. Parents pay a price in the long run. The tolerance for the painful consequences of crucializing varies from parent to parent. Some can tolerate much. For most, however, the pain becomes overwhelming and overbearing.

MONEY TRAPS

There are two major money traps: 1) Taking a cost-benefit approach to parenting; and 2) Striving to accumulate more and more money and material goods for the present and future benefit of the children. First, there are some parents who use an economic model as their guide in parenting. They talk about "investments" in children, long term and short term, whether that investment is health care, food, education, or music lessons. This implies (and they fully expect) some payoff surpassing the investment. They look forward to a "return." Perhaps it may be something as simple as good health for the child or something as elaborate as admission to a prestigious Ivy League college. This way of thinking is becoming more evident among young highly educated parents. We wonder whether the availability of home computer systems, with their sophisticated decision models, will make this kind of parenting easier!

Parents who take this approach make a fundamental error, however. First of all, they neglect to consider all the "costs" and "benefits" of parenting that are intangible, that cannot be quantified or translated into dollars and cents. Second, they do not recognize the intrinsic values of parenting in itself. If the economic cost-benefit approach were the decision-making model used to determine whether or not to have children, there would be very few people on this earth. There are some who apply this model and reach the conclusion, "I can't imagine why anyone would want to have children. It doesn't make sense." What they are saying, and we would agree, is that this is a bad *business* decision.

With our modern-day penchant for family planning, which is certainly advisable and responsible, there is a danger that parents may go too far and expect guaranteed results because they have planned so well. The era of "The Planned Child" has come into being and with it many expectations that may never be met because they are inappropriate.

Gary and Elaine were cost-benefit thinkers when it came to

parenting. A successful insurance salesman, Gary was very much concerned about his family's financial security. Money was very important to Elaine as well. Like other housewives in today's society, she tried to economize as much as possible. However, both Gary and Elaine liked nice things and their split-level home in an upper middle income Philadelphia neighborhood reflected this.

Elaine had decided to go back to work as a nurse so that she and her husband could afford to transfer their oldest son, Mark, to a private independent prep school in the city with a tuition of $3,500 a year. They felt that this would be a good "investment" for their ten-year-old because graduates of this school often "go on to great things, meet the right people, you know."

It took a while for Mark to make the adjustment from his public school to this new environment. He expressed his concerns to his parents and they were understanding and tried to support him. Mark was concerned that he couldn't keep up with the other students academically and that he might not be accepted because he was the "new kid in class." Mark worked hard, but also worried a lot. His father and mother bragged continuously about how well their son was going to do in life because of this fine education they were providing him.

Mark's first report card was less than spectacular. When Gary and Elaine saw it, they became upset immediately. "All this money and this is what we get?" Mark cried and felt that he had let everybody down. Gary warned him that he had better get on the ball. That night Gary and Elaine sat up and discussed the issue. The major concern was not Mark's feelings, not his academic success, but whether the $3,500 spent was a wise decision. At one point Gary even said, "Maybe we should put the money in CD's (certificates of deposit) instead. By the time Mark is twenty-one, they would be worth quite a bit. The money might be better than the education, particularly if he continues to get grades like this." Today Mark is still at the prep school and doing a little better academically. However, Gary and Elaine still ponder the wisdom of their decision.

The second money trap can be equally devastating and probably affects more parents. It is the desire or felt need to accumulate wealth for the benefit of the children. It is almost an instinctive drive among caring parents to want to leave something for their children, and the more the better. This usually begins to take on more importance as fathers and mothers approach mid-life and old age does not seem so far away. For some parents this need to "leave something" becomes an obsession. This obligation coupled with the enormous financial demands of child rearing often drive parents to spend substantial amounts of time attempting to earn money. Workaholism is rampant among burned-out parents. They do not know when to stop.

Again, the real issue here is one of degree. Obviously, it takes a lot of money to raise children today. However, the distinction between what is necessary and what is desirable is often clouded. Parents have a tendency to accept or even create more and more "necessities" for children, thereby creating the need for more and more money. Toys are a case in point. Jason, age eleven, would have "absolutely died" if he had not gotten his favorite video game set this past Christmas. He could never have faced "all the kids who are getting one." So Dad and Mom, who really couldn't afford it, squeezed out the several hundred dollars it took to get young Jason the set, saving him from this traumatic disgrace! All at a cost of $245. And there are two other children in the family who had their own Christmas expectations.

When good caring parents spend more time working simply to accumulate more money, they usually develop a sense of ambivalence. What's it all about? As they spend less and less time with their children and see them grow faster than they would like, they become saddened that they are being driven by situational factors beyond their control. "I would love to spend more time with my kids, believe me. There is nothing that I hate more than going to work in that hardware store every Saturday. But I have to if we are going to maintain this standard of living. I feel like sitting down and crying!" laments Mario, a father of three young children, ages ten, eight, and five.

Because burnout victims are basically givers and providers they fall victim to the money traps more than others. Often the major immediate trigger for the onset of burnout is the sheer physical exhaustion from overwork. This is one trap that will continue to be a major problem during the 1980s as the economic burdens of raising children continue to skyrocket.

THE GRANDPARENT TRAP

The impact of grandparents on the role of parents is often complex and ambivalent. Grandparents perceive themselves as beautiful people and form warm loving relationships with their grandchildren. Grandchildren generally have the fondest memories of their life relating to their grandparents. Arthur Kornhaber and Kenneth L. Woodward do an excellent job portraying the importance of the "vital connection" between the two.[1]

The problems generally arise in the relationship between the grandparents and parents. Difficulties occur when parents have not established their own authority role with the grandparents. This is usually due to uncut emotional, financial, or otherwise supportive attachments. There is a strong connection to the demands and expectations of the grandparent. As a result, a kind of "shared parenting" develops, which over the long run usually creates serious problems.

Most parents want grandparents to have a relationship with their children, but are usually sensitive to undue or inappropriate influence. The key causes of conflict center around either differing values or differing emotional states. Whether it be a simple issue such as giving the children more candy than you as a parent would like or something more complex such as religious beliefs, conflicts between parents and grandparents in relation to the grandchildren can be most painful. Most parents feel rather distraught when caught in these predicaments. Caring and sensitive parents often find the resolution of these conflicts very difficult and have a tendency to avoid or postpone addressing the problem until it becomes unbearable. They then usually handle it in an awkward way that exacerbates the problem.

Martha found herself in this situation with her parents, particularly her mother, who lived about twenty miles away in a suburb of Miami, Florida. Martha had been close to her parents all her life and generally had a pleasant and peaceful relationship with them, while having some disagreements from time to time. However, the subtle tensions, which were continuously growing in intensity, began

[1] *Grandparents/Grandchildren: The Vital Connection* (Garden City, N.Y.: Doubleday/Anchor Books, 1981).

to develop soon after her daughter was born. The grandparents were totally thrilled to have a grandchild and were very supportive of both Martha and her husband, Gene. Martha's mother visited her practically every day at first, but then cut down the visits to once or twice a week. When she could not visit, she would call her. During each visit or telephone call Martha received some advice on how to treat the baby. It usually began, "If I were you, I would . . ." After a while these words began to grate on Martha's nerves. When she was on the telephone with her mother, she would often hold the receiver away from her ear. When her mother was there in person, she would look the opposite way and roll her eyes in disgust and frustration, all the while feeling terribly guilty about her lack of tolerance. "If I were you, I would . . ." became her nemesis.

Martha's mother, while certainly well-meaning, took a rational intellectual approach in her recommendations to her daughter. She was not tuned in to the feelings that her daughter was experiencing: the concern, anxiety, stress, and physical exhaustion of being a new mother. She had probably forgotten or sublimated her own similar feelings of twenty-five years ago. She was able to take a much "cooler" approach this second time around in her vicarious kind of parenting. In a sense, it was her second chance at being flawless as a young mother!

In some ways, Martha thought that her mother was right and she was angry at herself for not being able to appreciate what she suggested. This ambivalent state of resentment, confusion, love, and hate toward her mother added a new dimension of pressure on Martha, which magnified the normal stresses of parenthood. Martha mentally planned all kinds of confrontations with her mother. "I will tell her right out to mind her own business," or "I will say, 'Look, Mom, everybody raises children differently, let me do my own thing,'" or "Please don't say 'If I were you' one more time. I can't stand it. You are driving me crazy." After fantasizing about each "showdown," Martha would feel totally guilty about it and begin to get very sad. Her husband would become upset because he saw his wife so dejected. They would then discuss her mother and eventually end up arguing about each other's families.

This went on for over a year until one day, after being examined by her physician, it was discovered that Martha was developing colitis. Following several consultations with her doctor and a recommended psychologist, it became clear that this condition was directly connected to Martha's bittersweet relationship with her mother. The conflict of Martha's love, caring, and sensitivity to her mother's feelings and her own physical exhaustion and worry over her new role as parent was literally tying her into knots. Martha told her psychologist quite early in their sessions and over and over again that she was convinced that her mother probably thought that she was a mediocre and ill-equipped mother. "Why does she feel the need to give me so much advice?" Martha said that this really bothered her and, in some ways, was gnawing at her whole self-concept.

With her psychologist's help, Martha has confronted her mother. While it was painful at first, they are now developing a much stronger positive relationship.

Alan had a similar problem, but has not been as fortunate in its resolution. His father, a businessman in his sixties, saw his grand-children, especially Alan's two sons, as extensions of himself. "They are chips off the old block . . . just like me. My connection with immortality." Alan's father often credited his grandsons' attributes to himself. "These kids can't go wrong with their genes." This grandfather not only took credit for much of his grandchildren's development, but he also actively engaged himself in their lives. Almost every weekend he stopped by and picked up the children and took them to a fast-food restaurant or a ball game. He bought them many toys, athletic equipment, and clothing. "The kids just love him. They hold him on a pedestal."

It was not unusual for this grandfather to contradict his son and daughter-in-law when they were trying to discipline the children. "Aw, leave them alone. They're just kids. They're okay." These occasions usually drove Alan and his wife up a wall. After his father left, Alan would go into a tirade. "How do you tell him to keep his nose out of things? You'd think that he would know this by now!" The children would usually take up support for "Grandpa" and both Alan and his wife became even more furious with them.

This could only go on for so long. On one Thanksgiving Day, shortly after the holiday meal, Alan's father stepped in one more time to rescue his grandchildren. Alan blew up and argued vehemently with his father. Grandpa was shocked and reacted in anger, "After all I've done for them. I'm only sticking up for my grandchildren. Can't I do that?" Totally enraged, he stormed out of the house, taking Alan's mother with him. The whole day was ruined.

Alan's relationship with his father has not been the same since then. It has become very cool. The children miss seeing their grandfather as much as they used to. When they see him, they feel awkward. Alan wonders to himself often whether or not he was too harsh. Or was he harsh enough? Was he too intolerant? Not understanding or patient enough? Or was his father really wrong? He feels uncomfortable not knowing the answers and he doesn't like the current state of affairs at all.

GUILT TRAPS

One of the most powerful and most common parent traps is guilt. Guilt, of course, is a relative thing and is very much related to self-expectations. Guilt sensitivity varies from person to person, but burned-out parents generally experience guilt to a much higher degree than others. They often feel that they never do enough for their children and they have a hair-trigger for the guilt response. Children or others who desire to control or influence the behavior of these parents get to know the triggers very well.

What are some of these triggers? A major one is the feeling that one is not giving the children enough attention. Whether it was the busy professional father, the working mother, the parent holding down two jobs, or the mother overactive in community affairs, the feeling was widespread. A whole repertoire of compensation for this lack of attention (methods to alleviate guilt) has been established. They range from simple soothing aphorisms such as "It's not the quantity of time, but the quality that counts" to systems of downright material payoffs: "I've got to take the kids to a real nice [expensive] resort this year. After all, I don't spent too much time with them." Most parents know that the best gift that they can give to their children is their attention and that the lack of attention can be devastating. The caring parent is most sensitive to failure in this area and usually feels very guilty about it.

A second common trigger for guilt is the feeling that the children are not getting enough material goods. Considerate, overzealous, and achievement-oriented parents place very high demands on themselves for providing not only superior food, shelter, and education, but also the very latest in toys, clothing, and furnishings. Fathers and mothers often work overtime or take on second jobs in order to provide that little "extra," the lack of which is often viewed as deprivation. It is often this extra work that spells the difference between stability and total exhaustion in parents. Parents often feel drained, irritable, and dispirited, that they are working harder and harder and getting nowhere, particularly in these days of high inflation.

A third sensitive area for the guilt-prone is public involvement in such children's activities as Little League games, school plays, recitals, and so on. Understandably, children generally want their parents present at these events. However, attendance often is logistically difficult or impossible due to work schedules or other responsibilities. When there are several children involved, this could literally become a nightmare. There are many parents who count the days till the end of soccer season. "Every Saturday and Sunday for ten weeks is tied up!" The caring, concerned parents who think that they should be involved feel terrible about missing an event or showing up late or leaving early. The amount of stress can be overwhelming when the parent has to deal with the saddened faces of the children they have disappointed. Many parents "can't bear the thought of letting them know that I won't be there." All kinds of schedule contortions are attempted to avoid these disappointments.

A fourth guilt trigger is comparisons with other fathers and mothers: "Ted's father took him to Disney World" or "Kathy's mom is a Girl Scout leader." Children sometimes explicitly or implicitly motivate their parents to do things for them by drawing on the accomplishments and kindnesses of their friends' parents. Many parents, particularly reactive burnout types, are quite sensitive to these comparisons. Of course, they never win the game because there will always be some parent who is perceived as doing more.

Another common guilt trigger is the "health hammer." It is the rare parent who is not concerned about the health of the children. Often it is the top priority of parents: "As long as they are healthy." Lack of good health, particularly if it was caused by negligence or inadequate care on their part, is the last thing that the parent wants to experience, whether it is a common flu episode, measles, mumps, or something much more complex and trying. To avoid this potential trauma parents will do almost anything. The caring parent will feel obliged to provide nearly any service and perform any task to prevent or alleviate illness in a child. The children come to expect this and it can become a trigger for parent guilt. "I swear I could have the bubonic plague myself, but if I heard my daughter coughing in her room at night, I would definitely get out of bed and go check on her!" one mother told us.

The last guilt trigger, which affects parents of teenagers more than others, is the possibility of revenge by the children. Some parents live in constant fear of being let down, disgraced, totally embarrassed, or financially drained by some act of their children. The possibility that this might be a defiant act makes them shudder. The following thoughts are common: "Will he go out and take drugs just to numb some of the pressures that I put on him?" "Will she go out and get sexually involved with some guy because she feels that she can't communicate with us?" Parents who have these fears to a high degree often feel like they are walking on thin ice; one false move and their children will go off and do something devastating. When something does in fact happen, their first response is, "What did I do wrong? Why did I cause this to happen?" This state of mind creates high anxiety and stress, quickly harming the sense of mutual respect and open communication necessary for effective parenting.

THE SEVEN DEADLY "SINS" OF PARENTING

There is a distinct set of parent traps that we refer to as the seven deadly "sins" of parenting: pride, lust, sloth, anger, envy, gluttony, and greed. Together and separately they often engulf parents, moving them into situations that trigger burnout or exacerbate it. In some cases they are even sought as the cures or ways to prevent burnout. It must be remembered that ultimately these traps do not stem from inherent vices but rather overdone virtues. Consequently, because all of these traps have an attractive side, they can become appealing and enticing for the parent. Fathers and mothers who are burning out are particularly vulnerable to them because of their tendency to overachieve. The sense of moderation and balance needed to prevent virtues from becoming shortcomings is often missing. It is important that you become aware of any vulnerability that you may have in these areas.

Pride

Burned-out parents very often have been involved in competition with friends, relatives, and neighbors, particularly in relation to their children. They cannot stand the thought of being an "average" mother or father. In their quest for being the best, they lose touch with reality. They develop an overconcern about how things look and many family decisions are made against that sole criterion. They begin to live two lives as parents, one public and one private. They expect their children to do likewise. This dichotomy, with its consequent shifting back and forth, causes a high degree of stress in itself. It detracts from the authenticity of family relationships and relationships with those outside the family.

Ed and Carol had been married about fifteen years and had a son, age eleven, and a daughter, age eight. They were comfortably settled in their quiet community in the suburbs of Baltimore. They were relatively close to neighbors and had some very good friends with whom they had been close for years. Ed and Carol had spent many enjoyable days with their friends before the children were born and when they were younger. They often counted themselves fortunate to have such good companions. However, during the past few years, they found themselves becoming more sensitive to the accomplishments of their friends' children and doing some comparing: report cards, success in sports, music ability, clothing, appearance, and so on. One evening on the way home from visiting friends, while the children slept in the back seat of the car, they began to discuss these feelings. "How did we get to this point? Competing with our friends?" Both Ed and Carol quickly agreed that they thought it was their friends who were really "starting it," with all their bragging about their children, especially "Larry, who responds to anything good about our kids with 'one better' about his kids." Both admitted that this had been grating at them for some time and they found themselves bragging much more when they were in Larry's presence. During the next few months, as Ed and Carol were becoming increasingly aware of it, the competition

seemed to skyrocket. At one point it was hard to tell who was initi-
ating and who was reacting. Ed found himself spending a lot of
time thinking about Larry's attitude and the more he thought
about it, the more furious he became: "I'll show him. My kids will
be so great that he won't know what hit him." Ed admitted to
Carol that he was really hurt that his old friend was acting in such
a competitive fashion. "I can see where he should be proud of his
kids. But I'm proud too and I'm not going to let him outdo me."
Ed reached a point where he couldn't wait to tell Larry about the
successes of his children, "just to see his face." Before long the children began to feel uncomfortable when visiting as their parents
continued to pressure them to outperform the other children in success stories. Much unspoken hostility had developed between the
two formerly close friends, who had been very supportive of one another as parents in the past. Ed felt alienated from Larry and it became obvious that the feeling was mutual. Today the two families
see each other occasionally, usually during one of the holidays, but
their relationship is rather superficial.

Lust

Sexual affairs are often viewed as a new beginning, a renewal, a
new life, or even as an act of entrepreneurship for the achievement-
oriented person. Parents who reach the higher stages of burnout are
more susceptible to extramarital affairs than those at the earlier
stages. They often feel that a major change is necessary in their
lives and a new sexual relationship is sometimes the method for
bringing this about.

While the physical pleasure may be rewarding and the diversion
welcomed, the emotional price in terms of human energy most
often magnifies the problem. This is particularly true if the sexual
encounter is linked with a romantic involvement, because some new
emotional connections begin to develop. It introduces a new set of
demands that generally cannot be coped with in the parent's current mental or physical state.

Jack was a "happily married" father of two daughters and one
son. A professor at a large urban university and a consultant, Jack
had been very successful and had high ambitions for himself as well
as his family. In many ways, he lived for his children. He worked

very hard, putting in extra time at the university on special projects. He also traveled extensively giving lectures on his research and writing. His wife complained that he was not home enough, but was supportive of his intense and busy professional involvement. Jack's rationale for all his work was his children's welfare.

Jack became more and more tired as he kept up this frenetic pace. On several occasions his physician told him that he had better slow down. He would for a while, but then gradually his pace would increase until he reached near exhaustion again. At times like this he would get depressed and wonder whether he would ever achieve his lofty financial goals for his family. He began to look forward to the day "when the kids will be on their own." These thoughts began to frighten him. "Am I beginning to resent these kids and see them as the cause of my exhaustion?" Gradually but steadily Jack began to delay coming home to all the "unappreciative demanders. They have no idea of what I'm going through and they could care less." He also began to view his wife, Ellen, as being too supportive of the children and not attentive enough to him. He saw her spending her evenings and weekends involved with the children's schoolwork, music lessons, and hygiene needs. She would usually flop into bed too tired for sexual relations. Jack often became hostile and Ellen responded by crying and whispering, "I'm just too tired. Perhaps tomorrow night." Occasionally, the roles were reversed and Jack was the one that was just "too tired." This situation continued for about two years with Jack and Ellen having sexual relations four or five times a month on the average.

During this period Jack was becoming more frustrated. "All this work. I'm killing myself, probably ruining my health, and even this is being taken away from me. They don't care about me. None of them. I might as well not even be here. I think that she is happy when I'm not around placing sexual demands on her." It was at this point that Jack began to be attracted to Julie, a professional colleague whom he had worked with for the past two years. He found himself scheduling more meetings with this attractive young woman, who had been divorced a few years earlier. Within a few months Jack found himself intensely infatuated by Julie. He felt "great" when he was with her, "refreshed, a new lease on life. She was vivacious and didn't drain me." Jack couldn't get Julie off his mind. He envisioned himself married to her, living separate from his wife and children, a thought that he could not have imagined a few years before. While he was frightened by these thoughts, he could not stop himself from developing his relationship with Julie. It was obvious that Julie enjoyed his company and attention. Within a few months Jack and Julie were involved romantically and sexually.

Julie fell madly in love with Jack. In some ways, Jack loved Julie, but he still felt that he loved his wife and certainly his children. It was obvious to Jack that his life was getting too complex. He looked for simple solutions, but there were none. "What a mess. How did I get myself into this?" The anxiety and the stress of managing his homelife while maintaining his affair with Julie soon affected Jack's physical and mental health. Upon the strong recommendation of his physician, Jack took a six-month leave from the university to rest. After psychological counseling, he broke off his relationship with Julie. He is closer to his wife and is convinced that if he had put some of his effort into his family relationships instead of work, he could have built an intimate web of relationships that would have supported him rather than depleted him.

Sloth

Sloth is generally expressed by a lack of ambition and a low degree of activity, a state of ambivalence where the parent has no clear goals. It is a period of no growth and often regression. Individuals who are suffering from sloth are generally unresponsive to their environment. They spend a lot of time sitting around daydreaming or watching television.

Often it is assumed that there is a high correlation between the number of tasks a parent has to perform and burnout. While unrealistic workloads and responsibilities can be a critical factor in burnout, having too little to do can be just as troublesome. Often the tasks become magnified if there is not enough to do. Parents procrastinate until the last minute and find themselves overwhelmed, making "mountains out of molehills." The apprehension that the parents feel in regard to procrastination is usually more burdensome than the actual performance of the task and causes a general feeling of being overwhelmed by normal household duties. Parents who suffer from sloth find themselves in a state of immobilization, unable to take the "parenting bull by the horns." They find themselves backed into the corner. They react by doing nothing. "Where do I begin?" "Why bother?" "There is no hope, not for me."

Nancy had reached this point about two years ago when she concluded that her life was pretty much out of her control. "I will never catch up." Her house was a continual mess. Her three teenage children were in and out so much that she would plop in a living room chair shaking her head in despair as she turned on the television to watch "anything that was on." She felt that this would give her a sense of freedom for a while before her husband came home from work. Nancy had gained fifteen pounds during the past year. She was constantly picking on sweets and chain smoking as she sat around the house. She didn't know where to begin. While she complained about having no time to get anything done, she actually resented those hours in the day when she was alone, when, in fact, she could get things done. She would start one project, like tidying up the family room, only to divert her attention to or from a phone call from a neighbor or friend. The calls usually lasted longer than she wanted. Nancy recalls never really enjoying them and "always feeling guilty about not doing more constructive things."

Nancy had reached a point where she literally hated getting up and facing the day. She felt guilty and defensive about her lack of productive activity. Every evening she would promise herself that "tomorrow I am going to get my act together and get going." Needless to say, she was disappointed by evening. She soon began to blame those around her (her children, her husband) for the condition that she found herself in. "If it wasn't for them, I could keep this place in shape." After several confrontations and in the middle of a tirade by Nancy her youngest daughter yelled out, "Mom, you're just a lazy slob. Don't blame us!" Nancy was enraged and struck her child. She had never done this before. That evening she thought about what her daughter had said. "It was painful to realize how correct she was. I knew that I had a serious problem and that it would ruin my family if I didn't correct it soon. The next day I made an appointment with Dr. ———." Nancy and her psychologist have been working closely during the past year. She has made great progress. She has lost fifteen pounds, is far more active, and procrastinates much less. She realizes that she must take one step at a time.

Her counselor found that Nancy had a tendency to magnify the importance of each parenting task to the point of being overwhelmed. She was afraid of failure and of disappointing her husband and children, so she opted to do nothing or very little. She could then blame her lack of parental success on circumstances rather than incompetence. Her model of what a good parent was supposed to be and do was unrealistic. She thought (rightfully) that she could never live up to it.

Anger

Some anger is temporary and passes with time. Other anger is long-lasting and can become a characteristic of a personality, forming a "state of anger." Whatever the length, most agree that anger is probably the most devastating of emotions. It can literally drain away human energy. It can be destructive and corrosive. It can lead to an outlook on life that feeds upon itself, generating more anger. It often leads to erratic mood swings and other neurotic behaviors.

When all is said and done, anger is the result of not getting what one wants. It is based on disappointment; the key ingredients in the anger formula are expectations and occurrences. Because parents who burn out have a tendency to hold unrealistically high expectations, they often see themselves failing to achieve expected goals and objectives. They generally do not recognize the unrealistic nature of these goals, and, as a result, are not aware of the underlying cause of their anger. Some parents are "seething continuously," sometimes actively and sometimes in a passive kind of way. The parents' disappointment often becomes obvious and spills over into the attitudes of the children, who, in turn, see themselves as the cause of this disappointment. This situation establishes a "chain of hostility," which feeds upon itself, destroying all who are linked to it.

Sam was a thirty-five-year-old father of two sons and a daughter. The son of immigrant parents, he had finished college evenings, majoring in accounting. He was now working for a large manufacturing firm in Fall River, Massachusetts. Sam felt that he had had "kind of a tough life . . . a lot of pressure and obstacles to over-come, but I did it." He prided himself on the fact that he had made some significant socioeconomic gains. He had even higher goals for his children. "The name of the game in this country is money and power. I want my kids to get all they can." Sam believed that the way you reached these goals was through educa-tion, hard work, and the right connections.

Sam's oldest son was in junior high school and the two youngest, a daughter and second son, were in elementary school. He had set very high expectations for his children early. They were encouraged to read, do their homework, and above all, get good grades, that is, perfect grades. He was convinced that these early years were criti-cal. "It is make or break time," he often warned. "Anything short of perfection is not acceptable." He was as strict about their behav-ior as he was about their schoolwork. "They have to toe the mark," he would say. "They'll thank me later."

Sam's oldest son had done very well in elementary school and the two younger children were following in their brother's footsteps. However, the first year of junior high school was another story. For some reason or other, the boy's first report card was far below what Sam expected or could tolerate: three A's; three B's, and one C. He went into a tirade when he saw this. His first reaction was to blame the teachers. However, after meeting and chatting with them the next day, he turned his wrath on his son. The scene was explosive, a lot of screaming and many warnings. The younger chil-dren got the message also. He told them that he was "really let down." For days after this episode, there was often complete silence at the dinner table as Sam sat there fuming. There was very little talk after dinner as well as Sam sat reading the newspaper or watching television. Sam's wife, Irene, tried to soothe him, but to no avail. He would push her away, muttering such comments as, "After all that I'm doing for them. They'll probably end off where my father was, behind the eight ball all his life."

At the second report card his son's grades were lower than the first: one A, four B's and two C's. The grades of the younger chil-dren had fallen off a little as well. Sam blew up! He sat his chil-dren down and screamed at the top of his lungs, "Look, you little dumbbells, you are going to get perfect grades next term or it's going to be all over for you! You'll see." He was livid and his wife was very concerned about his health. She thought he was going to have a heart attack. He told her that he just couldn't take it anymore. "This and all the pressures at work are just too much. I was counting on these kids to make me happy, but they are not coming through." A few weeks after this episode Sam's son's school counselor called him and his wife and asked if they could get together sometime soon. When they met, the counselor pointed out that many of the teachers had indicated a serious concern about his son's obvious anxiety and his developing apathy. "It's like he has given up. His behavior is surprising." One teacher who discussed the issue with him pointed out that the youngster responded, "I can't win. Why should I try? I can't be perfect and that's all that counts with my father."

Sam was surprised to hear this. At first he felt that his son had violated their relationship by going to a third person about his difficulty. However, after several long meetings with the school counselor and some of the teachers, Sam realized that something had to be done to turn the situation around. He has come to realize that his anger was not helping matters, but, in fact, exacerbating the problems. He is now trying to change his style, to control his anger and utilize this energy for constructive purposes. He can literally see his anger diminish as he lowers his expectations and makes them more consistent with reality.

Envy

Like anger, envy can be a powerful emotion, draining away tremendous amounts of energy. Envy is one of the more mysterious traps. Unlike jealousy, which is based on the fear of losing something that you have, envy is the distinctive urge to destroy or spoil something that another person has or has done in order to feel equal. It is often based on the fear of being disregarded or viewed as inadequate. Often people who have been deprived feel more envious than others. They regret and resent those periods of deprivation and the feelings that went with them. Because deprivation is often a relative thing (what do I have or not have compared to those around me?), individuals entrapped by envy feel a need to destroy physically or, more often, verbally, the accomplishments, possessions, or attributes of those around them. Sometimes the closer the envied parties are to them, the stronger the need to destroy.

Burning-out parents are particularly sensitive to how they are viewed by their children. After all, they are putting so much into their children they expect to receive some reciprocation. They have a tendency to be very sensitive to any praise or attraction their children may bestow on others. They feel that they deservedly have cornered the market on devotion. No one else has given as much and therefore no one else is entitled to as much in return. Sometimes they isolate their children and "protect" them from those whom they perceive as threats to their own total domination of their children's dedication. They often destroy those relationships. Children usually become confused when this happens and do not quite understand their parents' motivation. Children begin to hold back information concerning their true feelings and soon this breaks down the communication. The situation detracts from the authenticity and intimacy of the parent-child relationship.

In some cases, parental envy becomes a powerful tool for the children, especially older ones. Sensing this competition and the desire to destroy on the part of the parent, the child uses the exclusivity of their relationship as a leverage over the behavior of the parent. The message, although subtle, is, "If you don't do what I want, I'll become more fond of so and so." Parents who are easy prey for this kind of trap become very sensitive to the influences of relatives, teachers, coaches, friends, the parents of children's friends, and even clergymen. They put themselves in a double bind. On the one hand, they want their children to have good relationships with these kinds of people, but at the same time they fear that they may be compared to them and not measure up. The mixed signals that they send to their children create stress and confusion. If this continues into the critical teenage years, the ambivalence will become even less tolerable for the children. It will severely diminish the quality of the parent-child relationship further, frustrating the parent all the more.

Gluttony

Gluttony, another serious "deadly trap," is the compulsive need to take into our bodies some form of tranquilizer, whether that be actual food, drink, or drugs. As a relief for pain, we rely on them in periods of anxiety, when we are threatened, lonely, or depressed. The feeling of a full stomach becomes a replacement for security, intimacy, and love that may be lacking. Parents who burn out usually experience various forms of gluttony; that is, they have a tendency to take in more food, drink, or drugs than is reasonably good for them. Of course, gluttony solves no problems but simply adds to them. Parents find themselves in a vicious circle, eating or drinking more and more to dull the pain and disliking themselves more and more because of weight gain or drug abuse.

Al had this problem. The father of four young children who were born about two years apart, he often felt that he had never really controlled his own life. While he loved his family, he also realized that his marriage at nineteen and the ensuing rapid development of his family had not given him much time to prepare himself for fatherhood either financially or psychologically. Al found himself working two jobs to make ends meet. When he came home from work he "didn't want to hear any problems." To assure that he wouldn't he often stopped at a local bar in his Boston neighborhood to "tie one on." If he did not stop at the bar, he would drink several beers or more soon after he walked in the door. He loved his children but just couldn't "take all the confusion" at the dinner table and after dinner. "It was too much after working all day."

Al found himself drinking more and more to ease the pain. He lost respect for himself as he gained more weight. His "beer gut" and his morning hangovers made his getting out of bed every morning a "totally depressing experience." He wouldn't even look at himself in the mirror. If he did, it was from his neck up. Because Al felt this way about himself, he began to assume that everybody else did. Once an easygoing friendly person, he became defensive and obnoxious to his friends and relatives. He drank more, gaining over thirty pounds in two years. He continues his lifestyle to this day, often sharing his "plight" with fellow drinkers at the neighborhood bar. He has not been able to address the real problem honestly: the difficulty of rearing four children. His drinking partners have not helped matters, but, in fact, have added to his problem by their "sympathetic" ears. His wife holds out hope that someday he will be able to change. Al needs help, but at this point he will not seek it. He feels that "everything will be okay."

Greed

We have stated several times that one of the factors likely to create the tendency toward burnout is that of a lack of balance in the life of the parent. Some parents are consumed by their parenting role. The pitfalls or traps described in this chapter are all examples of the loss of balance. Greed is one of the most dangerous. The danger of this trap lies in the power of reward associated with it. Our culture places a tremendous emphasis on the acquisition of material goods. Greed can begin with a simple overbelief in the value of material things and then quickly become an obsession in itself. Greed is the all-powerful and all-consuming need for the acquisition of wealth or gain. It can manifest itself in many ways, including an obsession with increased social position or career promotions or political clout. In our study and research, we discovered many parents who either had fallen into the greed trap themselves or had a spouse who had been captured by greed.

Dennis was one of them. He was a man with a very pleasant personality who always had something nice to say about people unless the subject of money came up. Once that happened, he almost immediately developed an angry and defensive attitude and a "me against them" posture toward others. Dennis had grown up in a family where the mother constantly expressed her disappointments toward the father for not being a financial success. To this background was added Dennis' lack of success in school. After Dennis graduated from a local community college, he worked at several low-paying jobs and began to worry that he was doomed to the same henpecked existence as his father.

As he began to place pressure on himself to "establish a decent living," he met Linda, and after about a year they got married. Linda worked as a secretary and even though neither of them made a lot of money, their combined salaries came to more money than Dennis had ever earned. Almost immediately, Dennis set down rigid rules for the spending and saving of his and Linda's salaries. Linda balked at simply turning over her paycheck to him and having literally to beg for an inadequate allowance, but he convinced her that she wasn't disciplined enough to adhere to "their" vigorous saving plan. As time went on, Linda simply gave in and allowed

Dennis to control all aspects of their economic life. Eventually, Dennis got a good job as a salesman and because of his hard work and organized nature, he started to make much more money. Linda began to feel the "call of nature" and started to talk about wanting to begin a family. This wish was initially ignored and later ruled out by Dennis because they "just can't afford to have one income." As Linda continued to put on more pressure, Dennis finally weakened and soon Linda became pregnant and left her job. After that happened, all Dennis could talk about was what a shock the loss of her income was to his plans for accumulating wealth. Linda complained to her friends that Dennis took all of the fun out of her pregnancy with his constant harping about money. During this time, Dennis' friends were becoming increasingly irritated by his unrelenting desire to save money at all costs. If Dennis and Linda went to dinner with one or two other couples, he would complain throughout the meal about the cost. He became such a "drag" that slowly their friends began to reject and avoid them.

Dennis' response to all of this was to redouble his efforts to increase his income and put more of it into savings. Throughout their marriage, they bought houses, fixed them up, and sold them for profit so that they could get a more expensive house. At first, Linda had enjoyed it, but she soon discovered that this process was merely an extension of Dennis' program of saving money and moving up. He measured every request of hers for a household improvement or decorating suggestion by the standard of whether it would pay for itself when they sold the house. Linda began to fear that she would never be able to call a house her home because Dennis would soon sell it and move on in his determined progression toward more wealth.

When Bobby was born, Linda at last had her baby. She had some security and someone to love without thinking of money. But Bobby represented a new source of expense for Dennis and he began to resent Linda's requests for money to buy baby clothes and toys. Dennis also developed a new subject of conversation. He constantly complained about how much baby food was costing. There were new financial worries too. How would they ever afford private schools? Bobby would need expensive toys, clothes, and sports equipment. Dennis began to work harder. He was away more and more. Linda began to resent his being away and his miserly clamp on their money. She had almost no support or relief from the boredom and drudgery of infant care. They never went out unless he could "write it off," and this always required the presence of customers, so they were almost never alone during their nights out.

It wasn't that Dennis didn't know that there were problems. He was basically a good person and he dearly loved Linda and Bobby, but his desire for more money was driving a wedge between Linda and himself. It also caused Linda to become angry about being "stuck at home" and deprived of a full life because of Bobby. She began to feel tired all the time. Linda and Dennis fought more and unless they were picking at one another they rarely spoke. Linda knew something was very wrong but was afraid to ask Dennis for money to see a counselor. All the while, Dennis' savings account got bigger and bigger.

To this day Dennis and Linda remain enmeshed in the greed trap. Linda is progressing rapidly down the road toward Chronic Disenchantment, complete burnout. Dennis says that things will change as soon as they "have enough money." However, because of his greed that day will never come.

It is important that these traps be recognized if parents are going to avoid burnout or recover from it. Some of the traps are obvious and others more subtle. Some have been with us for a long time and some are more recent in their development. All of them must be addressed and understood at some point. We recommend that the reader spend some time thinking about and discussing the material in this chapter before going on to the next sections of the book. The following guideline may be helpful in doing this:

TRAP	MY LEVEL OF VULNERABILITY			MAJOR CAUSE OF VULNERABILITY
Time Use	High	Medium	Low	
Crucializing	High	Medium	Low	
Money	High	Medium	Low	
Grandparents	High	Medium	Low	
Guilt	High	Medium	Low	
Pride	High	Medium	Low	
Lust	High	Medium	Low	
Sloth	High	Medium	Low	

	MY LEVEL OF			**MAJOR CAUSE**
TRAP	**VULNERABILITY**			**OF VULNERABILITY**
Anger	High	Medium	Low	
Envy	High	Medium	Low	
Gluttony	High	Medium	Low	
Greed	High	Medium	Low	

My Most Vulnerable Area:_____

My Least Vulnerable Area:_____

7

Parent Burnout Recovery Plan

Since you have already taken the *Parent Burnout Index* (pages 40–41) you know where you stand. Burnout is either a problem for you or it is not. This chapter presents a treatment plan. Those of you who scored 40 or above in the index should follow the treatment plan very carefully for the whole six-week period. You may wish to read the whole plan through first and then go step by step one day at a time. Those of you who scored below 40 points should read the entire treatment plan in order to become familiar with its content, but you would be better served by focusing on the Bypass Plan in Chapter 8.

Some of you may be wondering if the number and ages of your children make a difference in your ability to recover from burnout. Our research and clinical experience have shown that while the ages and number of children can be a factor in the incidence of burnout, these two factors are not significantly correlated with the occurrence of recovery. Common sense, however, dictates that the ages and number of children will affect the style and ease with which you carry out these plans. The most significant effect of these two variables shows up when you are directed to share part of this treatment plan with your family. For instance, if your children are under five years old, the level of communication and sharing will differ from a situation with teenagers.

In designing the Recovery Plan we have attempted to take into

consideration as many family situations as possible: the busy schedules of working fathers, the time pressures of mothers who work
outside of the home, and the many unavoidable individual, family,
and social responsibilities of parents. We have designed the treatment plan and directions with the assumption that you will do
what we tell you and in a manner that is appropriate for you and
your family. Remember, the plan may appear to be designed to
make you self-centered. Nothing could be further from the truth.
However, the plan *will* instill a spirit of "selfish altruism," the realization that you must take care of yourself in order to regain peak
performance in parenting.

The choice to make changes is very often a subconscious one. Indeed, the treatment we offer for burnout is actually an attempt to
raise the following very important questions to the conscious realm.
Change is likely and the burnout cycle is threatened when you can
answer these three questions affirmatively.

QUESTION 1: *Will I become a balanced person with interests and
activities outside of the family?* One thing learned by many parents
during the Doubts stage is that they need more support than the
family alone can give them. Some parents had varied and full lives
outside of the family before their children were born. For them the
process of "reactivating" is much easier than for those whose lives
were rather narrow and withdrawn and who hoped that somehow
parenthood would finally fulfill them. They will have to build a life
that they never had before their children. But all parents have to
learn to build—or rebuild—varied and full lives outside of their
families, away from the responsibilities of child rearing.

QUESTION 2: *Will I pay more attention to my physical and
mental health as well as my personal growth?* This question relates
significantly to a parent's perception of his or her value as a person.
After all, the first law of nature is self-preservation. Many parents
misguidedly believe that their lives will be fulfilled if they can just
give more to their families. As they become tired and depressed,
they often respond with more giving. If this rigid pattern of behavior continues, they will speed rapidly down the road to burnout,
resenting it all the way. Recovery is unlikely. If, however, they
begin to take stock of the counterproductive nature of their past behavior and start to rest up, take care of themselves, and personally
grow, the burning out will have been a learning experience.

QUESTION 3: *Will I become closer and more intimate with those I love?* The answer to this question depends, to a great degree, on the answer to the second question. As parents burn out they lose touch with who they are. They get confused and feel separated and distanced even from themselves. If parents feel distant and pulled away from themselves, they cannot possibly be close and intimate with one another. A major task of personal growth and burnout recovery and prevention is for parents to get in touch with themselves and then begin to improve some of their specific characteristics. The choice to reunite—with both self and other people—is another move in a positive direction away from burnout. The choice to remain separated is a choice to continue toward total burnout.

THE NATURE OF THE RECOVERY PLAN

This plan is designed to begin to reestablish the balance between your feelings of responsibility as a parent and the ever-present need to look after your own physical and mental health. This is not an easy thing to do, especially when the two objects of our choices are our children and ourselves. Some anguish is inevitable.

At first glance this plan may appear to be rigid. It *is*. Being given a choice among several options often results in the selection of the one that seems most familiar and minimizes the discomfort. However, unless you make some *significant* changes in attitude and behavior, within no time at all you will have drifted back to your old patterns. The choice is up to you. You can perceive this plan as an imposition on your freedom for six weeks or you can see it as a highly structured supportive map that will make your road to recovery easier. We have taken the steps to make sure that you do not get lost in the process. Like all treatment plans, the prescription must be followed thoroughly. Some of the medicine may be difficult to swallow. You may not be used to it. Keep in mind that you are interested in recovery from parent burnout because your life is not going the way you want it to. Sticking to the same old patterns with only minimal change will not result in anything other than needlessly irritating those around you.

To effect a recovery a life reconstruction must take place. Like any responsible program of reconstruction it begins with small steps and will gather momentum as you begin to gain confidence and feel more energetic. This is a proven method and does not lend itself to making substitutions or following only the elements that feel easy to do. Be advised, there is nothing easy about recovering from parent burnout, but if one follows the plan as presented, thinks positively, and views the pain of burnout as a motivation to grow rather than as an excuse for self-pity and withdrawal, this plan will work.

Although the steps in this Recovery Plan start small and grow in difficulty and scope as the program progresses, there is a general pattern to each day in the six-week period. Keep in mind that it takes a while for parents to burn out and it will take a while for recovery.

Each day in the plan is built around the awareness and practice of three major components. The first is attitude. Burned-out parents tend to have a negative and discouraged attitude. They are dispirited. This view of life sets up a self-fulfilling prophecy. Some of the activities of each day are designed specifically to heighten awareness of this negative attitude and turn it around toward the positive.

The second component is behavior. Remember that parent burnout results in a process of increasing isolation. There will be activities every day aimed at creating and strengthening individual and group relationships. Some of the behaviors required may feel uncomfortable at first. Certainly, many of them will not feel natural initially. This is the place to begin practicing that new positive attitude. Have a little faith. Focus on your forward movement up and out of burnout and not on the temporary discomfort associated with trying new things.

The third component is affirmation. There is tremendous power in positive thinking. So much power, in fact, that regular affirmation of a positive attitude and new behaviors, however uncomfortable, will result in success. Success is not reserved for just a few. It is particularly likely for those who have experienced failure and pain. These people have the advantage of knowing very clearly what not to do. They have a head start. What may have seemed like failure was really very valuable learning.

The attitude exercise will be in the morning between your waking up and noon. This will require quiet reflection or meditating on questions each morning for ten minutes. New behaviors will be introduced and practiced in the afternoon between noon and 6 P.M. The affirmation exercise will be completed sometime between 6 P.M. and bedtime. At the end of each week there will be a commentary. The purpose is to present a cumulative review of what you should be thinking and feeling and how you should be behaving as you follow the treatment plan. We will also address some of the major problems that you may have encountered during that week.

THE EIGHT NECESSARY CONNECTIONS

The plan for curing parent burnout is built on eight important ingredients. They are connections with the environment and they are critical for overcoming the effects of burnout. The connections or ingredients are: information about parenting; a significant other; small group membership; goal-oriented activity; knowledge of self; attachment to money and credit; frame of reference; and a self-nourishing activity. Each of these is described below.

Information About Parenting

Parents need a constant supply of new information about parenting and they can obtain this through books, magazines, courses, or study groups. However, whatever the method used, it must be kept in mind that for something to be informational there must be *new* ideas, attitudes, and perspectives presented. Reading *Dr. Spock* twelve times doesn't do it!

Books have the advantage of being available when you need them. You do not have to go anywhere to get information from them and you can review certain parts whenever you have the need. Literally hundreds of books on parenting are available in bookstores and libraries. A bibliography of some quality books is given below. It is not exhaustive by any means, but it is a good starting point.

GENERAL

Appleton, William. *Fathers and Daughters.* Garden City, N.Y.: Doubleday, 1981.
Auerbach, Stevanne. *The Whole Child: A Sourcebook.* New York: G. P. Putnam's Sons, 1980.

Bartz, Wayne R., and Rasor, Richard A. *Surviving with Kids*. New York: Ballantine Books, 1978.

Brehm, Sharon S. *Help for Your Child*. Englewood Cliffs, N.J.: Prentice-Hall, 1978.

Brenton, Myron. *How to Survive Your Child's Rebellious Teens*. New York: Bantam Books, 1980.

Brooks, Jane B. *The Process of Parenting*. Palo Alto, Cal.: Mayfield Publishing, 1981.

Brutten, Milton, et al. *Something's Wrong with My Children*. New York: Harcourt Brace Jovanovich, 1979.

Digiulio, Robert C. *Effective Parenting: What's Your Style*. New York: New Century, 1980.

Dodson, Fitzhugh. *How to Parent*. New York: Signet/New American Library, 1970.

———. *How to Discipline with Love*. New York: Signet/New American Library, 1978.

Dreikurs, Rudolph; Gould, Shirley; and Corsini, Raymond J. *Family Council*. Chicago: Henry Regnery Co./Contemporary Books, 1974.

Eden, Alvin N. *Positive Parenting: How to Raise a Healthier and Happier Child*. New York: New American Library, 1982.

Faber, Adele, and Mazlish, Elaine. *How to Talk So Kids Will Listen and Listen So Kids Will Talk*. New York: Rawson, Wade, 1980.

Fraiberg, Selma. *The Magic Years*. New York: Charles Scribner's Sons, 1981.

Galinsky, Ellen. *Between Generations: The Six Stages of Parenthood*. New York: Times Books, 1981.

Ginott, Haim G. *Between Parent and Child: New Solutions to Old Problems*. New York: Avon Books, 1977.

Gordon, Sol, and Wollin, Mina McD. *Parenting: A Guide for Young People*. New York: Oxford Book Company, 1976.

Gross, Leonard H., ed. *The Parents' Guide to Teenagers*. New York: Macmillan, 1981.

Heffner, Elaine. *Mothering: The Emotional Experience of Mothering After Freud and Feminism*. Garden City, N.Y.: Doubleday, 1978.

Hersey, Paul, and Blanchard, Kenneth H. *Family Game*. Reading, Mass.: Addison-Wesley, 1978.

Kiley, Dan. *Keeping Parents Out of Trouble*. New York: Warner Books, 1981.

Maccoby, Eleanor. *Social Development: Psychological Growth and the Parent-Child Relationship*. New York: Harcourt Brace Jovanovich, 1980.

Palmer, J. O. *The Battered Parent and How Not to Be One.* Englewood Cliffs, N.J.: Prentice-Hall, 1980.
Princeton Center for Infancy. Edited by Frank Caplan. *The Parenting Advisor.* Garden City, N.Y.: Doubleday, 1977.
———. *Parents' Yellow Pages.* Garden City, N.Y.: Doubleday, 1978.
Salk, Lee. *Preparing for Parenthood.* New York: Bantam Books, 1975.
Silberman, Melvin L., and Wheelan, Susan A. *How to Discipline Without Feeling Guilty.* New York: Hawthorn Books, 1980.
Wright, Logan. *Parent Power: A Guide to Responsible Childrearing.* New York: William Morrow, 1978.

SPECIAL INTERESTS

Ashdown-Sharp, Patricia. *A Guide to Pregnancy and Parenthood for Women on Their Own.* New York: Vintage Books, 1977.
Atlas, Stephan. *Single Parenting: A Pratical Resource Guide.* Englewood Cliffs, N.J.: Prentice-Hall, 1981.
Berman, Claire. *Making It As a Stepparent: New Roles and New Rules.* Garden City, N.Y.: Doubleday, 1980.
Biller, Henry, and Meredith, Dennis. *Father Power.* Garden City, N.Y.: Doubleday, 1975.
Curtis, Jean. *Working Mothers.* Garden City, N.Y.: Doubleday, 1976.
Hawke, Sharryl, and Knox, David. *One Child—By Choice.* Englewood Cliffs, N.J.: Prentice-Hall, 1977.
Kappleman, Murray. *Raising the Only Child.* New York: New American Library, 1975.
Klein, Carole. *The Single Parent Experience.* New York: Avon Books, 1978.
Maddox, Brenda. *The Half-Parent: Living with Other People's Children.* New York: Evans, 1976.
Nobel, June and William. *How to Live with Other People's Children.* New York: Hawthorn Books, 1977.
Price, Jane. *How to Have a Child and Keep Your Job: A Candid Guide for Working Parents.* New York: Penguin Books, 1981.
Reynolds, William. *The American Father.* New York: Pocket Books, 1980.
Rosenbaum, Jean and Veryl. *Stepparenting.* Novato, Cal.: Chandler and Sharp, 1977.
Vail, Priscilla L. *The World of the Gifted Child.* New York: Penguin Books, 1979.
Visher, Emily and John. *Step-Families: A Guide to Working With Stepparents and Step-children.* New York: Brunner/Mazel, 1979.

In terms of parent education, there are two major sources of high quality: 1) P.E.T. (Parent Effectiveness Training), a parent training program widely available; and 2) PARENTING, a very effective program developed by the Red Cross.

In addition to utilizing reading materials and training, it is often necessary for a mother or father or both to have access to a "parent mentor." This should be a person with similar values to your own, with a similar temperament, someone whom you respect, and whose children are just a little older than your own. This is the person you call when you do not know what to do. Since your mentor has most probably been through a similar situation, he or she often can help you handle your parenting problem.

This is better than asking your own parents, who are less objective and who have to remember back twenty-five years to when they had a similar situation and they may selectively forget how important the problem felt at that time. In addition they tend to minimize the importance of your crisis, whereas your mentor usually knows exactly how you feel.

How can you find a mentor? Some possible sources are a relative (e.g., an aunt, uncle, cousin, brother-in-law, sister, etc.); a neighbor; a member of your church or synagogue; a friend at work in similar circumstances; a close friend.

Having a mentor is very helpful, but it is only half of the treatment. Real help and success in combating burnout are only possible when you become a mentor to someone else. As we know, the best way to learn something is to teach it.

While information is important, it is necessary to point out that parents must be aware of false, misleading, or self-serving information. There is a huge supply of information available to any parent who simply turns on the television set. However, this information (both advertising and programming) is carefully designed with one thing in mind: having the viewer buy something. Commonly called motivation, the goal of most television information is to prove to you that you are inadequate, unhappy, deprived, and less fulfilled than other people. Once you have bought this premise, television then offers you a product that will provide you with temporary relief. If you have any doubt about this, watch any typical evening of television with this knowledge in mind. How many nonbeautiful, nonperfect, and nondedicated mothers or fathers do you see in commercials? Much false and misleading information concerning parenting flows from the mythological "perfection model" of motherhood and fatherhood. Often parents are unaware of the profound influence of these myths on them and the guilt that they produce.

A Significant Other

Every human being must have at least one other person with whom he or she has an intimate relationship. However, it is important that the feelings and levels of intimacy be mutual. The significant other must be a person who knows you on a completely open and honest level. Who could this person be for a parent? It could be a spouse and often is. It could be another parent. It could be your best friend. It could be a rabbi, minister, or priest. It could be a neighbor. What is important here is that this relationship provides a warmth and a feeling that one is loved and understood.

There are times when parents find themselves without a significant other. This could be due to death, divorce, moving to a new location, or because they have grown apart from someone. During these times, parents sometimes turn to professionals for support, but it is usually only temporary relief. Developing another significant relationship must remain the long-term goal. The best source for a new significant other is often a small group where the members have a common interest.

First, find a topic that you are interested in or might be interested in. Next, call the local library and see if there is a group in your geographical area formed around your interests. An excellent source to give you some ideas is *The Encyclopedia of Associations*.[1] Third, contact the group's membership chairman and go to a meeting. From our experience in counseling parents and helping them join groups, the following are some of the more common organizations: service clubs (Lions, Kiwanis, etc.); bowling leagues; softball teams; church societies; PTA; civic associations; etc.

A common initial complaint on the part of parents is "I don't have the time to join a group. I am already up to my neck in work and I'm too tired to add anything else on." This feeling is perfectly normal. Keep in mind, however, that part of your resistance is the

[1] Detroit: Gayle Research Company, 1981.

quite natural tendency to avoid changing the pattern of your life. That pattern has led you into burnout. So take a risk, invest the time, and go do it. Being a member of a small group is the third necessary connection.

Small Group Membership

Membership in a small group provides a parent with a feeling of solidarity and unity—being a part of something larger than oneself. Another function of a small group is to provide support in times of trouble. This connection is the key to all of the others and unfortunately is usually the first connection that parents lose when their lives become troubled. There is so much shame and stigma attached to parent burnout that people who feel it pull away from normal associations and become increasingly more depressed and isolated. Using the small group for support is an important step toward recovery.

Goal-oriented Activity

Everyone must engage in at least one activity that has measurable standards of performance. Attaining some level of performance provides a goal toward which a parent can work. It is the feedback regarding performance at something that maintains a person's self-respect and self-esteem. Some examples of activities that provide a goal are most paid jobs, athletic competition, accomplishments in music, volunteer work recognition, hobbies with measurable outcomes, and the accumulation of money. One of the problems with parenting is that there are no commonly accepted standards for performance over which the parent has control. Being the parent of the captain of the football team or being the parent of a musical prodigy or being the parent of an Eagle Scout indirectly suggests that the parent has been successful in his or her role. Unfortunately, the reverse is also true. Being the parent of a drug addict, school dropout, or a cult member often indicates failure on the part of the parent. The risk of basing one's self-esteem on the accomplishments or failures of children is very high, because the children do not necessarily have the reputation of their parents in mind as they succeed or fail in life.

In this case, just being a good parent is not good enough. Parents must maintain their function as individuals and do something successfully that has nothing to do with parenthood.

Knowledge of Self

Every person must have a clear notion of who he or she is. This can be accomplished by making a simple list of twenty items that describe yourself. Some sample descriptive items are "I am intelligent"; "I am overweight"; "I am kind"; "I believe in God"; and "I like chocolate ice cream." The twenty items in the list do not all have to be positive and do not have to be philosophical or earthshattering in nature. The only two requirements are that they be true and precise. If a list of characteristics is overwhelmingly negative, some effort must be made to balance the list with positive terms, but stay with the truth.

If a person cannot come up with twenty items or the items are too vague, it is suggested that he or she turn to the significant other for help. Others often see qualities in us that are blocked from our view by current circumstances.

The purpose of this list of twenty items is twofold: first, it will force you to do some of the introspective work required and to shift the balance from focusing all your attention on your children to focusing on yourself. Second, it will provide an inventory of yourself that you can refer to at times of severe stress and self-doubt. This inventory can also serve as a benchmark. It provides the base on which you build your plan for change. It also serves as a written criteria for evaluating your growth in self-knowledge.

Attachment to Money and Credit

The system of commerce used by the Western world is one of the things that separates modern man from primitive man. People who do not have access to money must provide goods and services necessary to life on their own. Having access to money gives a person power that enables that person to command goods and services from others. A person who is adequately connected to a money supply does not even have to know a person who provides goods and services. His or her money is good anywhere. In order to be adequately connected a simple rule is that any adult given five working days must be able to have three thousand dollars cash in hand. This does not have to be one's own money. It could be borrowed from the bank, credit cards, friends, family, etc. But the further a parent is from having the money the more vulnerable he or she really is.

This connection is an example of how positive are the financial implications of the women's movement. The demand for equal credit, equal credit records, property titled in one's own name, etc., decreases the likelihood of financial dependence on someone else. The absence of this connection is no more or less important than any other, but the lack of money and credit is easily noticed.

Frame of Reference

Everybody must have faith in something to provide meaning for his or her life and to serve as a guide. This faith must be based on something greater than man in order to make it completely safe from attack by other men. Most people in the Western world use religion of some sort as their system of faith. Belief in God, however, is not required. A person could have a very strong ethical nonreligious set of beliefs.

This connection is unique in that out of the eight connections only this one cannot be given to you by someone else. Taking the leap of faith is a completely personal decision. One common characteristic of the burned-out parent is the lack of a strong belief system to guide his or her life. The vast majority of burned-out parents feel inadequate and unsupported because they have no stable foundation and must face each parenting encounter as a fresh situation requiring a risk and an energy-consuming decision. Because they have no frame of reference to routinize their decision-making these parents become easily and quickly exhausted.

Self-nourishing Activity

Parenting is an inherently unbalanced process in that in most cases more energy flows from the parent to the children than from the children to the parent. Common sense tells us that any time more of something flows out than flows in, sooner or later the source will run dry. Parents must come to realize that their energy supply is finite.

On a regular basis all parents need an emotional feeding. This may require engaging in an activity for the sole purpose of pleasing oneself. After all, the first law of nature is self-preservation. A common characteristic of burned-out parents is their exaggerated need to please their children and often at the cost of displeasing themselves. To maintain this connection the rule is very simple: for at least one half hour a day a parent should do something with nobody's benefit in mind other than his or her own. This is not permission to become totally selfish and ignore one's responsibility. Very simply, that half hour a day is reserved to guarantee the inward flow of positive feelings and refreshing energy. These activities do not have to be carried out alone. But the parent must very carefully make sure that if he or she engages in an activity with someone else, more energy comes in than goes out. Some examples of activities are sitting in a nice hot bathtub; taking a walk; gardening; quiet reading; listening to music; bicycling; or swimming.

These eight necessary connections fit together as the pieces that make up a line of defense against parent burnout. They are the medicine. Each one of them is necessary and it takes all eight of them as an interrelated system to provide adequate protection. The absence of any of these provides a weak link in the chain of defense and that weak link will sabotage any efforts to avoid or recover from parent burnout.

PARENT BURNOUT RECOVERY PLAN

FIRST WEEK

Monday

MORNING

Write down your first thoughts after you wake up. *Keep a daily log of these thoughts for review at the end of the plan.* You will be surprised at how far you will come. Answer these questions: Are you happy to be alive or do you dread this upcoming day? Do you feel tired or do you know that you have the energy to succeed today? Do you feel trapped or do you feel free? If you have chosen the negative alternative to these questions, take another look at your life. Are you controlling your energy? Or is someone else? Is it possible for you to choose the positive alternatives? Of course, it is. Do you know that your weaknesses are generally overdone strengths?

AFTERNOON

Make a list of all the people who can help you carry out this six-week plan.

EVENING

Before you go to bed, stand in front of a mirror. Look at yourself in the mirror and actually tell yourself how much better you feel because you are taking steps to gain control of your life. Remember the power of affirmation!

Tuesday

MORNING

Write down your first thoughts after you wake up. Answer these questions: Do you feel irreplaceable as a parent? Do you accept parental duties out of responsibility or out of obligation? Do you secretly believe that no one else can do quite as good a job as you?

AFTERNOON

From yesterday's list of possible helpers, select three and imagine yourself asking them to do something for you in your role as parent.

EVENING

Before you go to bed, stand in front of the mirror. Look at yourself and say, "I am not indispensable and I am comfortable asking for help because I am not superhuman."

Wednesday

MORNING

Write down your first thoughts after you wake up. Answer these questions: Have you overextended yourself at home? Do you feel persistent pressure—too much to do and too little time? Do you feel like your family relies on you for everything?

AFTERNOON

Gather your family together before dinner and explain to them that over the next six weeks you are going to be making some changes in yourself. Explain to them that this is going to be one of the most important things that you have ever done and ask them to help you. Let them know that at times you will be preoccupied with yourself. Reassure them that you love them as much as always and that after these six weeks are over your family will be closer and stronger because you will be a better person. End this activity by getting agreement from yourself and your family that this treatment plan will work. Many fathers and mothers have found that at first their families do not understand what they are saying and feel threatened by this. Their families may ask "Why change? We are happy." In some cases, the children may be totally unaware of or insensitive to the parent's suffering. They may even be denying it because acknowledging it is frightening. It is critical that children see some payoff for themselves or in their relationship with you as a result of your going through this plan. Examples of payoff for them could be less yelling by you, more patience, more energy, time to have more fun with them, or better communication. While the attractiveness of the benefits of payoff will be a function of the age of your children, the more concrete and specific the better.

One final note: If you have young children, gathering them together to explain something as complex as your feelings may be inappropriate. You know your children. You be the judge.

EVENING

Before you go to bed, stand in front of the mirror and say, "I feel like a weight has been lifted from my shoulders. My family is going to help me out of burnout."

Thursday

MORNING

Write down your first thoughts after you wake up. Answer these questions: Do you have one person outside the family with whom you can share everything? When is the last time you talked to that person? How do you feel when you are with that person?

AFTERNOON

Narrow down your list of three helpful friends and choose one to help you carry out the rest of this plan. Remember, you will be asking a lot from this person. So think carefully.

EVENING

Before going to bed, stand in front of the mirror and say, "I am so happy that my friend (Insert name) will help me overcome burnout."

Friday

MORNING

Write down your first thoughts after you wake up. Answer these questions: Do you feel guilty when you ask people for things? Are you afraid that you will lose your friend when you ask for help? If a friend asked you for help, would you resent him or her for it?

AFTERNOON

Call up the person you have chosen to help you and explain that you have chosen him or her out of all the people that you know to help you recover from burnout. Ask your friend if he or she will help you. If the person agrees to help, explain that for the next thirty-five days you will call and report your answers to the questions of that morning, describe the behavior that you will do or have done that day, and how you will affirm the new behavior in the evening. Tell the person that what you really need for the next thirty-five days is someone to listen, to be supportive, and above all else, to be positive. Also, tell your friend that you are likely to feel weak and unable to cope at times and you may need an occasional pep talk.

If the person says "No" to your request for help, it is not the end of the world. Remember that each failure you have, each disappointment you feel, and each apparent setback are more things that you have learned. Use this knowledge. Not everyone feels confident enough to make a commitment to help someone else. Maybe your friend did not feel up to helping you. Choose another who does. Go to the second person on the list and start the process again.

Any time you ask anyone for a favor you have placed yourself at risk. The person could say "No," say "Yes," but never get around to helping you, or say "Yes" and sincerely try to help and do a bad job. There are obviously plenty of people who do not want to get involved with the problems of another. You can minimize the risk by honestly assessing the willingness of each of your friends to get involved. If after all of that you are rejected in your request for help, try to view that rejection as not your failure, but the failure of the other person. Go on to someone else. After you find a friend willing to help you, remember to call that person every day.

EVENING

Before going to bed, stand in front of the mirror and say, "I am really going to enjoy my family tomorrow."

Saturday

MORNING

Write down your first thoughts after you wake up. Answer these three questions: Do you dread weekends? Do you find excuses for being away from your family on weekends (such as playing golf, going to the hairdresser, working at the office, going shopping, etc.)? Have you saved up all the hassles (e.g., doing the laundry, mowing the lawn, etc.) for the weekend?

AFTERNOON

Spend at least two hours engaged in an activity that includes the entire family, excluding watching television. Examples are: going shopping together; playing a game; taking a walk; working around the yard; running errands; and going out to eat.

EVENING

Before going to bed, stand in front of the mirror and say, "It was nice enjoying spending time with my family once again." Remember, even if it is not true, say it anyway because having said it, it is more likely to come true.

Sunday

MORNING

Write down your first thoughts after you wake up. Answer these three questions: How do you feel about your body? Pleased? Displeased? Why? Do you think that you get enough rest? Do you think that you get enough exercise?

AFTERNOON

Choose some physical exercise and do it for half an hour. Of course, it is recommended that you receive approval from your physician before engaging in strenuous exercise. These are some possibilities: walking, bicycling, badminton, tennis, jogging, calisthenics, swimming, etc.

EVENING

Before going to bed, stand in front of the mirror and say, "I feel that I am more relaxed and energetic. Therefore I am a better person and a better parent."

End of Week Comments: By now we have had you focus your attention on some of your basic feelings about being a parent and also indirectly on whether or not you feel worthy to ask a friend to help you. We have also had you bring your feelings about being a parent out in the open by having you sit down with your family and ask for their support. Finally, we have started you on a regimen of positive thinking. It is likely that you have two specific feelings as a result of doing all of this. You probably feel some anxiety. That is perfectly natural. This is new and you have completed only the first week of a six-week program. You are not really sure how all of this is going to turn out. The second feeling that you most likely have is a tremendous sense of relief. You have gotten your feelings out. You have communicated them to the people who should know about them and you have made every effort to gain the support from not only your family but also a friend who will see you through this process. Probably your greatest source of relief, however, is that once again you have taken control of your life. You used to have it, you gave it up, and now you are getting it back. Good for you!

SECOND WEEK

Monday

MORNING

Write down your first thoughts after you wake up. Answer these questions: Are you an energetic person? Do you expend a lot of energy in a normal day? Do you try to balance stressful and difficult tasks with tasks that are easy and enjoyable?

AFTERNOON

A goal of the Recovery Plan is to restore you to peak performance in parenting. The key ingredient in peak performance is a balance of energy and demand. However, the energy supply can be increased, in fact, must be increased, as the demands increase. Some of your activities increase energy and others drain your energy away. It is important for you to identify those aspects of your life that increase or decrease energy. It is your most precious resource.

Complete the following Energy Audit:
  Instructions: One important component of parent burnout is distress. Pleasurable and enjoyable activities allow you to take in energy, while unenjoyable ones deplete your energy. Keeping a log of

daily activities is a good method of identifying stress factors that
are specific to your role as a parent. To be most useful, this log
should be maintained over an extended period of time. However,
to obtain an index of your stressful activities, reflect back on an
average day last week. Assign one of the following scores to each
activity:

1   pleasurable
2   enjoyable but trying
3   required (but not pleasurable or trying)
4   not enjoyable; rushed; tension-producing
5   very unenjoyable

The scoring will allow you to identify those activities that give you
energy (the pleasurable and enjoyable ones) and those activities that
rob you of energy (the unenjoyable ones).

Sample:
      Date: April 5, 1982   Day of the Week: Monday

Activity	Duration	Score
Shower	7:00–7:15	1
Breakfast with Family	7:20–7:40	4
Drive Children to School	7:40–8:05	2
Do Laundry	8:10–8:30	3
Attend Meeting at Work	etc.	
Business Lunch		
Attend Little League Practice		
Listen to Children's Stories, etc.		

EVENING

Before going to bed, stand in front of the mirror and say, "I am
going to balance my days so that I usually have as much energy
coming in as I have to put out."

Tuesday

MORNING

Write down your first thoughts after you wake up. Answer these
questions: Do you understand that your energy is limited? Are you

able to increase those activities that give you energy? Are you able to decrease those activities that drain energy? How and when will you begin the increases and decreases?

AFTERNOON

Go to the library or bookstore and select some books from the list recommended on pages 143–45.

EVENING

Before going to bed, stand in front of the mirror and say, "I am going to do some reading on parenting this week."

Wednesday

MORNING

Write down your first thoughts after you wake up. Answer these questions: Where did you learn what a good parent should be? Where did you learn to parent? Have you learned anything new about parenting since you started this plan?

AFTERNOON

Read approximately thirty pages in the reading material on parenting that you have selected.

EVENING

Before going to bed, stand in front of the mirror and say, "I enjoy reading about parenting and thinking about why I do what I do."

Thursday

MORNING

Write down your thoughts after you wake up. Answer these questions: Are you a flexible person? Are you open-minded about parenting? Can you read the views of others on parenting without feeling threatened?

AFTERNOON

Read another thirty pages of your material on parenting. Continue reading from selections on the list for the next four weeks.

EVENING

Before going to bed, stand in front of the mirror and say, "I enjoy reading about parenting and thinking about why I do what I do."

Friday

MORNING

Write down your first thoughts after you wake up. Answer these questions: Since you have begun reading about parenting, what new attitudes do you have? What new behaviors are you demonstrating? What plans do you have?

AFTERNOON

Using the results of the Energy Audit, begin to do more of one activity that takes in more energy than goes out. Continue to add these kinds of activities to your daily schedule for the next four weeks.

EVENING

Before going to bed, stand in front of the mirror and say, "I am really going to enjoy my family tomorrow."

Saturday

MORNING

Write down your first thoughts after you wake up. Answer these three questions: Do you dread weekends? Do you find excuses for being away from your family on weekends? Have you saved up all the hassles for the weekend?

AFTERNOON

Spend at least two hours engaged in an activity that includes the entire family, excluding watching television.

EVENING

Before going to bed, stand in front of the mirror and say, "It was nice enjoying spending time with my family once again."

Sunday

MORNING

Write down your first thoughts after you wake up. Answer these questions: How do you feel about your body? Pleased? Displeased? Why? Do you think that you get enough rest? Do you think that you get enough exercise?

AFTERNOON

Choose some physical exercise and do it for half an hour. See recommendations from previous week.

EVENING

Before going to bed, stand in front of the mirror and say, "I feel that I am more relaxed and energetic. Therefore, I am a better person and a better parent."

End of Week Comments: During this past week you have begun the process of reestablishing the balance in your life. The first issue of balance involved assessing the intake and outgo of your energy. By now you must recognize and appreciate the limited nature of your energy. You know that you have only so much. You also know that either you will control it or someone else will. We are sure that by now *you* have chosen to control it because you recognize that it is the most valuable resource that you have. Energy is life. Losing control of your energy is losing control of your life. An effective parent cannot afford to do that.

Maybe you have had trouble finding the time to do the reading we have asked you to do. Remember, you must make time. Establish a reading pattern and stick to it. For example, you may do some of your reading early in the morning, during your lunch hour at work, or at bedtime. The key is to be faithful to your daily reading commitment.

Now that you have begun to reconnect yourself with the thinking of other people you are most likely beginning to encounter information with which you do not agree. You may find yourself vigorously disagreeing with some of the values presented in these books. That's great! The process of reading and agreeing or disagreeing is likely both to broaden your horizons and increase your confidence in your own judgment. As with the first week, we are ending with invigorating and relaxing physical activity. You are beginning to feel more alive.

THIRD WEEK

Monday

MORNING

Write down your first thoughts after you wake up. Answer these questions: Are there any groups of people that know you very well (e.g., family groups, church groups, work groups, social groups, etc.)? How often are you with these people as a group? Do you feel good when you are with them?

AFTERNOON

Make a list of all the groups of which you have been a member or would like to be a member. Remember, *The Encyclopedia of Associations,* available in most public libraries, is a good resource for you. Some types of groups to consider are civic associations; service clubs; athletic groups; political organizations; volunteer groups; school associations; church societies; etc. If you work outside the home and feel that you already do not spend enough time with your family, you may want to consider a group designed to initiate and support family activities. Some examples are: Indian Scouts, recreation clubs, Brownies, Boy Scouts and Girl Scouts, swim groups, church associations, etc.

EVENING

Before you go to bed, stand in front of the mirror and say, "I am strengthening my ties with at least one group."

Tuesday

MORNING

Write down your first thoughts after you wake up. Answer these questions: Are there any groups that would help you in your role as parent? Are you a different person now from the one you were before you were a parent? Are all the groups that you thought of yesterday appropriate for you now that you are a parent?

AFTERNOON

From yesterday's list of groups select three in which you would like to be active.

EVENING

Before going to bed, stand in front of the mirror and say, "I have become too isolated and I am becoming part of a group."

Wednesday

MORNING

Write down your first thoughts after you wake up. Answer these questions: Is your family jealous of your outside-the-family activities? Does your family have exclusive rights to all of your time? Are you still capable of managing a life of your own?

AFTERNOON

Tell your family that you may be spending some additional time with an outside group.

EVENING

Before you go to bed, stand in front of the mirror and say, "I am glad that my family understands my need for a life outside the family."

Thursday

MORNING

Write down your first thoughts after you wake up. Answer these questions: What do you expect to get from membership in a small group? What are your fears in interacting with a new group? How do you expect to feel as part of a group outside your home?

AFTERNOON

Choose a group to join (or rejoin).

Before you go to bed, stand in front of the mirror and say, "Being a member of my chosen group will really broaden my life."

Friday

MORNING

Write down your first thoughts after you wake up. Answer these questions: Whom will you approach in your chosen group? Do you already know this person? If someone asked you to help him or her join your group, wouldn't you be happy to help?

AFTERNOON

Take action to join the group that you have chosen.

EVENING

Before you go to bed, stand in front of the mirror and say, "I am really going to enjoy my family tomorrow."

Saturday

MORNING

Write down your first thoughts after you wake up. Answer these questions: Do you still dread weekends? Do you find excuses for being away from your family on weekends? Have you saved up all the hassles for the weekend?

AFTERNOON

Spend at least two hours engaged in an activity that includes the entire family, excluding watching television.

EVENING

Before going to bed, stand in front of the mirror and say, "It was nice enjoying spending time with my family once again."

Sunday

MORNING

Write down your first thoughts after you wake up. Answer these questions: How do you feel about your body? Pleased? Displeased?

Why? Do you think that you get enough rest? Do you think that you get enough exercise?

AFTERNOON

Choose some physical exercise and do it for half an hour. See recommendations from the first week.

EVENING

Before going to bed, stand in front of the mirror and say, "I feel that I am more relaxed and energetic. Therefore, I am a better person and a better parent."

End of Week Comments: You have spent this entire week thinking about, answering questions, and making decisions about the nature of your connections to at least one small group. At this point you are halfway through the Recovery Plan. The relationship between you and your mentor has most likely matured and it is likely that you have been as much of a help to your mentor as your mentor has been to you. The scope of your knowledge about parenting is much broader than it was before. In fact, you are now becoming a good resource person on parenting.

FOURTH WEEK

Monday

MORNING

Write down your first thoughts after you wake up. Answer these questions: What kind of a person are you? What were you like before you became a parent? In what ways are you now a better person?

AFTERNOON

Make a list of five characteristics that describe you to yourself.

EVENING

Before going to bed, stand in front of the mirror and say, "I am getting to know myself better."

Tuesday

MORNING

Write down your first thoughts after you wake up. Answer these questions: How many of yesterday's characteristics are negative? Can you think of five more positive characteristics that describe you? Which one of those five is the most positive?

AFTERNOON

List five positive characteristics that describe you to yourself.

EVENING

Before going to bed, stand in front of the mirror and say, "Being a parent has really broadened me as a person."

Wednesday

MORNING

Write down your first thoughts after you wake up. Answer these questions: In what ways has being a parent added to your positive characteristics? What characteristics of yours have been strengthened by some of the hassles of being a parent? Doesn't adversity often lead to increased strengths?

AFTERNOON

List five of your characteristics as a parent that describe you to yourself.

EVENING

Before going to bed, stand in front of the mirror and say, "Some of my negative characteristics are really overextensions of my strengths."

Thursday

MORNING

Write down your first thoughts after you wake up. Answer these questions: Couldn't being a worrywart be an overextension of love

and concern? Couldn't closed-mindedness really be an overextension of loyalty to an idea? Couldn't being picky be an overextension
of carefulness?

AFTERNOON

List five of your weaknesses (negative characteristics) as a parent
and indicate next to them the strengths from which they have been
derived.

EVENING

Before going to bed, stand in front of the mirror and say, "I am
glad that I now understand that most weaknesses are really overdone strengths."

Friday

MORNING

Write down your first thoughts after you wake up. Answer these
questions: Does your family know you better than you know yourself? Does your family see strengths in you that you don't see? Are
you a harsher critic of yourself than your family is of you?

AFTERNOON

Before dinner, share your list of twenty characteristics, developed
during the past four days, with your family. Communicate to them
how a negative characteristic can be the overextension of a
strength.

EVENING

Before going to bed, stand in front of the mirror and say, "I am really going to enjoy my family tomorrow."

Saturday

MORNING

Write down your first thoughts after you wake up. Answer these
questions: Do you still dread weekends? Do you find excuses for
being away from your family on weekends? Have you saved up all
the hassles for the weekend?

168 PARENT BURNOUT

AFTERNOON

Spend at least two hours engaged in an activity that includes the entire family, excluding watching television.

EVENING

Before going to bed, stand in front of the mirror and say, "It was nice enjoying spending time with my family once again."

Sunday

MORNING

Write down your first thoughts after you wake up. Answer these questions: How do you feel about your body? Pleased? Displeased? Why? Do you think that you get enough rest? Do you think that you get enough exercise?

AFTERNOON

Choose some physical exercise and do it for half an hour. See recommendations from the first week.

EVENING

Before going to bed, stand in front of the mirror and say, "I feel that I am more relaxed and energetic. Therefore, I am a better person and a better parent."

End of Week Comments: You have just completed identity week. There can be no doubt that you know yourself better now than even one week ago. We have focused your attention from outside of yourself in terms of groups and information about parenting to inside yourself for a look at the real you. Isn't it comforting to discover that you do not need to make gigantic and unsettling changes in yourself to modify your deficiencies. Merely toning down the strength of some of your most irritating traits will most likely reconvert them into positives.

By now we know one thing for sure. You are not lonely and you are not bored. You know your strengths and you know your weaknesses. You know that your "Achilles' heel" is not rooted in your weaknesses, but ultimately in your strengths. By now you are beginning to appreciate moderation.

FIFTH WEEK

Monday

MORNING

Write down your first thoughts after you wake up. Answer these questions: Do you do anything that can be measured or assessed as being well done or poorly done? How can you assess objectively how well you do as a parent? What did you do before you became a parent that provided you with positive feedback about yourself?

AFTERNOON

Make a list of ten things that other people have told you that you do well and that have measurable standards of performance.

EVENING

Before going to bed, stand in front of the mirror and say, "I enjoy getting positive feedback from others."

Tuesday

MORNING

Write down your first thoughts after you wake up. Answer these questions: Do you enjoy doing things even when you cannot do them perfectly? Do you avoid doing things because you cannot be the best? If you were to be graded at something, would a B+ be good enough?

AFTERNOON

Narrow down yesterday's list to the five items that provide you the most positive feedback.

EVENING

Before going to bed, stand in front of the mirror and say, "I will gladly accept positive feedback even if it doesn't tell me that I am the best."

Wednesday

MORNING

Write down your first thoughts after you wake up. Answer these questions: Is there anything that you can do that provides you with a lot of positive feedback? Can you do one thing often that people say that you are good at? Isn't it better to do one thing often and moderately well than one thing rarely and excellently?

AFTERNOON

Choose a parenting activity from the list that has measurable standards of performance and that you do frequently and moderately well rather than something that you do perfectly but rarely.

EVENING

Before going to bed, stand in front of the mirror and say, "I am going to enjoy all the positive feedback I get from my new activity."

Thursday

MORNING

Write down your first thoughts after you wake up. Answer these questions: How does your family respond to change? How will they adapt to a happier you? How will they respond if they like you the old way?

AFTERNOON

Before dinner tell your family all about your new activity and ask them to support you in it as much as they can.

EVENING

Before going to bed, stand in front of the mirror and say, "My family will be proud of how far I have come during these five weeks."

Friday

MORNING

Write down your first thoughts after you wake up. Answer these questions: Are you happier now than you were five weeks ago? Aren't you proud of yourself? Isn't your family proud of you?

AFTERNOON

Meet with or telephone your friend who has been helping you and tell him or her how much you appreciate the help. Ask if your friend has grown from the experience. This does not have to be a long and deep discussion, but, no doubt, it will be an authentic one and you and your friend will be energized by it and you will feel good.

EVENING

Before going to bed, stand in front of the mirror and say, "This will be the first weekend of the rest of my successful life as a parent."

Saturday

MORNING

Write down your first thoughts after you wake up. Answer these questions: Do you still dread weekends? Do you still find excuses for being away from your family on weekends? Have you saved up all the hassles for the weekend?

AFTERNOON

Spend at least two hours engaged in an activity that includes the entire family, excluding watching television.

EVENING

Before going to bed, stand in front of the mirror and say, "It was nice enjoying spending time with my family once again."

Sunday

MORNING

Write down your first thoughts after you wake up. Answer these questions: How do you feel about your body now? Pleased? Displeased? Why? Do you think that you get enough rest? Do you think that you get enough exercise?

Choose some physical exercise and do it for half an hour. See recommendations from the first week.

Before going to bed, stand in front of the mirror and say, "I feel that I am more relaxed and energetic. Therefore, I am a better person and a better parent."

End of Week Comments: By now you should have become very comfortable with this entire treatment plan. After all, you have been at it for five weeks. Should you expect that you are now the perfect parent? No. Should you expect that you will never have doubts? No. Should you expect that everything from now on will magically go the way you want it to? No. But, let's be honest. Don't you feel that your life has taken a turn for the better? The crucial question to ask at this point is "Are you still following some of your old habits by tending to overdo some of the parts of this treatment plan?" Keep in mind, do the best you can, but don't throw your life out of balance in the process.

Remember, now, in a week this treatment plan will be completed. Technically, at that point, you won't need to call your mentor. Obviously, then, this relationship that you have developed during the last five weeks will not go away nor should it. During the week coming up, give some thought to how you want to modify your relationship with this person.

SIXTH WEEK

Monday

MORNING

Write down your first thoughts after you wake up. Answer these questions: Could you come up with three thousand dollars in cash by Friday of this week if you really needed the money? If you cannot do this, how do you feel? Is it a source of worry for you in your role as a parent? If you are connected to this amount of money, how do you feel?

AFTERNOON

If you are not connected to three thousand dollars, sit down and develop a plan whereby you will be able to accumulate at least this amount in cash or have access to a cash advance of this amount within five days. Whatever the plan, it should be systematic and attainable within a twenty-four-month period. If you do have this connection, think about possible ways of increasing the amount.

EVENING

Before going to bed, stand in front of the mirror and say, "I am pleased that tomorrow I will begin an organized plan to make me and my family more financially independent. I will then worry less about the vulnerability of my family as I fulfill the goals of the plan."

Tuesday

MORNING

Write down your thoughts after you wake up. Answer these questions: Do you believe that you have to give to get? Could you have come this far by yourself? Will the new "you" be strengthened by helping someone else with parent burnout? If someone had offered to help with parent burnout, would you have viewed it as an imposition?

AFTERNOON

Make a list of five people whom you could help out of parent burnout. Then narrow down your list of candidates for help to one person to whom you are going to be of some help.

EVENING

Before going to bed, stand in front of the mirror and say, "My offer of help will be very much appreciated. Helping others out of parent burnout will also help me."

Wednesday

MORNING

Write down your first thoughts after you wake up. Answer these questions: How responsible do you feel for other people's problems? If you offer help and are turned away, how will you feel? Is it better to offer help and be rejected than not to offer help at all?

AFTERNOON

Decide beforehand how involved you want to be with the person whom you have chosen to help. Once you have made your decision, write a contract with yourself and put it somewhere handy to remind you of the limits that you have set.

EVENING

Before going to bed, stand in front of the mirror and say, "I am glad that I can help another person who is suffering from burnout. My own experience with this problem will be most beneficial for my success with this person."

Thursday

MORNING

Write down your first thoughts after you wake up. Answer the following questions: How would you like someone to offer unsolicited help to you? Is it reasonable to assume that someone else would want the same thing? What are you going to say to the person whom you have chosen to help?

AFTERNOON

Contact the person you have chosen and offer to help him or her with parent burnout. You may have some fears that this person may view your offer of help as an intrusion on privacy. However, if you keep in mind that what you have to offer is not primarily directed toward the removal of a flaw, but rather toward a *return* to peak performance in parenting, the threat of intrusion will be reduced significantly. You are simply dealing on a parent-to-parent basis. You are linked by a common bond of interest in effective parenting.

EVENING

Before going to bed, stand in front of the mirror and say, "My family will understand that in order for me to remain happy and the way I am now I have to try to help another parent who is burned out."

Friday

MORNING

Write down your first thoughts after you wake up. Answer these questions: How long will the results of this treatment plan last if you end it right here? Have the conditions which led you into parent burnout disappeared? Could you repeat this treatment plan again if you were in the same condition as six weeks ago?

AFTERNOON

Check to see if all of the eight necessary connections are now a part of your life:

———— Information About Parenting
———— A Significant Other
———— Small Group Membership
———— Goal-oriented Activities
———— Knowledge of Self
———— Attachment to Money and Credit
———— Frame of Reference
———— Self-nourishing Activity

EVENING

Before going to bed, stand in front of the mirror and say, "I will continue to use and reuse this treatment plan and help others use and reuse the treatment plan in order to prevent burnout from touching my life again."

Saturday

MORNING

Write down your first thoughts after you wake up. Answer these questions: Do you still dread weekends? Do you still find excuses for being away from your family on weekends? Have you saved up all the hassles for the weekend?

Spend at least two hours engaged in an activity that includes the entire family, excluding watching television.

Before going to bed, stand in front of the mirror and say, "It was nice enjoying spending time with my family once again."

Sunday

Write down your first thoughts after you wake up. Answer these questions: How do you feel about your body now? Pleased? Displeased? Why? Do you think that you get enough rest? Do you think that you get enough exercise?

Choose some physical exercise and do it for half an hour. See recommendations from the first week.

Before going to bed, stand in front of the mirror and say, "I feel that I am more relaxed and energetic. Therefore, I am a better person and a better parent."

End of Week Comments: Well, you have made it. You did what we suggested that you do. As you know, success breeds success. You probably feel so good about your growth these past six weeks that you can't wait to help other parents who feel like you do. There is no doubt that many parents can benefit from your help.

You now have tremendous power to affect family life in a positive way. One of the aspects of helping others that you may have overlooked, however, is that by helping them you may also be helping yourself. The easiest way to maintain this new sense of tolerance in your life is to help others achieve it. You may wish to do this on a personal one-to-one basis or you may decide to initiate a more widespread self-help program for burned-out parents. If you choose to do the latter, the Parent Burnout Workshop plans described in the Appendix should be useful. *Keep in mind that you do not need a professional to lead these workshops.* These programs are designed for parents who want to help themselves. The information provided in this book is sufficient material for a successful self-help workshop. However, if you feel that you need more information, please feel free to write to us at Loyola College; 4501 North Charles Street; Baltimore, Maryland 21210.

8

Bypassing
Parent Burnout:
The Inoculation

If you are a dedicated and caring parent—and therefore a prime candidate for burnout—you may have experienced many of the burnout symptoms even if you haven't reached the danger point. For you, it is vital to take preventative action. The Burnout Bypassing Plan presented here applies not only to parents who have not yet burned out, but also to those who have followed the treatment plan and want to avoid burning out again. The Bypassing Plan focuses on wellness and, more importantly, on growth.

The key point of the plan is this: keep life moving in a forward direction. There is no holding pattern for parents. Those who do not progress and feel the pressures of parenting closing in on them are headed for the swamp called "burnout." They are reactive people and generally abandon control of their own destiny. Proactive parents, on the other hand, take control of their destiny and allow themselves to grow. They reject the notion that health is simply the absence of illness. Instead, they identify their own potential and develop it. There are at least ten important areas to focus on in the development of the parents' personal growth plan.

One of the common characteristics of healthy, vibrant, and energetic parents is their well-organized and *balanced* life. They keep the parenting role in perspective and manage the rest of their life in a way that increases the likelihood of fulfillment. One of the natural laws governing all systems is entropy: anything that is left unattended or unused or unmanaged will break down over time. Automobiles need tune-ups, metal outdoor furniture needs painting, rooms need dusting, and lawns need mowing. The same is true for people and their relationships. Therefore, it is critical for growth that parents first develop a very clear understanding of *themselves*, start exercising a positive proactive orientation, and gain a fuller understanding of their relationships with their family members. Once that is firmly established, they must begin a regular maintenance plan to keep all of these achievements in top working order.

HOW THE BYPASSING PLAN WORKS

This plan is not as structured as the Burnout Recovery Plan. What we present here are the ingredients of a plan that can be used throughout your life as a parent. We have found that instead of receiving a rigid plan from us, it is more effective to have you make the choices concerning which areas of growth you will pursue first. We want you to include all of these in your lifelong pattern of growth as a parent.

Select one of the growth areas each week for the next ten weeks. Complete the exercises fully. If you care to, share the process and the results with your family. If your children are old enough to understand the exercises, have them complete them also. However, do not pressure them to share the results. If they really want to, they will.

The information and self-knowledge that will result from this Bypassing Plan should inoculate you against the burnout-producing hazards of parenting. However, all of us need a "booster shot" now and then. We recommend that you undergo an introspective checkup at least once a month after you complete this plan. A good method for doing this is to review the symptoms of the first two stages of parent burnout as outlined in Chapters 1 and 2: If you are beginning to have some of those feelings and exhibit some of those behaviors, then you need to increase your level of self-awareness and take control of your life again. Reviewing the exercises in this chapter will help you do that. You may notice that some of the treatments of the Recovery Plan are also a part of the prevention plan. While the processes may be the same, the purposes differ in each case.

1. UNDERSTANDING YOURSELF

Parents are often "programmed" with feelings of inadequacy. They maintain their low self-esteem because it affords them sympathy and attention from others; it allows them to lean on others; and because it is risky to change and may incur some family member's disapproval.

Fortunately, parents are retrainable, but they must work hard to overcome some of the attitudes and behaviors that have become ingrained. They do not have to become victims of their past styles. However, few positive changes will occur if they do not adopt some new approaches to child rearing.

It is critical that parents renounce the love, affection, and approval of their children as "needs." Rather, these are to be treated as unexpected rewards, bonuses, or windfalls. Parents must work at taking care of themselves, knowing that the quality of their parenting will, in the long run, be a function of their own physical, mental, and emotional well-being. Parents must expect discomfort to accompany this change in attitude from reactive to proactive. Like any radical shift, growing pains are inevitable.

The first step in understanding yourself is to find a time and a place where you can focus all of your conscious thinking on yourself. Ask yourself these questions: "What am I really like? What are twenty facts about me that I can tell myself?" List them on a piece of paper. Peggy, a mother of two, made a list that included the following items:

1. I am a kind person.
2. I am intelligent.
3. I am ten pounds overweight.
4. I love ice cream.
5. I like the outdoors.
6. I am glad that I have my children.
7. I wish that I could travel more.
8. I am not very patient.

As you can see, the list does not have to be full of earth-shattering items. The idea is to begin to introduce yourself to yourself. Now that you have your list, think about and record the events or personal influences in your life that have resulted in each of your twenty items. If you come to an item and cannot possibly pin down a source for it, then pass by it and move to another. Once you have your list and the events and people that you think may have contributed to each item, you have the option whether to continue on to the third part of this exercise for understanding yourself.

The third part of this exercise is to select someone and read your list to that person. It could be a family member, friend, or neighbor. This task is designed to expand your external relationships as a way to prevent parent burnout. Once you have shared your list, discuss those factors that you have identified as the causes of the items. If there are some items that you would like to strengthen, devise a strategy to do that. If you want to eliminate or decrease the importance of items that you see as weaknesses, develop a strategy for that as well. Your strategy for growth or diminution should follow the pattern presented below:

My overall goal is: _____
  (e.g., to lose ten pounds in the next month)

Constraints and barriers to this goal are: _____

_____

_____
  (e.g., I have to attend many social functions that require eating)

Attainable objective: _____
  (e.g., to lose ten pounds during the next *two* months)

My methods to reach the objective: _____

_____

_____
  (e.g., follow a prescribed planned weight-loss diet)

Select among methods: _____

Implementation plan: Start _____ End _____

Methods for monitoring progress: _____

_____

(e.g., daily morning weighing)

This structured format allows you to translate your goal into concrete action. It also helps you to clarify nebulous or vague goals.
The idea is to become more proactive and build on your strengths
and modify your handicaps. Think positively and keep in mind that
there are no limits to your growth potential.

2. BOOSTING SELF-CONFIDENCE

Accepting oneself at less than perfection levels is essential to self-
confidence. Techniques for enhancing self-confidence are being
willing to admit, then redo or undo mistakes; avoiding competitive
comparisons; and eliminating zero-sum thinking (the belief that
there is only a finite supply of success and if someone gains then
you lose).

Parental self-confidence will be enhanced proportionally to the
willingness to try, to risk; the difficulty of what is undertaken; and
attitudes toward failure. We stated earlier in the book that one tendency of burning-out parents that is likely to get them in trouble is
"crucializing." All parents have made mistakes and have done a
few things that they wish they could take back. Most often parents
who feel this way are more negatively focused on their wrongs and
shortcomings than those children whom they have supposedly
harmed. Children are generally resilient and forget quickly. However, parents dwell on memories of past errors and lower their self-
confidence.

They may have adopted an expectation that they will be the
sculptors of their children's lives. When the kids do not conform to
the plan mapped by their expectations, parents often ponder the
question: "Where did I go wrong?" The widespread belief that
they could retain control and great influence over their children's

personalities, behaviors, and choices frequently leads mothers and fathers to blame themselves and swallow large doses of guilt for some unidentified deficiencies in their performance as parents. Such frustrated expectations and the resulting guilt are prime fuel for burnout.

Rita was full of "supposed to's." She lived her life as a parent as if it had been written as a script for a play. She read all the latest parenting books and magazines. She attended parenting seminars and lectures as often as she could, trying to learn more about how she could be a better mother to her four young children. Scrupulous in her self-accountability, she had become more frustrated as she tried to live up to what she constructed as the image of the good parent. She had gleaned all the best qualities presented in her studies of parenting and constructed a hybrid model of the ideal mother. This became her frame of reference—an intellectualized construct that did not, nor could not, exist.

Rita attended one of our seminars held in the Washington, D.C., suburbs. After she explained her situation, we asked her to try a little exercise. She was to write a one-page description of her day as a parent—her behaviors, her thoughts, her feelings. We asked her to pretend that this would be published in the Washington *Post* with her name attached. She was to call this Version A. We then asked her to write another similar description of her day as a parent, but this she would share with only her best friends. This was called Version B. Lastly, she was to write a similar description, but this was to be read by Rita alone, shared with no one, and quickly shredded. This was Version C. After this exercise, Rita was to ask herself three important questions: Were all three versions the same? (Usually the answer was "No.") If not, which was the most accurate? (Usually, the answer was Version C.) Where did the others come from, particularly Version A? (The answer often centered around what we thought others expected of us—the established protocol for parenting behavior.)

We asked Rita to think about the discrepancies of the three versions. How did she feel about Version C? Would she share it with anyone? Why? Why not? Was Version A really possible? Was she living an unnecessary dual existence as a parent, one public life (Version A) and one private life (Version C)? Wouldn't this split parenting personality eventually take its toll?

The part of crucializing mistakes that often lingers is worrying about how someone feels about us after we have wronged him or her in some way. Sure, we have apologized, but we did not *really* set the record straight. Now is the time. If it is possible, find the appropriate time to undo some past wrongs. You will most likely be surprised and relieved at how well the results turn out. Develop a specific plan and tackle each item one at a time.

Start by going to someone whom you see all the time and tell this person that you want to clear up something that has been on your mind for a while. Then, review the incident in question, state your perception of what really happened, and see if he or she is harboring any resentments stemming from your past conflict. If the person does still feel some anger, then try to come to some compromise or agreement in as nonthreatening a way as possible.

Next, move on to someone who is important to you but whom you don't see very often. Getting around to your past conflict may be a little more difficult because you do not have the context of an ongoing relationship to rely on. The straightforward approach is the best. Tell this person what you told the person in the above example, go through the process, and continue on to the next person.

Now that you have come to grips with some of the confidence-reducing parts of your past, it is time to begin a practice that will elevate your level of self-confidence. There is an old adage that "what goes around, comes around." This simply means that if you do something enough, it will be done to you. For the next two weeks make every effort to bolster the self-confidence of others. Be as positive as you can and really extend yourself. What you will begin to feel is a gradual but sure return of your own confidence in yourself. Don't expect all those that you have helped to return your positive attitude in an outward fashion. However, focus on how you feel about yourself. Give it a try. It will work.

3. SEEING THE POSITIVE SIDE OF STRESS

As we have seen in Chapter 4, there has been much interest and research on the topic of stress during the past few years. Unfortunately, the term generally has a negative connotation. As you recall, this was not the view of Dr. Hans Selye, who pioneered much of the research on stress and its impact on the quality of life and relationships. Whether the stressors commonly experienced in the parenting role are viewed as eustress (good stress) or distress (bad stress) is largely up to the parent. Stress is an individually perceived phenomenon. Parents who are highly functioning tend to view stressors as challenges that they can overcome. Other parents might tend to view these same stressors as insurmountable threats and just give in. How do you generally cope in the world? What is the context of your stress? What is the nature of the stressors? If two out of these three factors are essentially positive for the parent, it is likely that he or she will experience stressors as external challenges. The opposite is true if two of the three factors are negative for the parent. In this case parents will view the stressors as robbers of their energy.

Stress is not reality. Stress is merely your response to the events of the world as they occur around you. The choice to perceive these events as either overwhelming problems or motivating challenges is up to you.

For example, if you received a call from one of your child's teachers telling you that your son or daughter was failing miserably in a certain subject, you could perceive that as a hopeless situation bringing shame and disappointment to both you and your child. You could also perceive this as a challenge presented not only to the child but to you as well. Families are likely either to fall apart or pull together in a crisis, and this is most likely something they have control over. The situation of your child flunking a subject in school could bring you closer.

One important measure for stress analysis is the level of contentment that you feel in your environment. Answer the questions listed below with a "Yes" or "No" answer:

_____ 1. All in all, are you happy with the behavior of the members of your family?

_____ 2. Are you happy with your role as a parent and family member?

_____ 3. Are you happy with the level of cooperation in your family?

_____ 4. Are you satisfied with the level of skill that you display as a parent?

_____ 5. Does your role in the family make full enough use of
            your skills and abilities?
_____ 6. Does your day-to-day life allow you to develop your-
            self mentally?
_____ 7. Is your day-to-day life fulfilling?
_____ 8. Are you relatively free from heavy financial worries?
_____ 9. Is your physical health good?
_____10. Is your children's health good?

Award 1 point for each "Yes" answer. If your score was 7 or above,
then you view your environment and your life as essentially positive. If the score was 4 or below, then you view your life and environment as negative and nonfulfilling. In either case, the solution
to developing a more positive and fulfilling view of the context of
your life is to expand it beyond the limits that you currently feel.
This expansion could itself be viewed as stressful, but you will
choose to view it as a challenge.

It is important to keep in mind that managing stress centers
around three issues. We call them the *ABC's:* Attitudes, Behavior,
and Coping. First, it is important to develop a proactive and
growth-oriented attitude. You must believe that you can control
your own destiny. You are not totally trapped by past events or
programmed into a fully determined future. You must also develop
an attitude of "healthy selfishness," that is, you must realize that to
serve your children well you have to take care of yourself. Chronic
unselfishness is a neurotic attitude. You do no one any good, yourself or your children or your spouse. Second, these attitudes must be
translated into behavior. This is the difficult part because we often
have to overcome ingrained patterns. What are some of the behaviors that flow from the above-mentioned attitudes? Clearly, one is
the need for *you* to decide what will make your day successful. You
must say to yourself every morning, "Today will be a success if I do
the following three things: _____
_____." You must free yourself from
looking for the judgment or approval of others or using the criteria
of theoretical models to determine your success as a parent.

Sufficient sleep and time-outs for emotional breathers are critical
for managing stress. The amount of energy available must at least
equal the demand for energy. It is a simple formula, but one often

overlooked. Spouses have to cover for one another regularly. Single parents must get some helpful coverage from their parents, friends, or neighbors. The totally selfless parent, who disregards his or her own well-being, will sooner or later become the ineffective parent.

A third important behavior for managing stress is the need for some self-nourishing activity, an activity in which more energy comes in than goes out. Physical exercise is one very good means. Jogging, bicycling, walking, swimming, or tennis are all useful and appropriate, depending on your own physical condition and makeup. Boating, travel, and music are other possibilities. For some, work can be a self-nourishing activity as long as there are times when more energy comes in than goes out. For instance, there are people who work long hours, but at the end of the day, even though they are fatigued, they are relaxed. The key is to recognize these as valuable and necessary methods for increasing your own well-being and your effectiveness as a parent. They are not optional, but mandatory.

Lastly, coping skills are an integral part of stress management. There are three specific areas of coping that are critical for parents: the changing nature of children; the ambivalence of parent-child relationships; and the presence of imperfection. First, it is important to recognize that effective parenting is like trying to hit a moving target. Just when you think that you understand what should be done as a parent and begin to act, the situation changes. The fastest pace of human change occurs during childhood, not only physically, but also emotionally and socially. During certain years children sometimes seem to change by the minute! Tolerance for change is a necessary coping skill. Adapting to change can be painful. However, the rewards can surpass the costs if change is viewed as exciting growth.

The ambivalence of parent-child relationships can also be painful. The sometimes erratic shifting of feelings of love and dislike of children can be confusing and most stressful. "The children get on my nerves and I scream at them. Within a few minutes I feel guilty and find myself hugging them. Every time this happens I feel depressed and totally screwed up," explained one mother from New Jersey. As children mature and become more independent or develop friendships or go off to college or the world of work, parents often feel a sense of accomplishment as well as loss. "I was thrilled when my daughter was accepted to Yale, but I quickly became very saddened because I knew I wouldn't see her very often and we are very close," said a Richmond, Virginia, father. Coping with this constant state of conflicting feelings is critical for effective stress management.

Being able to recognize, accept, and live with the presence of imperfection is necessary as well. Family life is bound to be replete with "loose ends," shortcomings, and ambiguity. Successful parenting does not follow a fixed formula or recipe. The complexity of child development cannot be reduced to a simplistic set of "steps." The parental goal of, or hope for, a family life that is characterized by perfection is sure to lead to disappointment and fuel the gnawing perception of failure.

4. UNDERSTANDING ANGER AND USING IT CONSTRUCTIVELY

Parents must understand that anger is a basic, normal, universal, and unavoidable reaction of displeasure. It usually involves some misunderstanding as well as unmet expectations. It generates an internal energy force that can be controlled if one chooses. It is important for parents to understand that anger generally entails a "slap on the ego," a contradiction of a belief or self-concept. It is very often expressed toward those who are important to us. Love and anger are flip sides of the same coin. It is necessary for parents to encourage and respect healthy expressions of anger from children. Such expressions are natural. Those who have no anger are either indifferent, anesthetized, or incapacitated. As with any behavior, coping with anger gets easier with practice and normally improves relationships.

There is one situation that brings about anger more quickly than anything else: not getting what you want. It can be most corrosive as it slowly attacks our internal organs. Intense uncontrolled anger can literally kill. Anger drains away the energy supply and peak performance becomes affected. Anger must be recognized, harnessed, and controlled. In order to begin to understand your anger more, make a list of ten things that make you angry. Include at least three items that relate to your children. Keeping in mind that you are angered by not getting what you want, look at your list and write down what you specifically wanted in each case. Now comes the critical element of this exercise. Try to be objective and ask yourself if each of the things you wanted to happen, and that did not happen, was a reasonable thing to expect. If you determine that they were reasonable, then were they reasonable to expect from the people or circumstances involved? If so, was it reasonable to expect that what you wanted happen every time? By now you have probably answered "No" to at least one of these questions. In that case, you have several choices. You can modify your wishes somewhat so that you will probably not be as angry again, or you can increase your demands so that you will get even angrier, or you can do nothing and stay as you were when those things on your list occurred.

Try to imagine yourself as a more tolerant and forgiving person. Would the lateness or forgetfulness of your spouse or a messy house make you as angry as you usually get? It probably would not. In short, you can control your anger by controlling your wishes. As a final task of this exercise, write a list of the personal qualities of the most tolerant and integrated person that you know. Begin adding these qualities to your behavior one at a time until they feel natural for you.

5. PRACTICING POSITIVE THINKING

Parents who think negatively rarely meet with success. They affirm the future, but in negative ways. Those who are likely to succeed are those who think positively. More than just a good attitude, this requires active daily affirmation. Practicing affirmation simply requires that parents look themselves in the eye in the mirror and tell themselves repeatedly that they are succeeding at whatever they are trying to do.

Think back to those days just before you became a parent. Make a list of those expectations that you had of yourself as a parent and of your children. Since those earlier days you have become wiser and more realistic. Rewrite your list in light of what you want right now. Finally, put priorities into the list by ranking the items from the most desirable to those you desire less.

Get into the habit of thinking in positive terms. Reflect on the priorities in your list each morning for a few minutes. The truth is that you are already affirming every day now. You may be waking up and telling yourself how tired you are or how bad the traffic will be or what difficulties you will have with the children. These are affirming the negative and they subtlely set up a prophecy that is likely to come true.

All of this can change. Start with your first priority and tell yourself that what you want has already occurred. Actually say to yourself something like, "I am happy that I had an enjoyable day with my kids." Repeat your positive prophecies again and again, day after day, until they come true. In most cases they will come true sooner than you think.

6. DEVELOPING INTIMACY SKILLS

It is critical for parents to maintain a high degree of intimacy with at least one other person. Intimate communication usually involves self-disclosure in each of the following four areas: facts, preferences, beliefs, and feelings. As a relationship becomes closer and more open we are willing to disclose and accept more about feelings and beliefs.

The primary personal trait for developing intimacy is self-confidence. To this end, parents have to develop self-reliance; accept their own mistakes not as failures, but as learning experiences; and try to carry on relationships without playing games.

We have suggested in the Burnout Recovery Plan that each of us must have an intimate relationship with at least one other person. That person must also feel that he or she has an intimate relationship with you. The relationship could be with a family member, a friend, or a neighbor. Begin by sharing with someone two facts about yourself that are not obvious and that the person does not already know. For example, you may care to recount some story from your childhood relating to your relationships with your grandparents or you may reveal one of your most closely guarded ambitions. Then be willing and open, but not demanding, to listen to two facts that they might care to share with you. Once you have become comfortable doing that, move on to sharing two preferences (things that you like more than other things) with someone. For example, you may point out that you would rather read than watch television or that you would rather spend money on clothing than traveling. The sharing of the preferences begins to communicate your values to the other person. Having similar values helps in the development of an intimate relationship.

Sharing two of your beliefs is the next step. For example, you may share your ideas about religion or politics. This moves you out of the realm of the rational and conceptual, and places you in a position of making statements that you will not be able to fully defend. For the other person to accept you, he or she will have to agree with, or at least tolerate, your beliefs.

Lastly, we move on to the heart of what intimacy is all about. Share two feelings with your intimate. For example, you may point out that you fear rejection by him or her and are most happy when you are praised by that person. These shared feelings must be genuine and they should relate to how you feel about that individual. This is the riskiest step of all for many people. Most people are hurt when their feelings are ridiculed or ignored or rejected. However, true intimacy requires honesty and the sharing of feelings. If you have trouble getting this far, take a risk, and ask someone whom you trust to help you.

7. LEARNING THE NATURE OF LISTENING

The most precious gift that parents can give their children is their attention; however, it is also one of the most difficult and most energy-consuming activities. Parents often do not understand the dynamics of listening. They think of it as something passive and cannot understand the exhaustion that results. Active listening is critical for effective parenting and parents must understand the importance of these key elements: eye contact; physical feedback; and empathic statements. There are five kinds of listeners: 1) Those who listen to only what they want to hear; 2) Those who listen for the central theme or ideas in the message; 3) Those who focus on the source of what they hear (*who* says it is more important than *what* is said); 4) Those who are in tune with the speaker's emotional state (e.g., fear, joy, hostility, etc.) as well as the content of the message; 5) Those who are listening to find if what is being said either agrees with or counters what they already think.

Listening requires the expenditure of energy and, performed correctly, it requires that you direct your attention toward the speaker so that he or she knows that you are interested. Physical gestures, particularly facial expressions, are an integral part of active listening. The nonverbal feedback that you give to the speaker is critical.

Starting tomorrow begin to listen to your children more actively. When your children speak, look at them, show them that you are interested, do not interrupt them, and let them know that you have understood. Be prepared for some discomfort and pain as you expend the energy needed for successful listening. As hard as it may be at first, really listen. The results will be worthwhile.

Try this little exercise for improving listening. Ask your spouse or a friend to listen to you in as distracted a way as possible (for example, looking over your shoulder, looking out the window, walking around the room, etc.). Tell that person some life experience that you think is absolutely fascinating or important. As you relate your story focus your attention on how *you* feel. After you have done that, just imagine how your child feels if you tend to be a person who listens in a distracted manner.

8. DEVELOPING ASSERTIVENESS

It is important for parents to feel comfortable expressing themselves freely and assertively. To avoid hurting others, especially your own children, some of you often assume a nonassertive style. You may abdicate your guidance and direction roles. Children, especially younger ones, feel uncomfortable in this situation. In fact, they often beg their parents for direction. If you do not articulate this direction, one of the most basic needs of children, security, is not fulfilled.

To express yourself assertively does not mean that you have to act and communicate aggressively with your children. Being assertive simply requires that you recognize and admit your own perceptions and feelings about a situation. For example, if you are angry because your child failed to carry out a responsibility, to whom does the anger belong? It belongs to you. The blame might rightly rest with your child, but yelling and pointing the finger will usually cause a negative reaction in the child. This reaction, coupled with your anger, makes the situation less controllable. The assertive way to handle this problem is to state a *feeling* in terms of yourself: "I'm disappointed," followed by the *situation* that caused it, "that the trash wasn't taken out," followed by a *reason* for the feeling, "Because it didn't get collected, it will pile up, and will make this house look like a mess." The key to assertiveness is to leave the "you" statements out. Try not to attack the child directly, detracting from his or her dignity, but focus on the behavior that was performed or not performed.

The next time the need arises for a parental command, try the assertive approach. Express your feelings, with the accompanying reasons, clearly. Focus your attention on behavior. Let your children know that while you may not be satisfied with their behavior today, you still believe that they have the potential to perform better tomorrow.

9. ANALYZING PROBLEMS THOROUGHLY

Parents often have the answer to many problems inside them, but do not have a systematic way to get to those creative solutions. Creative problem-solving is blocked because it is locked into old ways of thinking; parochialism; inflexibility in the face of evidence; adherence to cherished beliefs; too much attention to detail; and a lack of imagination.

Parents have to loosen up their mental machinery and develop their creativity. They have to believe that they can control their own destiny.

Many problems that exist in families have developed over a long period of time and seem to take on a life of their own. Issues such as low school grades, disrespect for parents, drug abuse, poor sleeping habits, and sibling rivalry tend to be long-standing problems. The nonproductive tendency of many parents is to seek an instant solution to these and other problems without giving careful enough attention to the problem itself. Parental problem analysis is worth the time involved. It should follow the procedure outlined here: Step one is to describe the problem in terms of what is going on that we do not want, or conversely, what is not going on that we do want. Step two is to state in what way the problem situation could be worse and in what way it could be better. Focus on the worst and best cases. Usually a problem situation lies somewhere between. Step three is to begin to determine what causes are keeping it from getting better. Undoubtedly, some of the proposed causes will involve things that we have no influence or control over. These factors are eliminated from consideration. For those causes that remain, carefully propose solutions, one at a time, which should involve taking specific action. The actions should then be translated into an organized plan.

Paul is a seventh-grader and even though he has always had good grades and has high intelligence scores, his grades this year are far below what is normal for him. The problem, then, is that his grades are below his usual level of performance. The optimum situation would be all A's. The worst case would be all F's. Paul is between the two, but tending toward the F side.

His parents should begin to determine what causes are keeping Paul from moving toward the A's. Maybe Paul is bored. Maybe he has fallen behind in his work and cannot catch up. He could be depressed. He could be anxious about performance. He could be spending too much time flirting with the girls in class and not paying attention. Perhaps subconsciously he sees failing as a way of getting attention. Then they should consider what is keeping him from getting all F's. Maybe he likes certain subjects. Maybe he has maintained some pride in himself. He could want to please his parents. He may need certain grades to be allowed privileges.

Take each cause, one at a time, and propose solutions. For example, in regard to boredom, they might "spruce up" his curriculum with something he would like and that would serve as a challenge. If he has fallen behind in his work, getting him extra help to catch up might do the trick. If Paul has been helping in the process, it would be good to continue with him in putting together a comprehensive plan. If the parents have been doing this without Paul, they might bring him into the process as they build the plan. In either case, rewards must be assigned for attempting the plan and penalties for holding back. This process of systematic problem-solving may seem too tedious, complex, and time-consuming. However, with practice the process gets easier and eventually becomes ingrained in the parenting style.

10. TIME MANAGEMENT

Most parents realize that time is one of their most precious resources. However, many parents do not know how to manage their time. And good time utilization often makes the difference between becoming a determiner of one's destiny or simply a reactive person. Parents must internalize the fact that while most mothers and fathers do not feel they have enough time, all of them have all the time there is, i.e., twenty-four hours a day, no more and no less. The key factor will be the *management* of this time, not the amount.

Parents can grow in this area by doing the following: (a) List and prioritize their long-term and short-term goals; (b) do a Time Use Audit; and (c) compare time use with priority of goals. This exercise will allow parents to know whether or not they are using their time in a manner that is consistent with their goals.

Time-management Exercise

1. Stop and think for a few moments. . . . Write a list of the three most important goals in your life. These are probably long-term goals and general in nature. They are viewed as *critical* for your happiness. Examples might be: to have happy and healthy children; to be financially secure; to see to it that your children are well educated.

2. Next, translate these three goals into more immediate objectives. What do your goals mean for you over the next five years? Over the next year? The idea is to establish short-term goals that will eventually bring about the long-term ones. Examples might be to help my child develop strong study skills by the end of the sixth grade; to save $15,000 by 1988.

3. It is also necessary to consider goals and objectives that are viewed as *very important,* even though they may not be considered *critical.* These will be next in priority in the event that you should reach your critical goals. For example, building a new family room for your house may not be critical, but it might be very important for family fun and togetherness.

4. After your critical and very important goals, list your *desirable* goals. These are third in priority. An example might be traveling across the country by automobile with the children.

5. Next is the Time Use Audit. Completed properly, this task takes approximately three weeks. Select Monday and Wednesday of the first week; Tuesday and Thursday of the second week; and Friday,

Saturday, and Sunday of the third week. For each day keep a log of your time use. This should focus on identifiable blocks of time. We recommend breaking the day into half-hour segments:

Time Use Audit

Time	Activity
6:00–6:30 a.m.	
6:30–7:00 a.m.	
7:00–7:30 a.m.	
7:30–8:00 a.m.	
8:00–8:30 a.m.	
8:30–9:00 a.m.	
etc.	

One word of caution: Do your Time Audit for longer than one week. Any single week may be an exceptional week in one way or another and may provide an inaccurate picture of time use.

6. The next step is to compare time use with goals and priorities. Do you find yourself spending your time pursuing your critical or very important goals? Do you spend the bulk of your time on activities that are not even mentioned in your goals list?

7. The last step is an analysis of the consequences of your comparison of goals and time use. There are three possible conclusions: (a) Your time use is consistent with and supportive of your goals and you most probably will control your destiny; (b) your time use is inconsistent with and not supportive of your goals and you most probably will not control your destiny; (c) either your time use or goals have to be modified.

If your time use is consistent with your goals or if you modify your time use to make it consistent, you then have a framework for organizing your daily activities. Once this framework is established, it is recommended that you do the following every day: (1) Make a list of everything that you should accomplish in your day; (2) Then determine the priority of each item. Label with an *A* everything that absolutely must be done today. Label as *B* all those items that would be better done today but can wait until tomorrow. Place a *C* next to all those items that should be done today if time permits, but may have to be done later. This priority-setting process is very important because you will do the A's, B's, and C's before anything else. This analysis will give you the information that you need to develop a daily "To Do" list. All of this will increase the probability of your controlling that precious resource, time, and channeling it toward what you deem as productive ends.

One last word of caution. If you truly value time as a precious resource, then you will view time robbers as you would those who might steal your money. Identify potential time robbers, be aware of them and your own vulnerability, and develop plans to protect yourself from them. As some of you may know, an overtalkative neighbor or friend can literally clean you out of time on a regular basis. Make your list of potential robbers, anticipate, and prepare accordingly.

The ten areas of growth described above are the building blocks for the prevention of burnout. However, there is one critical skill that is essential for effective parenting and the prevention of burnout: communication. We have touched upon this important competency throughout the book, but we believe that it deserves some special attention.

COMMUNICATION: THE LIFELINE OF THE PARENT-CHILD RELATIONSHIP

The critical skill for parenting is communication. It can often make the difference between success or failure. While many parents recognize this or learn it the hard way, very few have been *trained* in communication. However, this skill is most necessary in the prevention and alleviation of burnout. The consequences of not communicating effectively with children are all too often severely stressful. Communication is, in fact, the lifeline of the family and it is a most fragile one.

Like other skills there are degrees of development and communication is improved by continual practice. We wish to highlight a few important points that may help you improve this all-important skill.

In any communication we have a person sending a message to a receiver, who in turn gives the sender some feedback letting him or her know that the message was received. Simple? At first glance, yes. Until we consider some important implications the complexity of the process can be elusive.

Figure 3

THE COMMUNICATION PROCESS

This is a simple model which includes
all of the key ingredients of communication:

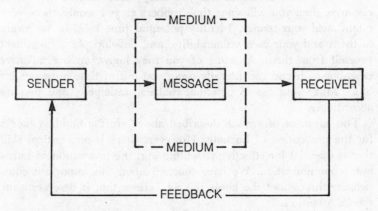

First, every message has to be encoded (that is, put into words or
"packaged" in some way), sent through a medium or channel (e.g.,
conversation, letter, etc.), and decoded (that is, interpreted) by the
receiver. The probability of distortion in the process is very high. In
fact, it would be wise for parents to assume that the message will be
distorted in some way. There is bound to be misinterpretation and
misunderstanding. Parents cannot avoid it, but they can reduce its
occurrence. To do so requires an understanding of some of the
major barriers to communication.

A few of the more easily recognized obstacles to effective communication are meaning discrepancies, stereotyping, prejudices,
faulty assumptions, an unwillingness to self-disclose, and differences
in frames of reference.

Meaning discrepancies occur when there are several meanings for
the same word. When we consider that there are over 14,000 meanings for the 500 most commonly used English words (a ratio of
28:1), misinterpretation is quite possible! For instance, the word
"set" has over 190 meanings. There are many other similar examples.

Stereotyping is the use of a general term as if all members of the
group represented by the term were the same. Stereotyping seems
inevitable because we have more persons, places, or things than

words. Therefore, we have to classify. However, problems arise when a particular person does not have the characteristics of the group. Parents who assume that all teenage daughters are "boy crazy" will have difficulty communicating with their children just as the parent who assumes that all ten-year-old boys love baseball will have difficulty.

Prejudices and biases also serve as major barriers to effective reciprocal communication because they prematurely block out messages that contradict preconceived notions. Often through the process of selective perception parents screen out those messages that challenge what is in place in their fact, value, or belief systems. What supports the parents' mental status quo is magnified and what does not support it is minimized.

Faulty assumptions often result when parents make inferences beyond the facts at hand. Some of these assumptions result from laziness or lack of time to analyze an issue thoroughly, from wishful thinking, from association, or even from suspicion. One parent whom we interviewed assumed that his daughter had to be promiscuous when he learned that her best friend had become pregnant out of wedlock. As he put it, "You know, birds of a feather . . . She must have been messing around too. No one will convince me otherwise." Can you imagine what difficulty his daughter has had communicating with him?

Parents sometimes are reluctant to disclose or reveal too much about themselves to their children. For example, they may be reluctant to show any emotion (fear, joy, sorrow) or admit to any past shortcomings (a low school grade, difficulty with friends, lack of ability in sports) for fear of disappointing their children or lowering their drive and motivation. When this situation exists it is difficult for children to sense any real empathy on the part of the parent. This seriously blocks communication as the children conclude that "my father [or mother] could never understand how I feel." Communication is very much affected by the authenticity of the parties involved. When genuineness is absent, communication is seriously wounded.

Another major barrier to communication between parent and child is the difference in frames of reference. Often discrepancies exist in relation to ambitions as parents look at the whole picture and know how important hard work and perseverance are for suc-

children do not share the experience and history and
re not internalized and legitimized the work ethic to
gree. What appears as a lackadaisical and carefree
eanor often infuriates parents, making it difficult to maintain
the mutual respect needed for two-way communication. Instead,
there is a lot of finger-pointing, yelling, and judging. "Here I am
trying to teach them how to get ahead and they could care less," is
the lament of many fathers and mothers.

An important point to keep in mind is that every message that is
transmitted has both a cognitive (mental) and an affective (emotional) dimension. Some individuals, as senders and/or receivers,
focus on the cognitive side and others focus on the affective side,
but neither dimension is ever fully eliminated. For example, a father saying "Very good work" to a child may not be communicating his approval to the degree he thinks if his daughter is a
perfectionist and would really want to hear "Superb!" "Excellent!"
"Super!" or "The best I've ever seen!" "Very good" to her may
mean mediocre. It is important for parents to be sensitive to the
emotional impact of their messages and to bear in mind that emotions are unique and irrational. They often do not make sense to
others.

It is also important for parents to remember that younger children depend much more on feelings and emotions than cognitive
processes and the equation shifts as the children progress in age.
There are also some critical points where the difficulties of the shift
in the balance are intensified (e.g., the "why's" of age three; pu-
berty; and late adolescence). Some examples of the several stages of
the equation would be the infant and parent who communicate entirely by touch, the ten-year-old boy or girl who may want to climb
onto Mommy's and Daddy's laps while chatting with them, and the
postadolescent and parent who relate almost entirely at the cognitive levels like any two mature adults.

Parents who attempt to communicate purely at the cognitive
levels, particularly with younger and adolescent children, have
many great difficulties and clog the lifeline of communication.

An equally important issue is the recognition of both verbal and
nonverbal communication. Verbal communication is what parents
directly say or write. It is at the conscious level. It is explicit and

we are aware of it. Nonverbal communication is what parents transmit indirectly or implicitly by their tone of voice, facial expression, and posture. It can be at the conscious level, but more often it is at the subconscious level. Within the family often over half the communication is of the nonverbal form. Parents can transmit their pleasure or disappointment by a simple glance at the children. Children likewise convey their innermost feelings by their facial expressions or the manner in which they walk or sit at the dinner table. Silence itself can be a powerful nonverbal message!

The total communication system between parent and child, then, is an intricate and sensitive network of verbal and nonverbal signals and cues. When the two are consistent and supportive of one another, the message is reinforced and often strengthened. When the verbal and nonverbal messages contradict one another (e.g., a father mouthing interest in a child's tales of school while looking totally bored), the child has a tendency to believe the nonverbal message. This lack of consistency of messages severely detracts from the effectiveness of the communication and sharply reduces the authenticity of the communication as well as the relationship. Nonverbal communication is a powerful tool. Parents cannot ignore it if they try. Messages will be conveyed even to the point where children know the mood parents are in by the way they open the front door as they return home from work in the evening. The key is to control and to use this tool effectively to help reach goals and build relationships.

Parents must remember that communication is very sensitive to perception; what children perceive to be true is true for them. Perception, in turn, is very much influenced and constrained by the needs one is trying to satisfy. These needs, in turn, serve as motivators. Anything that contributes to their fulfillment is valued. Anything detracting from their satisfaction is viewed as a threat. The importance of oxygen to the suffocating person is magnified far beyond its value to one who has all the air he or she wants. So, too, children magnify those items that they perceive as meeting their needs. The youngster who needs the sense of belonging will greatly overvalue Mom's or Dad's withdrawal of affection and support. The teenager who is seeking self-autonomy will overvalue what he sees as attempts to detract from his control over his own destiny.

Parents have to get in the shoes of their children as receivers. The more they know their children's needs the more able they will be to encode their message so that it will be decoded effectively.

Parents must not forget that when they are communicating with their children they are competing for attention. It is naïve for parents to assume that they could or should always have undivided attention. However, the more attractive and appropriate the message, the higher the degree of probability of success. Most parents feel helpless in this area. "How am I going to compete with the blasting radio?" or "I just don't know the lingo, the terms that the kids use today. They think that I am 'square' and they don't pay attention." Parents with these attitudes make one mistake. They assume that they have to be the *sender* of messages. They forget the other side of communication, *listening*. It is in the area of listening that they can compete and win. They can be quite sure that no one has as much interest in their children as they do. No one will be willing to listen as much as they can.

It is very difficult for children to dislike a parent who listens to them. It is a pleasant experience and children want to go back for more. Most children feel good about being listened to. Their parents' attention is the best gift that can be given to them and they know it. Parents have to recognize listening as a powerful communication tool.

Effective parenting is hardly possible without effective communication. If there is weak communication, there will be weak parent-child relationships. So often burning-out parents separate themselves from others, their friends, neighbors, relatives, and spouses because they do not have the energy for interactions. As burnout proceeds, they become less motivated to communicate. This situation accelerates the burnout as they turn inward and become lonely and detached.

Effective parents, on the other hand, are wired to their families, friends, and neighbors. They are in touch with their current environment and are supported by it. Through their sending and receiving of messages they are able to develop a loving growth relationship with their children.

The Bypassing Plan presented here includes all of the components for the prevention of burnout. The key is to study and understand the ingredients, value them as important for your well-being as a parent, and incorporate them into your daily life. It may take some practice because some of these concepts may be new to you. Think about what you need, follow the recommended exercises, and plan to practice each of these one at a time during the next ten weeks. Throughout your implementation of the Bypassing Plan, keep in mind the importance of communication as the vital thread of parent success and growth. Remember, these ingredients will be important for your continued growth throughout your life as a parent.

9

Special Situations and Parent Burnout

While, in a way, all parents are in a unique and special situation, there are several particular circumstances that merit attention and focus. In our research on the parent burnout phenomenon, we discovered several special situations that we consider major in the burnout experience of a number of fathers and mothers. Some of these special circumstances have been around for a long time and others are the result of recent social and economic shifts. Several situations stood out as having the most serious impact: single parents; stepparents; adoptive parents; parents of "latchkey children"; parents of exceptional children; parents of only children; and parents of twins. Each of these special conditions carries its own particular set of problems. In our discussion of each situation we present some insights and recommendations for alleviating these problems. Case studies based on interviews with parents in these special situations are presented as well. In Chapter 10 ("Parent Burnout Resources") we present organizations, as well as magazines, that are very good sources of information and help for parents who find themselves in one or more of these circumstances.

SINGLE PARENTS

Two years ago, Larry and Lynne and their two children were viewed as a "typical" American family. They lived in a modest three-bedroom rambler in the suburbs of Boston. While inflation and the rising cost of living gnawed away at Larry's income as a mid-level manager for an electronics corporation, he still managed to provide his family with some of life's extras: night classes for his wife at a local college, two-week family vacations every summer, and private schools for the children, Marie and Kenneth. Lynne was a proud homemaker with visions of embarking on a career in business once her degree was completed and the children were well into their teens.

Today, Larry lives three thousand miles away in Seattle, Washington. He has married a woman he met during a legal separation from Lynne, a separation prompted by increasing financial strife, Lynne's mounting desire for independence, and his series of brief, but frequent extramarital affairs. Larry shied away from accepting another middle-management position in order to launch a lifetime dream of starting his own business. While his dream has provided Larry with the rewards of "being my own boss," the initial costs of building his own enterprise left him seriously in debt. Consequently, he is finding the monthly outlay of support payments for Marie and Kenneth an increasing burden. He is often late with the payments and alternately feels guilty about his negligence and resentful of this obligation. His second wife has one child by her previous marriage and Larry now views himself as responsible for supporting two households, one in Boston and one in Seattle.

Lynne and her children still live in the suburban rambler, but it no longer looks like a house out of the pages of *Ladies' Home Journal*. Lynne does not have the time, energy, or inclination to maintain a spotless household. Her plans for completing college have been put on hold. After the divorce, she could only find a low-paying secretarial job. The reduced family income would not accommodate the college's tuition costs and furthermore, Lynne felt she should spend her evenings at home with the kids. Public schools have replaced the children's private school education.

Lynne particularly grieves over that change in her children's lives. "Kenneth and Marie had been through so much anguish over the divorce. They didn't understand why their father was no longer with them. I couldn't make them understand. And then on top of it all, they had to change schools. I worry about the quality of education they're receiving but more importantly, I worry about how much turmoil in their lives they can sustain," Lynne laments.

Lynne describes her new life as "very routine." After working all day, she comes home to fix dinner, spend some time with the children, and catch up on household chores. Apart from her job, she is rarely away from the children. Very infrequently, she will catch a movie with a girl friend, but she begs off most social invitations, claiming she is too tired or that her house "is in a shambles" and requires her cleaning skills that evening.

"I feel too guilty going out and enjoying myself while the children are left with a baby-sitter. I've taken away most of what they have known as a family and I certainly can't further deprive them of my time and attention," she says.

Although Lynne admits to having severe bouts of loneliness, she shudders at any suggestion of dating or interest in another man. Again, she contends that involving herself with another man would be "simply too cruel, too hard for the children to accept." Her few attempts at meeting men have left Lynne guilt-ridden and vowing to maintain a celibate life, at least until the children are in their teens. Marie is now eight and Kenneth is ten years old.

However, secretly, Lynne deeply fears spending the rest of her life alone and she occasionally will admit to having a wellspring of anger and resentment toward her children and her circumstances as a single parent. "I have to do everything," she sighs when her children are not present and the burdens of parenthood have congealed into a series of minor crises. "I have to work to make the money to clothe and feed the children, then I have to come home to fix their meals, listen to their woes, discipline them, encourage them, keep the house presentable, and there is no one else to help. If I don't do something, it simply doesn't get done," she concludes.

Larry and Lynne's stories are paralleled in millions of homes throughout America today. Over 8 million children under the age of eighteen currently live with one formerly married parent. An estimated four out of every ten children will live in single-parent homes for at least part of their childhoods. The single-parent home is not a new phenomenon. However, the incidence of children living with only one parent has dramatically increased. Today, almost 4 million single-parent households result from separation and divorce. Approximately the same number results from death and unwed motherhood.

Many single parents regard their status as very workable and, in fact, preferable. Parental stress and the prospects for burnout do not double or necessarily even increase simply because one half of the parenting team is absent. Countless single parents report that their confidence in their abilities to be a good parent increased after a separation or divorce.

"It's a grave error to assume that single parents are more likely to become frazzled and unable to cope with their lives and children," said Rachel, a mother of three who has been divorced for four years. "Although it is true that the responsibilities of raising children alone can appear overwhelming—especially in the first year following a divorce or separation—it is not true that single-parenting is a no-win, all-giving proposition," she said, citing her success in her new-found career, increased interest in the people and world around her, and consequently, her improved, closer relationship with her children.

"My problems with my marriage were inhibiting my ability to be a good mother," Rachel claims. "I was so involved with trying to patch the relationship with my husband together that I ignored the kids. I found their demands petty and exasperating. I am more relaxed with them now. We have our difficult times but at least now it's without all the rage and anger which was intended for my husband but misdirected at the kids. I'm a better parent now," she concludes.

Unfortunately, not all single parents can share Rachel's assessment that the solo road is better than a dual-parent responsibility for raising the children. And even parents who are apt to deem single parenthood as "better" are not likely to term the experience "easier."

Many single parents who were prepared for the double dose of responsibilities did not realize the sense of personal deprivation they would encounter. The lack of solitude is particularly evident in the lives of single parents. There's always one more page of homework to correct, one more face to be tucked under the covers, one more skinned elbow to nurse, and a dozen more questions to be answered. And as the single parents are quick to point out, there's only one available parent to fulfill these demands.

Obviously, coping with the mere logistics of single parenthood is quite a task and fraught with problems. Yet, it is often the emotional side of being a single parent that provokes more anxiety and concern than the financial and limited time worries.

As Morton Hunt and Bernice Hunt report in their book *The Divorce Experience:*

"The most painful experiences for single parents usually involve young preschool children. Young children are helpless, grief-stricken, fearful and, above all uncomprehending. The single parent tries desperately to explain, reassure, but the children stare wide-eyed, baffled, wounded. They whine and fuss, wet their beds, become picky about food, and uninterested in their toys. Some cry, some are deathly silent, some are panic-stricken when the babysitter arrives, some run for the phone everytime it rings, hoping to hear the outside parent. Part of what they do is annoying to the single parent, part is heartbreaking, all of it is guilt provoking."[1]

Older children and teenagers of course are no less upset, angry, or saddened, but they may use more complex methods of dealing with their emotions. They may rationalize by saying, "The split would have come sooner or later; it was just a matter of time," or they may deny the reality of divorce by claiming, "It isn't really forever; they will get back together soon," or they might withdraw from the situation contending, "Their problems have nothing to do with me. It's their issue." Regardless of the children's reaction to divorce, separation, or the death of a parent, the result for the custodial parent is the same: a nagging sense of guilt.

The guilt is twofold for the single parent. First is the guilt that results from the custodial parent's belief that he or she is depriving the child of a secure and happy childhood because both parents are not present. Second, single parents feel guilty because of the anger and resentment they inevitably harbor because the parent's pursuit of happiness must be compromised.

"I have raised my four children for the last twelve years alone. Now I feel it is their father's turn to do some of the raising," said one divorced mother. "I feel I've postponed my hopes and desires for a long time and now I want some of the freedom my spouse has enjoyed before I get too old to take part in some aspects of life," she continued. "I sometimes want to deposit the kids on my ex-husband's doorstep and walk away," she confessed, but admitted,

[1] *The Divorce Experience* (New York: McGraw-Hill, 1977), p. 170.

"Every time I think such thoughts, I tell myself only a wicked, horrible, unfit mother could imagine such dreadful things."

Single fathers face many of the same conflicts between careers and their children that women confront. In fact, in some cases, this particular dilemma may come to weigh more heavily on fathers with custody.

A thirty-eight-year-old widower says, "I was upwardly mobile, as they say—on the ladder of career success when the sudden death of my wife left the full-time care of three sons to me. I found it difficult to do everything—learn to cook, keep house, go to PTA meetings, and pursue my career goals. I found my employer to be sympathetic at first, but as time wore on, he grew impatient with the family demands which kept me from aggressively climbing that career ladder. I sensed he viewed me as lacking in ambition, having a mixed-up sense of priorities, and certainly not a man who would ever be willing to devote the needed attention to the job. He was right, in some ways. My family did and still does come first. As a result, I settled for a less than stellar career. I know I made the correct choice but I resent that the choice had to be made at all and at times, I resent the boys for keeping me from the top of that ladder."

This father's testimony indicates a feeling common, yet often masked, to many single parents. They frequently carry around an unspoken sense of failure—failure that their marriages did not last, failure that their career dreams will not be realized, failure to provide a "complete" home for their children. The self-inflicted charges of failure are almost limitless for a single parent.

Whether the state of single parenthood is caused by death, separation, or divorce, it brings about a major loss (regardless of how welcome it may have seemed earlier), which directly impacts on the children and adults alike. Furthermore, that loss must be managed when the single parent can least afford the extra demands made by children. Time and energy will be at a premium while the single parent tries to establish a new routine at home, maintain a career, and meet the emotional needs of the children.

The continual drain on time, energy, and emotional reserves provides a framework of stress, and possible burnout, for the single parent. While single parents are not necessarily more prone to burnout, the array of demands and responsibilities that they may face more often than dual-parent families does warrant special attention and requires the single parent to pay special heed to signs of stress and the need for developing a life that is separate from their many parental duties.

If you are a single parent, the command to reestablish balance in your life is likely to fit you more than almost any other parent. If you are single because of divorce, you have most likely traded the strain of a bad marriage for the new strain of being solely responsible for decisions that relate to your children. Where the attention and dependency that children shine on parents once was spread between you and your spouse, it is all focused on you now.

The six-week treatment plan that we have prescribed for all burned-out parents is appropriate for you too, but you must add one critical element to your life in order to be able to gain maximum benefit from the plan. *You must have help.* The logistics of being a single parent require that you have access to help with the job of father or mother. This source of help doesn't have to be permanent and always available (even a spouse doesn't always fill that bill), but he or she must be there enough to allow you to maintain a sense of your own life and to meet your needs.

You may wonder where these helpers will come from. Here are some suggestions. Try trading child care back and forth with friends. One young widow we interviewed alternates one Saturday or Sunday a month with a married couple who are her close friends. One Saturday or Sunday she will care for her own and their children and the next time they will keep their children and her son and daughter. This system has worked well for over two years and both the parents and children love it. Second, use baby-sitters if you can afford it and can find sitters whom you trust and who are reliable. Ask your own extended family. Grandparents, aunts, sisters, brothers, cousins, might relish the chance to get to know your children better. You may have a close friend with no children who likes your children and whom they like. *Do not be afraid to ask.* Your friends may actually want to help, but may be reluctant to ask to help you for fear of being accused of "butting in."

It is absolutely necessary that before you take any of these suggestions, you be willing to let go of your children and allow them to develop attachments to other adults. Feeling threatened by their having relationships with other adults will be counterproductive. Being jealous of other adults will hurt your chances of getting help with the care of your children. It will also make your children over-dependent on you.

After you have sought and found help, establish an appropriate balance between work (if you work) and time spent with your children. Establish a pattern and follow it as much as possible so the children will get used to it and feel more secure. Your children must know that they come first with you. Once you have proven that to them, they are less likely to continually test the limits of your love. If they know that you really would drop everything to attend their school play, they will understand if you feel the need to miss one occasionally.

Finally, establish a "we're a team" atmosphere in your family. The truth is that you really do need to work as a team in order to replace your spouse logistically. The team can wash the car, do housework, help move furniture, and do household repairs. Allow your kids to become experts in certain areas of family life and "run" the team. Do not be afraid to delegate the responsibilities or to lavish the praise for work well done.

If you can incorporate some of these recommendations into your parenting role, you will manage your life in a more balanced way and eliminate or prevent burnout.

STEPPARENTS

Twenty years ago a step-family was rare enough to be noticed in the community. Today increased divorces and remarriages have made the step-family commonplace and its needs better understood. This composite family not only faces the usual difficulties experienced in the natural family, but its potential for trouble is compounded by the number and complexity of the relationships that may be involved. The firm expectation on the part of those parenting this conglomerate that "we will be one big happy family," and the stress that may ensue from trying to accomplish that goal, can rapidly lead to burnout.

The goal of the "happy family" may not be an unrealistic one, but the expectations that induce stress and subsequent burnout frequently cause parents to act unrealistically because they minimize the complicated relationship of step-family members. For instance, the parent of a step-family may very well be a natural parent and a stepparent at the same time. This may lead to a "I love 'em like my own" overstatement in reaction to the feeling, held secret and perhaps even denied to oneself, that there may be little or no love for the stepchild. At the same time, there may be an abundance of love for the natural child. Superhuman efforts to compensate for this hidden feeling to help ward off guilt might be attempted. The energy that goes into bending over backward in this effort to overcompensate can be mentally and physically exhausting and will, no doubt, lead to strong feelings of resentment.

Another common result occurs when there are no natural children of a stepparent. The stepparent may feel inadequate about assuming a parenting role or may be seeking too much love from the stepchild. This can lead to an attempt at "superparenting." This could take the form of enthusiastically expending energy or, perhaps, being the passive "yes" parent who lets the kids walk all over him or her in hopes of being rewarded with love. A feeling of parental entrapment and anger may be the result if the child does not respond in the anticipated appreciative and loving way.

In addition, other people often influence how the stepparent acts. Exhaustive attempts to love and care for stepchildren may be undertaken fearing that "My husband won't love me if I don't love his children." Or, "What will his family and friends think of me if I don't do the right thing for his children?" The "Hansel and Gretel syndrome" has convinced many generations that the stepmother is wicked and cruel to her stepchildren. There are many who consciously or subconsciously believe the tale and so all the more need to be Supermom or Superdad.

Natural parents, on the other hand, can burn out practicing the juggling act of keeping the children happy while trying to please a new and not too child-crazy spouse. This situation can bring about a most stressful and painful values conflict, the resolution of which is seldom easy and usually awkward.

The natural parent may also have a need to prove himself or herself a good parent in the new family relationship, particularly if the past family life has left strained relationships with the children. "Now you'll see how great a dad I really am," says the father who needs to feel himself a more capable parent than his ex-spouse.

"Now we'll be a real family," says the mom who feels guilty about her perception of her children's past unhappiness. Focused in this way, the natural parent sets up expectations that place unrealistic demands on his or her behavior.

Parents and children coming into a step-family do so with differing values and life experiences. As with the natural family, there are differences in the viewpoints of the two generations, but, before the step-family was formed, each natural parent had been used to orderly family life in particular patterns. He, for instance, may think that 10 P.M. is a fine bedtime for a nine-year-old and she may believe that 8 P.M. is late enough. Not only can this place a strain on the relationship between the parents, but the children, used to certain values and routines, now are faced with two sets of codes and habits, which may be in conflict. Before the issues are resolved, the result is often confusion, tension, and stress.

The internal complexity of the step-family is not its only potential trouble spot. External forces make family relationships even more complicated: the hostility of an ex-spouse concerned about the care of the children; the intrusion of an ex-spouse's moral or behavioral viewpoints, particularly when they conflict with the step-parent's; the possibility of as many as four sets of grandparents; or in the case where the natural parent has died, the child's strong need to remain "loyal" to the deceased parent and never bestow love on an unwanted replacement.

"I never thought it would be like this. All I wanted was to be a good mother, I mean to Bob's kids as well as my own. Now we fight often, or worse, don't talk. I usually feel edgy, depressed too, I guess, and often I want to scream, or cry, or maybe just run away." Amid the ensuing tears Jan unfolded the story of how she, at twenty-seven, divorced and with a six-year-old, had married Bob three years ago. He was thirty-four, divorced, with two children, ten and nine. After being married for about one year and having only Jan's child in their home, Bob's two children, much to the expressed delight of Jan, moved in too. The move was not happy for one of Bob's children, who had wanted to remain with her natural mother. This seemed to start the problems. "No matter what I do that little girl just causes trouble," sighed Jan. "I do everything to make her happy. She takes so much time. Bob doesn't know what to do either, and his first wife keeps making pointed suggestions as to how we should do this and that for her." Bob's parents were also very vocal regarding how the step-family should function. "They shower attention on Bob's two children, even giving them things we don't want them to have, like too much candy and television. I try to please them and go out of my way to do what they want, but I guess I resent it. Everyone wants to tell us how to do things, but they want *us* to do it. If we could move far away, like to California, maybe we could raise the kids okay."

Jan and Bob were becoming "yes" parents, attempting to be obliging to children, ex-spouses, and grandparents, and the result was that the anger that they felt began to be directed toward each other. They both felt trapped, helpless, and overwhelmed by the demands of others. "I feel like a pie being cut into too many pieces, and everybody wants a slice," was Jan's way of describing her feelings. Burnout was evident in both of them. Counseling took some time, but gradually Bob and Jan began to recognize the underlying problems and to learn how to deal with them.

In the internal family structure Jan was able to realize that in "expressing delight" about Bob's children becoming part of the family she was overlooking the realities of the relationships involved. "Delight" does not deal realistically with the resentments, insecurities, and the yet unfelt love issues that exist in newly forming step-families. Jan and Bob were now able to look at and discuss these feelings between themselves, and with their children, and to acknowledge that this was a beginning point from which new ties could form if honesty prevailed. The family began to develop ground rules together; responsibilities were shared and respect shown. The trapped and beleaguered feelings began to diminish.

Externally, Jan and Bob, particularly, began to be less sensitive to the demands and influences of others. Both realized that if they were to become a strong family, they were going to have to take responsibility for decision-making. Many of the old ties had to be broken and some new relationship ground rules with grandparents, Bob's ex-wife, Jan's ex-husband, and friends had to be developed. This has been difficult. But Bob and Jan are succeeding and are looking forward to the birth of a new family member.

Denise's story takes a slightly different twist. "What's wrong with me? I know George loves me, but I'm not sure, I just feel, well, sorta numb. No future, no life, I'm not a person anymore. I just do everything mechanically. Maybe I made a mistake." These were Denise's opening comments as we interviewed her. She is forty-six, divorced, and had married George, forty-four, several months before, moved into his house where he had been raising his four teenage children since his first wife died two years ago. Denise has a grown daughter who has lived in a midwestern city far away for some time. Interviews with George revealed these feelings: "Maybe we got married too quick. I just thought that Denise was great, the first woman I felt anything for since my wife died. She was a wonderful woman, great with the kids. I expected that Denise would be too, but she's not. I'm still doing everything for them. She's no mother! Makes me mad. All she does is give me the silent treatment and won't do anything that I ask her. We're not a family. We're not even friends anymore."

George and Denise had known each other only four months before they married. Questioning revealed that they had never discussed their expectations of each other, or what their roles would be after they were married. George's expectations were based on his experiences with his first wife. He thought that Denise was similar to her and that Denise would assume the mothering role, slipping into the family and picking up where his first wife left off. In essence, though he cared about Denise and wanted her as a mate, he also expected to have a mother for his children. The fact that she did not meet these expectations made him angry and resentful of her. The responsibilities of caring for his children after his first wife's death tended to make him feel overwhelmed before he married Denise, and this feeling increased after the marriage. His disappointment and frustration began to spill over into his relationship with his children. For their part, the children cherished the memory of their mother, missed her, and were not sure that they wanted anyone to try to replace her. This feeling became stronger when Denise made little attempts to gain their affection. And when they experienced their father's increasing anger toward them after his marriage to Denise, their resentment was magnified.

Denise did not dislike the children, nor did she mind sharing a home with them. "It's just that, I guess, I've already raised my child, she's been on her own for five years now. I have a good job, responsible, you know, and, well, I guess I married George for adult companionship, and neither one of us considered how his kids would fit in. I guess I assumed that they would go on with George as their daddy and I'd just be there too. I'd forgotten what kinds of demands children place on you when they're growing up. When I came into that house, well, it was overwhelming. I guess that I just retreated inside myself."

This whole family is now in counseling. The children, well into their teens, did not want the replacement mother that their father envisioned, and once able to share that and have that feeling respected by him, they were better able to relate to Denise as the friend and support that she really wanted to be. George has been able to realize that his desire to have his family the way it used to be when his first wife was alive was also unrealistic. He has come to accept the fact that his first wife is gone and that this new family, if it is to survive, will have to find its own form and develop its roles based on the needs and feelings of the real people involved.

These two cases illustrate some of the many complexities faced by parents and children in a step-family structure. In many ways parents of a composite family are the most susceptible to burnout because the demands placed on them can come from many sources with differing agendas. The expectations that "I will love my stepchildren [even if I do not]," the denial and guilt that surround the issue, the need to overdo efforts at getting along, and the feeling of being "used, trapped, and angry" can accelerate the stepparent on the road to burnout.

Stepparents who succeed in avoiding burnout or alleviating it generally demonstrate certain important attitudes and behaviors. First, they accept feelings. Perhaps the major producer of stress in a step-family is pretense. Pretending (and then overcompensating) that everything and everybody are wonderful and that everyone in the family loves everyone equally is often unrealistic and not even to be expected. Second, they share feelings. It is important for the children in a step-family to know that no one is going to be angry at them if they express love, say, for their natural fathers while living in the homes of their stepfathers. Those parenting a step-family have the same need for openness and respect. For instance, Jan, in the first case, might say to her resistant young stepdaughter, "I know that you love your mommy very much and that you like to be with her even though you are living here with your daddy and me. I understand that because I love my daughter very much and I like to be with her. I also like getting to know you. Bet we can have some fun doing things together. Bet we may even be real friends." This is an honest statement, shows acceptance of the feelings of stepparent and stepchild, and invites the formation of a positive and growing relationship. Acceptance of the feelings of all concerned eases stress and anger, and begins to create a bond of mutual respect within the family. Comfortable relationships and even love can come from this beginning.

Third, successful step-families decide on roles and responsibilities. A family needs to develop its unique ground rules. In the case of the composite family, well-considered rules can help to unite the family and turn chaos into order. Parents of a step-family need to decide what role they wish to play, and form that role in a way that will be compatible with the children's needs. For example, Denise preferred the friend role in relating to George's children. This was congruent with the children's wishes and George was eventually able to live with it as well. The family then was able to function in its own unique way.

Lastly, effective stepparents approach family matters in a relaxed manner. Parenting in this situation is often like walking on eggshells. Once feelings have been explored and shared, the ground rules established, and the new relationships have begun to develop, a climate of calm should be fostered. Not making every issue crucial or perceiving it as a threat to the fragile nature of the step-family is important for the authentic development of the new parent-child relationships.

Having recognized the need to have the four attitudes and behaviors just discussed function within the step-family structure, how do stepparents establish these elements within the home?

Deciding who is in charge is the beginning point. As mentioned earlier, each stepparent may come into the marriage with different values and behavioral standards. These differences need to be discussed and negotiated by the couple privately so that a new and agreed-to set of rules for this family may be formed. It is important that both parents in the step-household be in charge, and that they present their leadership in a united and consistent way to the children. The stress felt by any parents when children are able to out-maneuver Mom's "no" by securing Dad's "yes" is self-evident, but in a step-family this "divide and conquer" strategy can be disastrous since it may put the children in charge and sabotage the attempt to form a secure and anchored new family. Every family needs fair, reasonable, and consistent ground rules and for the composite family these ground rules can serve as a powerful unifying force.

Next, with the two parents in charge, a regular family meeting should be held, perhaps weekly at first, and more frequently if a problem arises. An agenda of things to be discussed should be created, allowing each family member to contribute. For instance, Johnny may want to have family dinner at five-thirty on Wednesdays because of baseball practice. Mary doesn't think it is fair that she had to do homework before watching television, Mom is out of patience from asking the kids to pick up their clothes, and Dad wants to talk about vacation alternatives. Out-in-the-open discussion, where everyone is listened to with respect, and where decisions are made based on the needs of the individual and the family as a whole, tends to reduce tension, deepen respect, and strengthen that step-family's values.

Sometimes outside help is needed to enable the step-family to become more harmonious. There are many resources from which to choose, and finding the most appropriate one is important. Frequently it is not professional help but the sharing with other stepparents who have similar concerns that will best serve the purpose. This can relieve stress and presents new approaches to problems. Forming a stepparent support group can bring very positive results. How can you find other stepparents to form such a group? There are several ways. Ask the school principal, adviser, or guidance counselor to give you names or to contact other parents on your behalf with the suggestion of forming a group to meet monthly. Clergymen may know of others wishing to be part of such a group. Be sure to talk with several clergymen to secure enough contacts. If a Parents Without Partners chapter exists in your area, there may be those in their former membership who have remarried and are now part of a step-family; notices giving a phone number can be effective when placed in local community newspapers or on bulletin boards. The best group size is four couples, though three to five is entirely workable.

If professional help is desired, the selection of the person to help you is of critical importance. In many parts of the country step-family counseling *per se* is not yet an active specialty. However, a helper who specializes in family or marriage counseling could be of assistance. In selecting that helping person, interview him, asking questions such as: What are his attitudes toward step-family life? Family values? Does he place his value system on how your family should function, or does he see his role as enabling your family to chart its own way with his guidance to point out pitfalls? How does this helper approach teaching the family to communicate with each other? The person you select may come from any of the helping professions—social worker, mental health counselor, psychologist, psychiatrist, clergyman, etc., but of prime importance is his openness with you in regard to his credentials and his helping philosophy, and your feelings that this person understands the stresses you are attempting to deal with and will be able to work with you within the framework of your values.

In conclusion, dealing honestly with feelings, mutual respect, clarification of roles, joint decisions about responsibilities, and seeking help if needed are elements that help the step-family relieve the stresses that it may face and go a long way in preventing burnout.

ADOPTIVE PARENTS

"I will never forget the day we brought her home. I was euphoric and on cloud nine. I thought to myself, 'It finally happened after all these years.' " These were the words of Edith as she began to describe her life over the past years with Janice, now eighteen, her adopted daughter. "She really knows no other parents, of course. She has been with us since she was two years old. Everything has been fine up to now. I don't know what has gotten into her. I can't understand it. I do know one thing. I won't be able to take this much longer." What Edith was referring to was Janice's recent interest in determining her real identity, including who her natural parents are and eventually meeting them. "In a way I kind of knew all along that this day would come. This possibility has always gnawed at me. In fact, if you really want to know the truth, it has bothered me quite a bit all these years. I guess that I would sublimate it, but it was always there. I could feel it."

When Janice first expressed interest in this a few years before, Edith and her husband were understanding and sympathetic to their daughter, but inside they were totally crushed. "After all these years of intimacy, devotion, hard work, and worry I suddenly felt like a stranger, on the outside looking in. I suddenly found myself thinking, 'Blood is thicker than water and she doesn't even have my blood'—a terrible thought I couldn't have imagined having even a month before."

Edith found herself dwelling on this issue more and more. The image of her adopted daughter, whom she loved so much, meeting her natural mother was totally overwhelming. It became a living nightmare for her. What would the mother be like? Would they embrace? Would they develop an intimacy that would supersede their own? Would she eventually reject my husband, who has worked his whole life for her, and me as well?

The household grew more tense with each passing day as Janice could sense the disappointment and worry in her parents. Often there were long silences at the dinner table and during the evening hours when the family sat in the family room. "At times I felt like there was a stranger in our midst, in some ways a traitor or spy who was secretly more loyal to another person. It was a very eerie feeling and I am sure that Janice felt vibrations of our fearful thoughts. I was becoming exhausted, and I resented Janice more and more for this mental and physical torture she was putting me through. I knew that she could sense my resentment and I really didn't care."

Janice did indeed respond to this change in attitude and behavior on the part of her mother. One evening, as Edith and her husband sat in gloomy silence watching television, responding with one-word answers to Janice's questions about their day, their daughter snapped the television off and in a fit of rage screamed, "Look, you two. You are angry because I want to know my real mother and father. What's wrong with that? You should know by now that I love you. I am grateful to you for all that you have done. But let's face it, I filled your needs too, you know. You needed a baby and I was available. So get off my back!" Janice then stormed out of the house.

Edith was totally devastated by these last words. She sat there in tears, hysterical. She sobbed all evening and couldn't get herself to go talk to Janice, who had come back a few hours later and had

gone to bed. The next morning Janice greeted her parents at breakfast and apologized for her conduct the evening before. She asked
that they forgive her but she also pointed out that she did not in-
tend to abandon her goal of finding her natural parents. She explained that it was "just something that I have to do. I feel this
tremendous drive inside of me."

The next few weeks were very difficult for Edith. Her first
thoughts were to seek legal counsel to determine whether or not
Janice could be stopped. However, she soon abandoned "that crazy
notion." Her concern soon began to affect her physical health. She
found herself often feeling dizzy and nauseous. After several of
these episodes, including one severe attack when she was driving on
the freeway, she made an appointment to see her physician. He de-
tected that her blood pressure had soared and that she was heading
for complete exhaustion. She broke down and cried in the physician's office. After hearing about her plight he referred her to a
psychologist who specialized in counseling adoptive parents. Edith
is now in counseling. She has come to accept the fact that her
daughter's feelings and needs are instinctive and natural. These are
normal desires and they in no way reflect on her daughter's level of
love and respect for her.

Her expectations of how her daughter should or should not
think, feel, and behave are unrealistic. Edith has come to realize
that her fear of being rejected is totally unfounded and is really a
"disaster fantasy" and she is also becoming convinced, but more
slowly, that there is no need to look back and reconstruct past decisions. She and her husband have nothing to regret. They did nothing to bring about this difficult situation. It is beyond their total
control. What they have to do is learn to cope with the ambivalence and complexity of the reality they find themselves in. The key
for them is to accept this new experience, share the fulfillment of
their daughter's need with her, and bring themselves closer to her
by doing this. Their needs and her needs are in conflict. And, once
again, especially in this case, as good loving parents, they can
allow their daughter's needs to take precedence.

Following the advice of their counselor both Edith and her husband have developed a much more genuine, empathic, and mutually respectful relationship with their daughter, Janice.

PARENTS OF "LATCHKEY CHILDREN"

Latchkey children are those who come home from school to an empty house to care for themselves until a parent arrives. Some return home with siblings, others are completely alone. In all cases, these children spend some time each schoolday without adult supervision. Most of them wear a house key on a chain around their necks, thus the term "latchkey children."

There is no reliable estimate of how many latchkey children there are nationwide, since most are coached to be discreet by anxious, often guilt-ridden parents. Estimates range between 2 and 6 million. One thing is certain: the phenomenon is increasing rapidly. Causes for this dramatic surge are a high divorce rate, crippling inflation, and increasing numbers of unwed mothers and working women.

More and more women are entering the labor force out of financial necessity. Fifty-eight percent of mothers of school children are working and estimates are that two out of every three will be in the labor force by 1990. Many of these mothers leave their children to care for themselves after school. Some try day care-type programs initially, but often switch to self-care when costs become prohibitive, children balk at childish programs, or claim to be too old for "glorified baby-sitting." For most parents in this situation self-care is undoubtedly more attractive. First, transportation is no longer a problem. While getting a child from school to a sitter or day care center often involved public transportation, taxi cabs, private bus companies, or favors from friends, getting children home from school is less complicated. Most children walk or are delivered safely to their door by school bus free of charge. Second, parents of latchkey children no longer have to leave work at a specified hour and rush to a closing day care center. Delays at work or traffic problems can be handled easily with a telephone call home. Third, children at home can help with household chores and ease the burden for parents returning from work. Older latchkey children are often responsible for setting the table and starting dinner. Finally, self-care is without financial cost. But it does extract a price from both child and parent.

Betty is a thirty-nine-year-old secretary in Washington, D.C. She and her husband, Franklin, have a ten-year-old daughter, Karen.

Franklin is a salesman for a large computer firm and he spends much time traveling, leaving Betty and Karen to care for themselves. Karen gets home from school everyday at 3:30 P.M. She cares for herself until her mother arrives home two hours later. During this time Karen cleans her room, does homework, and watches her favorite television programs. Karen is self-sufficient and does not mind staying at home alone, "unless it's dark."

When asked how long Karen has been taking care of herself, Betty replied, "Only two years. Before that I didn't work. I just stayed home and played mother. At first I loved it. Franklin and I got married at twenty-one, the year I graduated from college. We didn't have Karen until I was twenty-nine. We didn't think that we could have kids. So when I found out that I was pregnant, I couldn't wait to quit work and be a full-time mother. But when Karen started school I felt a loss in my life. I needed to be needed and I wasn't. Well, not as much anyway. But I still stayed home because that's what my mother did. By the time Karen finished the second grade I was itching to get back to work. I didn't have to work. I mean we didn't need the money. We could use it, but we didn't need it. I just needed something to do. So I found a job at a local hospital as a secretary. I was overqualified, but it was close to home. I did not like it that much, but it was something."

When asked how she felt about leaving Karen alone, Betty responded, "Guilty. Terribly guilty. Before I went back to work, I was always there when she came home from school. We could talk about the day or do something special, you know. Bake cookies or go shopping. Now I wasn't there and I still felt that I should be. She was only eight years old then. I tried to talk with her when I got home. But it just wasn't the same. To her school seemed so far away and there was just so much to do before bedtime. I felt a distancing and it was my fault. I guess that I felt doubly guilty because I knew I didn't have to work. At times I'd ask myself who was more important, my daughter or I? Now that's a tough one."

We asked Betty if she was afraid of leaving Karen home alone. "At first I wasn't. We live in a pretty good neighborhood and she has always been exceptionally well behaved. I didn't expect her to break anything or get into trouble. . . . Then one afternoon Karen went to a friend's house after school. I took the opportunity to go grocery shopping. When I got home about 6:30 P.M., the front door was half-open. I shouldn't have gone in, but I did. There was a man at the top of the stairs. When he saw me he ran for the front door, pushing me out of the way as he left. The house was in a shambles, but nothing was missing. It seems like I came home just in time. The police never found him. Anyway, I never felt that Karen was safe after that. I would have nightmares about that man breaking in when she was home alone. . . . If anything would ever happen to her, I could never forgive myself."

Betty is quick to point out other problem areas for the parents of latchkey children. "I never noticed how often they canceled school until I started working. It seems like every week there is either a snow day, a holiday, or a teachers' meeting. The summers are a real problem. Karen has to stay home alone all day, and I don't like to do that. I often have to find a place to park her. And that's not always easy. You can only ask friends to do so much. Keeping her busy for three months is beginning to border on the impossible. I start worrying about it and making plans in April. Last summer she was a pool rat. I often dropped her off at the pool in the morning and picked her up after work. I know that she got tired of being there, but she never complained."

In addition to fear and guilt, parents of latchkey children experience other pressures unique to their situation. Most feel frustrated by their inability to control their children's behavior when they are home without supervision. As one mother of a ten-year-old boy noted, "I tell my son not to watch certain TV programs. But when I'm not there he watches them anyway. Then he calls me up frightened." Another mother of two boys experiences a similar problem. "I tell my sons not to fight. But when I'm not home they get into it over the least little thing. I don't know how to control them when I'm not there."

Other parents are frustrated by the lack of contact they have with their children after school. The telephone is their lifeline to their children and when parents cannot reach their children they get frightened. "I'll tell my son to come home right after school. He should get there by three-thirty," the mother of an eleven-year-old boy commented. "Yet when I call, sometimes he's not there. The first thought that runs through my mind is that something has happened to him. So far nothing has. He's just hanging around with his friends. But it scares me just the same." The mother of a twelve-year-old girl also had problems maintaining telephone contact. "I try to call my daughter from work to see if she's all right; sometimes I want to let her know that I will be getting home late. But I can never get through. She is always on the telephone. When this happens I can feel my heart racing and I am sure that my blood pressure goes up."

Many parents of latchkey children feel the added pressure of trying to entertain their children from a distance. "I try to think of things to keep my daughter busy," said a mother of a nine-year-old who spends one hour alone every afternoon. "But it's hard to think of things that are safe and that she can do herself. I don't want her sitting and watching television every day." Another parent also found entertaining her daughter a problem: "I feel bad enough as it is leaving her alone after school. But when she calls me up and says 'I'm bored' or 'I'm lonely,' I feel terrible. However, I could never tolerate having other children in the house with her. That would be even worse."

The key word for parents of latchkey children is "priority." The dilemma that most find themselves in can be alleviated, if not resolved, by the recognition of the mutually exclusive nature of the values of home child care and working outside the home. For some the priorities are a matter of options and can be chosen freely. For others there is no choice because of financial need or career development or strong personal growth needs. Parents of latchkey children must come to understand and accept emotionally that the situation that they find themselves in is not of their own making entirely, but is the consequence of a dichotomy between two important and equally valid needs. The stress that results from this tension must be recognized and managed in order to avoid burnout.

If you are the parents of latchkey children, what can you do? We have several suggestions. First, fathers and mothers must sit down with their children and explain the situation. Children should know why this situation exists: that you have to work to help with family expenses; that you have a career, which you want to develop; that you help other people who depend on you in your work; etc. Second, you must develop rules for your children and they should be written down and posted conspicuously (for example: "Be sure to keep the door locked; don't let *anyone* in the house; don't tell anyone who calls on the telephone that you are home alone"). Third, instruct your children in emergency rules and procedures. It would be good to run some practice drills for fires and other emergencies. Fourth, develop security strategies that include door and window locks as well as external lighting. Fifth, organize in-home activities that include chores as well as pleasurable tasks such as crafts projects or creative games. Sixth, consider having your child get involved in community recreation or library programs. Well-supervised programs that take your child out of the house even once a week will decrease the time that your child will be home alone. Lastly, it is important for you to come home immediately after work and find out how the day went for your children. If there is more than one child, make sure that each has the chance to talk with you individually. We have found that if latchkey children feel that the relationship between their parents and themselves is getting closer, the situation will be viewed more positively.

Parents of latchkey children could be prime candidates for burnout. The balancing of work and home life, the guilt, and the constant worry could add up to create a nightmarish existence. However, with some good planning and effective communication, burnout most certainly can be avoided.

PARENTS OF EXCEPTIONAL CHILDREN

As discussed earlier, parents hold a set of expectations for themselves based on a number of personal and societal images of what makes a "good parent." Similarly, parents also have a set of expectations for their children. For example, they may expect that their children be healthy, well adjusted, smart, friendly, or any one of a thousand qualities. But what happens when these expectations are not met? What if the child is frail or contracts a serious illness? What if the child is hyperactive? Or what if the child does not learn as quickly as the other children?

When parents' expectations of their children are not met, the immediate most common reaction is, "What did I do wrong?" Children's shortcomings or problems, regardless of how unrelated they are to the type or quality of parenting the children received, are first viewed by the parents as somehow a result of what they did or did not do.

Despite the countless influences external to the home that may affect the lives of children today, parents continue to feel primarily responsible for whatever malady, accident, or unfortunate circumstances befall their children. The net effect is that parents believe and expect that they are the sole guardians of their children's behavior and lives. And when something goes awry, the parents assume "It must be my fault." When the reality falls short of the parents' expectations of their children, just as when their expectations of themselves are not met, disillusionment and disappointment are likely to result.

This feeling can be greatly exacerbated when parents have a child or children who are having special difficulties maturationally, intellectually, emotionally, physically, or socially. Remember, it is estimated that in the United States today approximately 40 percent of all school-age children are not capable of performing up to grade level for one reason or another. Some are simply not mature enough for their grade. Others are held back because of physical or psychological problems. Some have specific learning disabilities, or problems in social behavior. Of course, the extent of the child's problems and the coping ability of the parents will combine to determine the levels of distress. Nonetheless, the parenting of a child with one of these problems, however "mild," can add a significant amount of stress to the parents' lives. The stresses of parenting can be exaggerated by any of the following factors:

- The period of dependency of the children may be extremely prolonged. In some conditions it may be permanent. The parent can be facing infancy forever.
- There is a great amount of daily care necessitated by special feeding, handling, and sleep problems.
- Round-the-clock care greatly inhibits planned social or personal time away from the child.
- Children are even less capable of appreciating parents' giving, and, depending on the problem, may not develop social smile, language, or relationship with the parents until much later than normal, if at all.
- Children are more vulnerable to illness and accidents because of their problem. The hyperactive child will have more cuts, bruises, and broken bones as a result of impulsivity. The child with learning problems may develop nervous disorders associated with frustration.

- Parents feel guilty for "having done this" to their children, even if the problem is not inherited. Mothers especially feel this way about brain-injured children or accident victims.
- Parent guilt may extend outward, that is, they perceive that other people consider them responsible for their children's difficulties. This is most often seen with emotionally disturbed or autistic children because these disorders are considered "social-psychological" in nature by the general public.
- The intensity of rearing children is amplified by the often difficult-to-manage behaviors that are a result of the child's immaturity for age, personal frustration, and limited coping resources.
- Parents often feel the need to "overprotect" their child, increasing their anxiety and sense of responsibility.
- Parents do not always agree on the child-rearing technique that should be employed with children with special problems: should the child be protected and coddled or forced to make his or her way without special help?
- In mild problem areas (e.g., undisciplined behavior), parents do not always agree that the problem exists. This causes fighting and guilt between parents, as the father may view the mother as too easy and the mother may see the father as too harsh.
- There is increased financial burden as a result of the need for medical, psychological, and social services. Parents can feel guilty, too, that other children in the family are not given the resources they would have otherwise received.
- Finding competent professional services is often a time-consuming and frustrating task. These may not be available in all communities and parents have to drive long distances regularly, involving much time, energy, and money.
- Mothers who had planned to return to their careers after the birth of the baby find themselves unable to return to the workplace because of guilt and inability to find competent care for their child.
- Because siblings can resent the attention given to the child with the problem, parents may find themselves trying to cope with the misbehaviors of their other children. Young children will often attempt to recoup lost attention from a parent by some form of misbehavior.

Nancy's story is a case in point. She was thirty-two and the mother of two children when she brought the younger child, Lee, to the diagnostic evaluation center seeking a residential placement for her son. The older boy, Billy, thirteen, was doing well, but Lee was a real problem.

Lee was the product of a difficult pregnancy, and Nancy had been hospitalized for four months during that time as a result of a major car accident. Lee was born on time, but was fussy and difficult from birth. Nancy, already parenting another child, did the best she could with him. His fussiness gave way to tantrums, withdrawal, crying fits, breath-holding, and running away as he got older. School and the pressures it brought only increased Lee's behaviors and he was placed in a special classroom for part of the day. Academically, he was not far from average. Lee was diagnosed as a brain-injured child at the center.

Nancy accepted the diagnosis almost gratefully. For the last eight years she and her husband had been attempting to parent this child, feeling all the while that their poor techniques were responsible for his difficulties. They had some help from her mother and sister who lived nearby, but as Lee got older, he became too difficult for her relatives to manage, especially when they had other responsibilities. Lee could not be left on the street to play with other children. He would run away (for the fun, he'd say), or play "chicken" with the cars. He had no sense of danger. Nancy attempted to get after-school day care for Lee so she could work and help with the family expenses. This was successful for a while, and she was able to secure an interesting job with an insurance company. However, within three months Lee's behaviors became more than the center's staff could handle.

At the time Lee was brought in for evaluation, Nancy was on the verge of having to quit her job because she could find no competent care for this child. She had tried private sitters. They would last a day, maybe two, before refusing to stay with him. Having a sitter come to their house met with the same results. No one wanted to be responsible for a child who would disappear from the home if not constantly watched.

Nancy was burning out. From her point of view she had nowhere to turn. She could not work, or go back to school as she had planned. She had no free time. Weekends were worse than the rest of the week. Personal life was reduced to nothing as Lee's behavior took all her attention. Lee's father had long since left discipline to the boy's mother. The alienation and desperation were such that Nancy petitioned the school district for residential educational placement for Lee. She really did not want to send him away, she said, but she felt like she could no longer go on parenting him full time. She had also begun to beat him and she was desperately afraid of her rage.

Because Lee was considered only mildly handicapped, the school system would not consider a residential placement and they told her so. Rage turned inward, as guilt and depression overwhelmed her. She had not liked the solution of sending Lee away, but now there was no solution. She was also personally concerned at this time that the school system thought that *she* was the child's problem. She and her husband argued more as the stress of this problem coupled with tight family finances became more burdensome. Nancy was in a desperate situation. She was about to quit her job, unable to help herself or her husband, and beginning to have difficulties with the older boy, who was just approaching adolescence. Nancy was burning out rapidly. Fortunately, the clinical diagnosis of brain damage was enough to begin to lessen some of the guilt felt. The diagnostic center also provided methods of behavior management and parent counseling as part of the service. She and her husband were helped to see her role in Lee's problems more realistically. Additionally, Lee was placed in a more appropriate educational setting and began to improve under that program. Fortunately, he was also a child for whom medication was helpful in controlling behavior.

As a result of the better parenting techniques, her new understanding of her responsibilities and controls, and the new school environment, Nancy was able to turn her life around and avoid total burnout.

If you are the parent of an exceptional child, you need support, help, and people with whom to talk freely about your situation. Some of the support services that are available today were not in place even three years ago. This is a result of federal legislation, Public Law 94-142, which guarantees handicapped children special services through the public schools. Children must be evaluated before they become eligible for services, however.

You can find help in many ways. Prevention is, of course, better than cures.

Here are some ways to *avoid* burnout.

1. *Acceptance.* This is the first, and probably the hardest, task. As a parent of an exceptional child, under most circumstances, you are not going to have your expectations of a perfect child met. Children are not perfect to begin with. Exceptional children, however, have aspects of imperfection that are not as easily ignored. As the parent of a child with special needs you must come to grips with the painful reality that this child will probably always be different. Knowing this and accepting it are two different things. We wish it were not true, and become angry when it stubbornly *is* true. This is normal. It is part of the acceptance cycle, outlined by Elisabeth Kübler-Ross in her work *On Death and Dying*.[2] It has four stages:

A. DENIAL: We refuse to believe the truth; the child *is* handi-capped.

B. ANGER: How could this happen to me? Why him? Why *our* child?

C. GRIEF: This is a tragedy.

D. ACCEPTANCE: This is how it is, let's get on with life.

These stages usually emerge in sequence. Inability to accept the truth about our child is usually a symptom of the denial stage. Eventually, most of us will come to grips with the truth about the condition. Symptoms of burnout can be distinguished from this, however, by their pervasiveness and worsening over time. Burned-out parents can be helped if they come to grips with the loss of expectations that they are experiencing, and with the true feelings of injustice and defeat. It *is* unfortunate that any child has to have disabling conditions; it is the case nonetheless. Feelings of sadness about the plight of the child are understandable, but the sadness must eventually be replaced by the knowledge that all persons have potential, some higher than others, and that the handicapped child needs special help to reach his or hers. Friends and professionals can help parents by recognizing their level of acceptance and allowing ventilation of natural feelings.

[2] New York: Macmillan, 1969.

2. *Locating help.* As the parent of an exceptional child you have more services and supports available to you than ever before. Federal law requires each state to hold "Child-Find" searches. This means that every state must actively seek out exceptional children and offer assistance in locating appropriate facilities, services, treatment centers, and schools. Usually, the state agency that handles this can also make referrals as well. Federal law also requires that all handicapped children be served from birth through age twenty-one. As a result, there are infant stimulation programs available that will provide appropriate education and competent professional guidance. You must take as much advantage of these programs as possible for the sake of your child and yourself.

3. *Getting Personal Support and Self-acceptance.* Burnout will be avoided if you feel comfortable admitting your feelings. Much of our guilt, if not all of it, stems from thinking that we "should not" or "must not" feel a certain way. The fact is that parenting of an exceptional child in general is hard. Feeling bad and angry and hurt is normal.

Various parent support groups are available to parents of exceptional children. Many are formed locally and organized around a particular handicap. An example is the Association for Children with Learning Disabilities. These groups can be informational/educational or they may be more therapeutic. In the latter case, the parents meet as a group to voice their concerns, confusions, anxieties, and frustrations. And everyone knows just what you are talking about. It often helps to hear another's solution to a problem you cannot see any way around.

4. *Professional Help.* Professional counseling is another way to avoid or eliminate burnout. Many professionals have experience with exceptional children, and can provide you with more appropriate child-rearing strategies and management techniques. This type of help is often available through hospitals, rehabilitation centers, and psychological consulting groups.

Psychotherapy may be required to assist a person in dispelling guilt and anger. Talking to a professional may be necessary, especially if you are feeling powerless to change anything in a positive way. Sometimes merely being able to speak openly and truthfully about the situation is helpful.

The key to recovery from and prevention of burnout for you as the parent of an exceptional child is recognizing the exceptional amount of physical, mental, and emotional energy needed to care for your child and taking advantage of all the individual, group, organizational, and governmental support that is offered and made available to you. You cannot do it alone nor should you. You will be better able to translate that exceptional love that you have for your special child into peak parenting performance if you take good care of yourself.

PARENTS OF ONLY CHILDREN

"This child wears me out! It just seems that I never have enough time to get everything done. Of course we want everything to be just right. I just don't know how parents with lots of kids manage. One child is a full-time job for me." This Los Angeles mother's exhaustion and frustration are not unusual among the parents of only children. Why when there is only one to take care of should these feelings exist? It generally has to do with all the parenting energy being poured into one child. Where the parents of the large family may face its potential burnout problems simply because of the numbers and the complexity of the relationships, the parents in an only-child family may encounter burnout for just the opposite reason: smallness and a more intense relationship. At most the only-child family consists of three people. In the single parent/only-child relationship, of course, there are only two.

At some point every parent is the parent of an only child (except in the case of parents of multiples). It is the first experience of parenting, those first few months in the life of the firstborn child, that exemplifies the potential burnout problem.

Take the case of Melissa and Raymond. They anxiously awaited the birth of their first child, read all the books, took all the courses, and waited and dreamed. "When Marcia was born we were beside ourselves. She was so beautiful, so delicate, a real little doll," said Melissa. "We could hardly wait to get home with her, to take care of her and have her in her own little bed. We wanted everything just right for her. After all, she was perfect, a perfect little treasure. We sure did enjoy her, of course, but now that I look back on it two children later, boy, were we worrywarts. We were afraid that she might break! And did we get ourselves up-tight trying to be perfect parents and have her be the most perfect little doll that ever lived."

Most parents of firstborns spend great energy in overconcern for their child's safety and well-being. The stress comes because many new parents feel inadequate, and yet expect themselves to be perfect in all that they do for the child, and, as the child grows, hold unduly high expectations as to how the child should behave. This overconcern usually disappears after the arrival of another child. This, however, is not true in the case of only-child parents. They tend to keep that "firstborn attitude" and remain overprotective. The only-child parent is forever in uncharted waters. Second, parenting the only child often means more time available to do everything perfectly. There is another subtle pressure at work here. Society, and frequently family and friends, attaches a stigma to those with only one child. "What's wrong," they say, "aren't you getting along? Can't you have any more? Isn't it a shame that little Billy has to grow up all alone?" These kinds of comments can make the only-child parent feel guilty. As a result, there is overcompensation once again to create the perfect child and to prove that they are really swell, normal, and capable people. In this mental state parents may find themselves as victims of the trap of crucializing. "Susie didn't eat much dinner, why did I let her have that cookie?" "I should have had Bobby wear his raincoat. Suppose he gets a cold?" and so on. As we have seen, years of this kind of self-blame can wear any parent down and increase the likelihood of burnout.

Third, as a spinoff from the high expectations of themselves as parents of an only child, is the intense desire that their child be a model son or daughter. In needing to prove their worthiness and capability and to overcome possible guilt, there is a strong need for the visible evidence of their brilliant parenting to be reflected in the behavior, characteristics, and accomplishments of their child. Many parents of the only child regularly go overboard. After all, everything is vested in Jimmy or little Judy! In some ways, the child is expected to "produce the results" of several children.

"I'm so angry at her. We do everything, give her every advantage, but lately she just isn't doing anything well. In school her grades are slipping, her music lessons—well she doesn't even practice the way she ought to. I just don't understand. I spend every minute I can arranging for her activities. My husband helps, too. Really, all day Saturday is devoted to what she needs. We try so hard. What's wrong with her?" The child that Monica is discussing is her eleven-year-old daughter, Sheila. Monica and her husband, Steve, are both professionals: she a lawyer and he an architect. Both work at their careers full time and both are very successful. Sheila was a much desired child and no further children were planned. As our interview proceeded it became evident that while the basic relationship among the three family members was sound, disappointment and anger surrounding Sheila's recent behavior were causing problems for all three of them.

The problems stemmed from expectations. Monica and Steve saw their role as parents as their most important job. "It's up to us to see to it that Sheila has every advantage, every opportunity, and that she makes use of them. We decided long ago that raising one child well was better than doing a lesser job with several," she quickly added.

There is nothing wrong with Monica and Steve's feelings and thoughts. However, the intensity and scope of their ideas are the root of their problem. If the child's success is really perceived as the indicator of the parents' success, then that can be a disaster for all. In this case, Sheila, in an eleven-year-old way, opted out of her parents' success game. Fortunately, the family was willing to explore the reason why. Sheila was feeling subtle but nonetheless heavy pressure from her parents. An only child in that situation usually has two choices: to fulfill the parents' expectations, perhaps abandoning her own independence; or to rebel either in an active-aggressive fashion or by causing a passive-aggressive slowdown, as was the case with Sheila.

Sheila's slowdown caused her parents to look at their role and to realize how really weary they were of it. The distress that they felt from years of orchestrating Sheila's activities, the all-day Saturday routine, the constant seeking and expecting of perfection from Sheila and themselves, the overwhelming time commitment that did not provide for shared fun, were making life exhausting for all. And everyone resented it. Through family counseling the family members have been able to communicate their feelings, fears, and wishes. Sheila, at eleven, was able to do more on her own. Saturdays became "fun with friends" day, and new activities were adopted and some old ones dropped by her choice. Monica and Steve relaxed more and began to see their role as listening to Sheila and helping guide and support her in the choices she increasingly made for herself. The end result has been less stress and more growing together.

While Monica and Steve had a problem with seeking perfection, Carol and Paul were overprotective. "Johnny's all we have and he means the world to us. When he was little he was sick a lot, colds, allergies, you know. We lost his older brother when Johnny was two, and, well, it was very hard for a long time. I can't help but worry, I know I shouldn't, but—what if something happened to Johnny?" That's a hard and painful place to be. Further discussion indicated that Johnny, seven, was indeed a very sheltered child. When a child has been sickly, and especially when the parents have lost another child, it is difficult for them not to be overprotective. At the same time, this overprotection, with the time demands and the anxiety, was keeping the parents exhausted. From that came resentment and then guilt. A fear arose, prompted by that guilt—"What would happen if . . . ?"

Carol and Paul have been in counseling for some time. They have been able to become more accepting of their first child's death, though the loss will always be felt—and they are beginning to realize that Johnny's childhood health problems are not unusual or life-threatening and do not relate in any way to their other child's death.

They are also becoming aware of why many parents of only children feel the need to overprotect their child, and in small ways, they are beginning to help Johnny become more independent. He is now in Scouting and will soon join a Saturday craft program. Beyond this, Carol and Paul are exploring the feelings involved in their overprotective attitude. As their overprotection diminishes, their exhaustion lessens, and so does their resentment of the demands overprotection imposes. The burden of guilt and fear, for them attached to resentment, is also decreasing. Carol and Paul are now in a parents' study group so that they can keep in touch with how other parents cope. This is raising confidence, reducing anxiety, and diminishing feelings of inadequacy.

For parents of only children, participation in a child study group is a helpful tool, since, as with Carol and Paul, it enables the parents to weigh their concerns in relation to what they learn from other parents. Child study groups are frequently formed within churches and throughout school systems. If one does not exist in your community, you may be able to form one. Ask your pediatrician or family doctor for help in contacting other parents and for suggestions about topics and guest speakers for meetings. Notices in community newspapers and on bulletin boards announcing a meeting date and speaker will draw people, and churches and other community facilities are frequently willing to sponsor such groups if one does not exist.

Another way for parents of an only child to keep in touch with others is to become a class parent or a Scout leader, thus taking field trips with many children in his or her child's age group while also sharing these experiences with other parents.

For the parents of only children burnout prevention begins with the awareness that the energy devoted to the needs of an only child may be expended in a disadvantageous manner. If that energy is used for the child's growth toward wholesome self-awareness, confidence, and independence, then that only child can be very fortunate. However, if parental energy is used to overprotect and seek perfection in everything relating to the child, this not only diminishes the child's chances for a productive and rewarding adult life, but it causes the parents constantly to place unrealistic demands upon themselves. Parents of only children must be aware of their unique potential vulnerability.

PARENTS OF TWINS

There are many who assume that being a parent of twins makes one automatically more vulnerable to burnout. However, our research has shown that while there are unique stressors for these parents, there are advantages as well.

Expectations are one of the major stressors that parents of twins mention. Twins have a greater chance of being born prematurely than single babies. They also tend toward low birthweight. The chance of threats to the mother's health during pregnancy and childbirth is twice that for mothers of a single baby. Almost every mother told us that not only was she aware of these facts, but people kept reminding her of what kinds of problems twins could bring. Since all of the parents that we interviewed knew well in advance that they were expecting twins, they had a lot of time to worry about the dangers and stresses that were facing them. On the other hand, many of the parents stated that they felt relief that they were going through a phase that they would likely not have to repeat. Many of the parents had set a target of two children for their families, and they now knew that once the twins were born and developing, they could relax and enjoy their "completed" families.

When we asked about the doubling of work that caring for two infants required, almost all of the parents acknowledged that in the beginning there were more diapers and more feeding duties and more problems with sleep, but they generally played down the "special" nature of their circumstances by pointing out that plenty of parents have children very close together and are faced with the same kinds of work. This comparing of themselves to other parents applied to the increased expenses too. The effect of having the twins need all the same things at the same time was somewhat more troublesome than if they had been fifteen months or more apart, but not overwhelming.

The two elements of being the parents of twins that were brought up again and again as potential burnout factors were the exclusionary relationship that the twins often developed with each other and the way that the parents were treated by other adults. Many parents of twins were treated as odd and even endowed with expectations by others that tended to rob them of their individual identities.

The parents we interviewed reported to us that on the average, at about nine months of age, their twins began to work together as a team. They were not always consistent, though, and their demands for attention would seem to randomly shift from a coordinated effort of team strategy to a determined rivalry between them. The parents had great difficulty switching their gears from honoring their twins' exclusive devotion to each other at one moment and then only seconds later treating them as individuals. During our interviews, there was a lot of kidding and laughing about this aspect of raising twins, but many of the parents reported that when these problems were actually happening, they caused much frustration. Almost universally, these parents stated that the only way to handle this unpredictable problem was to "roll with the punches" and not take the rejection of their twins too seriously.

The second major problem, that of being treated as different and "special" because of being the parents of twins, went much deeper as a potential burnout factor. It placed a strong external force on these parents to disregard their individual identities and take on an externally created role as their identity. This tendency of others to put a new identity on these parents extends far beyond their own homes. Many parents reported that at parties and other social occasions they were introduced as the "parents of twins." From that point on, conversation remained focused and limited to their special parent situation. People also made vast assumptions about how tolerant and noble they were. The mere fact of an accident of multiple birth seemingly endowed the parents of twins with additions to their identities that often did not fit or belong there.

There was a positive effect of the assumptions of others that many parents of twins were subjected to. All of the pressure to be a special and extra-tolerant and capable parent/manager had a positive effect on the self-confidence of many of these parents. They reported that they received so much respect and unwarranted admiration, that they were actually bolstered by these positive messages about their level of skill. They did not want to let others know just how inadequate and frightened they were, and their behavior and coping skills were greatly elevated.

Most parents agreed that organization seemed to make the difference in handling the duties of parenting twins. They spoke about developing systems and patterns of doing things that helped the family operate as a unified whole. They also stated again that the logistical problems of twins were not very different from having children close together in age.

Another condition of raising twins that did seem to cause problems to the parents was the twins' adolescence. In many ways, twins are alike, but during adolescence, the rapid changes that they go through negatively affect their predictability to the rest of the family. There is a tendency to equate the physical growth of adolescents with their mental and emotional growth. These areas of growth happen independently of one another and often can cause problems if there are assumptions made about the level of any of them based on the others. Often physical development may take place ahead of mental and emotional growth or vice versa. This is a particularly sensitive problem with identical twins, because although their physical appearance and development are reasonably similar, their emotional and mental development may be very different.

An additional concern of adolescence becomes exaggerated with twins. There is a strong tendency in adolescents to look inward and become ego-centered. They are doing this as a way to try to become used to all of the changes that they are experiencing during this period. Most adolescents see themselves as unique. They feel that they are different from other kids and that nobody can adequately understand them. They have a real need for privacy and to be treated as individuals. Twins experience more problems with this aspect of adolescence; people tend to treat them alike because in many ways they are alike. This puts extra pressure on parents of twins because they have to be careful to respect the individual needs of their twins and because they have twice the likelihood of making mistakes than parents of single children.

Many twins are driven by two conflicting desires: on the one hand, they feel an intense bond to each other. This bond may cause them to be around each other a lot and also to want to confide in only one another. On the other hand, each twin wants to develop a sense of individuality. They are often angered by being mistakenly identified as one another. We recommend to parents of twins that they recognize these two inherent conflicting drives and learn to be tolerant of the contradictory actions of their children. Withhold comments like, "But yesterday you demanded matching sweaters and today you don't even want to be in the same room with each other. What's going on?" This kind of statement will only intensify their level of internal conflicts.

Parents who would have normally been prone to burnout are simply pushed harder and faster by the happenstance of being the parents of twins. Those who have a balanced and healthy perspective on parenting are able to manage to control their time and energy in such a way as to prevent burnout.

10

Parent Burnout Resources

We have stated earlier that one of the tendencies of parents who are burning out is to withdraw from the family and society in general. This tendency is particularly troublesome because it cuts the parent off from many potential sources of help that exist in most communities. Detailed below are nine common resources that have been helpful to many parents. We have also described the process of seeking help from each source.

There are a few general comments about seeking help. When seeking help for parent burnout, remember that not all helping sources know what burnout is. It is best to describe your specific feelings and behaviors to them rather than presenting yourself with the burnout label. Let the helper diagnose you as burned out. Keep your wits about you in your search for help. Do not panic. It took a while to get to the state that you find yourself in and a little more time will not devastate you. If you get the feeling that one of the sources that you have contacted does not seem to be helpful or respectful of your current state, move on to another. Getting the right help is critical, even if it means getting it a little later.

Keep in mind that you are ultimately responsible for yourself. You will have to work with the helper. Therefore, rapport is all the more important. Be specific about your problems and set some goals for how you would like to feel and behave when help has been received. The clearer you are on this the better for you and your helper.

PEDIATRICIAN OR FAMILY DOCTOR

The pediatrician or family doctor is usually the first line of defense that many people turn to when they are feeling troubled. These professionals often have vast experience in dealing with the family problems of their patients because these problems so often lead to stress-related symptoms. Many have become quite expert in counseling and giving advice. They often can help a parent by quickly assessing the situation and giving specific guidance. There is one area of caution, however. Some physicians respond to the pressure of their patients for a quick fix by prescribing tranquilizers. Remember, these pills do not kill germs and rarely "cure" the problem. They make the patient feel better and relaxed so that he or she can make necessary changes with less discomfort. Tranquilizers have their place for short periods of excessively high stress, but if used for too long they can become a habit-forming crutch.

When seeking help from your physician explain your feelings openly, clearly, and fully. Do not hold information back. Do not be ashamed of any feelings you have. You can be sure that your physician has heard it all before. You may get advice right there in the office, or you may be referred to one of the other professionals detailed in this chapter.

SOCIAL WORKERS

In most areas, social workers are licensed professionals who have advanced training in helping people whose problems involve the environment around them. They are found in many settings. They often work in public and private agencies that direct their services to families and children. Many hospitals include social services departments which are staffed by social workers. Finally, there are social workers who maintain private practices just as do physicians, dentists, and psychologists. A listing of private-practice social workers can be attained through the boards of social workers in each state and can also be found in the Yellow Pages. Many of these professionals are specifically trained to counsel individuals with parenting problems.

MINISTER, PRIEST, OR RABBI

There are many parents who seek out a religious counselor for advice. Ministers, priests, and rabbis generally have many years of experience in family problems and issues. In addition to religious expertise, there are a growing number of them who have received specific training in family counseling techniques.

It might also be pointed out that more and more geographical areas have seen the development of pastoral counseling centers, which are often staffed interdenominationally. A major service of these centers is the provision of low cost counseling for parents and other family members. Most churches or synagogues would have a listing of such centers in a specific geographical area.

PSYCHOLOGISTS

Psychologists are another excellent source of help for the burned-out parent. They can be found in mental health agencies, hospitals, social services departments, school systems, or in private practice. Some psychologists focus their attention on individual problems, others prefer to work with groups or whole families. The more prepared a client is to state the nature of the problem and the expected result, the more effective will be the counseling. Psychologists are certified or licensed in most states, and are easy to find. Some good sources are referral by a trusted professional (e.g., physician, minister, etc.); the state or local psychological association; or a local university.

COMMUNITY MENTAL HEALTH CENTER

There is a comprehensive network of community mental health centers throughout the United States. They are operated by state and local governments and offer a wide range of mental health services to outpatients in the community that they serve. A complete listing of these centers can be found in the telephone book under the "Mental Health" heading of the appropriate governmental agency. These centers have two major advantages: their fees are quite reasonable and they often operate "support groups" to help people with similar problems. Parental support groups are growing in number and popularity in many communities.

CHILD STUDY ASSOCIATIONS

There is a large network of Child Study Associations across the country. These groups are started and operated primarily by parents who voluntarily come together to offer mutual support to one another. They often sponsor education and discussion sessions that teach parents about a wide array of issues relating to child rearing. While the focus of these associations is often younger children, they also serve as excellent referral sources for problems with older children. These associations can usually be located through the local public school system or through the white pages of the telephone directory under "Child Study Association."

EDUCATORS

Schools are becoming a more valuable resource for parenting problems. Because of the increased recognition of the role of parents in the educative process, schools are reaching out to communicate with and help parents more than they did in the past. Many teachers, counselors, and administrators are well trained in child development and adult-child relationships. They are a most useful, but often underutilized, source of help for parents. In addition, more school systems now have large and sophisticated psychological services departments, which are staffed by psychologists and other helping professionals who have high degrees of expertise in parenting problems. These departments are also valuable resources for reading materials, films, and tapes. Parents should view their local school as a potential resource for the entire family and not just the children alone.

INFORMATION AND REFERRAL SERVICE

Most communities have an Information and Referral Service that is a clearinghouse for individuals with problems who want help. Their function is to disseminate information about what services are available for specific problems. They usually make an appropriate referral once the counselors who answer the telephone have understood the nature of the problem. Information and Referral Services are located through the white pages of the telephone directory under the local governmental agency.

ORGANIZATIONS AS RESOURCES

There are hundreds of organizations that are designed to help parents or professionals who work with parents. Almost all of them provide reading materials and many will be able to serve as resources for specific parenting questions or needs. Some even provide counseling, speakers, and consultants.

The organizations listed below are those that we consider the most useful for parents experiencing burnout or who are interested in preventing it. The list is by no means comprehensive. The organizations are classified according to the following categories: general; child abuse; parents of exceptional children; single parents; adoptive parents; stepparents; and miscellaneous.

GENERAL

American Academy of Pediatrics
1801 Hinman Avenue
Evanston, Illinois 60204
  Promotes increased attention on health care for children; provides materials for parents on preventative care.

The American National Red Cross
(Contact the local Red Cross chapter in your own geographical area.)
  Provides parenting programs and courses. Has recommended readings and other services of help for parents.

Center for the Study of Parent Involvement
693 Mission Street
Suite 500
San Francisco, California 94105
  Collects and provides information on parent involvement; offers training for parents and professionals on parenting. Newsletter and other materials available.

National Association for Mental Health
1800 North Kent Avenue
Rosslyn, Virginia 22209
   Provides information for parents and educators to help them recognize the early symptoms of mental illness in children. There
   are local groups and they can provide information on services
   provided. Materials available.

National Institute of Mental Health
5600 Fishers Lane
Rockville, Maryland 20852
   Provides information on resources available for help with mental
   illness in children. Information on depression and child abuse
   and other areas available. Write for publication list.

National Self-Help Clearinghouse
Graduate School and University Center
33 West 42nd Street
City University of New York
New York, New York 10036
   Provides information on self-help groups as well as a referral ser-
   vice. Speakers bureau. Newsletter, books, and reports available.

Parents Choice Foundation
P. O. Box 185
Waban, Massachusetts 02168
   Provides parents with information concerning games, books, rec-
   ords, television programs, and movies for children.

Princeton Center for Infancy
306 Alexander Street
Princeton, New Jersey 08540
   Does research and develops materials for parents and professionals. Collects research results on parenting techniques. Developed the *Parent's Yellow Pages,* a comprehensive resource
   book for parents.

Profession of Parenting Institute
1609 Poplar Street
Philadelphia, Pennsylvania 19130
   Conducts workshops on methods to "professionalize" parenting.
   Some materials available.

CHILD ABUSE

Child Abuse Listening Mediation
P. O. Box 718
Santa Barbara, California 93102

The purpose is to help parents who may be in danger of abusing their children. The focus is on prevention and there is a twenty-four-hour listening service available each day (Hotline Number: 805-569-2255). A bilingual listener is available as well. Materials on parenting problems available.

National Committee for Prevention of Child Abuse
332 South Michigan Avenue
Chicago, Illinois 60604

Operates child abuse treatment programs. Materials and speakers available as well as reading lists.

Parents Anonymous
2930 West Imperial Highway
Suite 332
Inglewood, California 90303
or
250 West 57th Street
Room 1901
New York, New York 10019

The purpose is to help rehabilitate child abusers. Relies on support groups. Services are free, confidential, and available twenty-four hours a day through a hotline (Hotline Number: 212-246-6300).

PARENTS OF EXCEPTIONAL CHILDREN

American Association for Gifted Children
15 Gramercy Park
New York, New York 10003

Prepares materials for assisting parents with special problems they may encounter in rearing gifted children. Materials available.

Association for Children and Adults with Learning Disabilities
4156 Library Road
Pittsburgh, Pennsylvania 15234

Purpose is to help those with difficulties in learning. Many local chapters available. Parent discussion groups, newsletter, and referral service provided. Check with local school system.

Autistic Services Center
101 Richmond Street
Huntington, West Virginia 25702
Makes available a list of written materials on autism and other emotional problems. Also is a resource for information on schools, hospitals, and camps. Has national Autism Hotline (304-523-8269 or 304-525-8014).

Council for Exceptional Children
1920 Association Drive
Reston, Virginia 22091
Interested in assisting all exceptional children: gifted and handicapped. Refers to other agencies that focus on special needs. Several publications.

Deveraux Foundation
P. O. Box 1079
Santa Barbara, California 93102
A residential and day treatment center for children with psychological, speech therapy, perceptual and motor skill, and job skill needs. There are over twenty-five separate centers across the country. Publications and brochures available.

National Foundation for Gifted and Creative Children
395 Diamond Hill Road
Warwick, Rhode Island 02886
Purpose is to educate the parents on the importance of the early identification of giftedness. It counsels parents to assist them in understanding the special needs of talented children. Testing and counseling services provided.

National Special Education Information Center
P. O. Box 1492
Washington, D.C. 20013
The center has a list of parent organizations and other groups servicing children with special needs (for example, deaf, blind, retarded, etc.). Publications available.

Toughlove
Community Services Foundation
Box 70
Sellersville, Pennsylvania 18960

This is a network of parents of teenagers who are problems. Focuses on developing discipline for children. Support groups meet regularly and there are regional programs to train parents to establish new local groups. Publishes newsletter and manual. Speakers bureau.

SINGLE PARENTS

National Committee for Citizens in Education
Wild Lake Village Green
Suite 400
Columbia, Maryland 21044
Studies the problems of single parents and gathers data on school programs that assist single-parent families.

Parents Without Partners
7910 Woodmont Avenue
Bethesda, Maryland 20814
Devoted to the education, interests, and assistance of single mothers and fathers and their children. All states have local chapters. Materials and training programs available.

Single Dads Hotline
P. O. Box 4842
Scottsdale, Arizona 85258
Provides a referral service to the major fathers' rights groups. Has a large library of materials on fathers' rights, the psychology of parenting, etc. Materials and publications available.

ADOPTIVE PARENTS

Committee for Single Adoptive Parents
P. O. Box 4074
Chevy Chase, Maryland 20815
Provides information and help for single persons who have adopted children. Publishes *The Handbook for Single Adoptive Parents* and other materials.

Families Adopting Children Everywhere
P. O. Box 102
Bel Air, Maryland 21014
Focuses on providing support for adoptive parents and provides materials. Monthly newsletter.

STEPPARENTS

Stepfamily Association of America
900 Welch Road
Palo Alto, California 94304

Serves as a support network for stepparents. Provides information on issues and problems that affect stepparents. Materials and workshops available.

MISCELLANEOUS

Mothers Are People Too
P. O. Box 9956
Asheville, North Carolina 28805

Provides support for mothers experiencing postpartum depression. Holds monthly discussion groups. Publishes training manual.

National Organization of Mothers of Twins Clubs
5402 Amberwood Lane
Rockville, Maryland 20853

Purpose is to provide a forum to allow parents of twins to exchange ideas and experiences. It is a national network with many local chapters. Newsletter available.

Parents of Gays
Box 553
Lenox Hill Station
New York, New York 10021

Provides assistance to homosexuals and their parents in understanding and accepting one another. Helps parents maintain their love for their homosexual children. Regional groups. Newsletter and other written materials available.

To receive additional information, write directly to the organization. If you do not receive the assistance that you need or if you have special problems or interests and do not know where to turn, we may be able to refer you to the appropriate resource. Write to us at the address given on page 177.

MAGAZINES AS RESOURCES

The following magazines often include material that may be of use for parents who have particular needs or want to further develop their parenting skills. Once again, it is a selective list and is not comprehensive.

American Baby Magazine
575 Lexington Avenue
New York, New York 10022
 Focuses on the "how to" of parenting. There is a special emphasis on medical information. Personal parental experiences are recounted and interviews with specialists included.

Exceptional Parent
296 Boylston Street
Boston, Massachusetts 02116
 This magazine includes information for parents who have the responsibility of taking care of children with physical, emotional, or learning problems.

Families
The Reader's Digest Association
Pleasantville, New York 10570
 Includes feature articles on contemporary parenting issues, challenges, and problems. A special section for fathers and mothers respectively. Letters section.

Family Journal
W. J. Wheeler Publishing
RD 2 Box 165
Putney, Vermont 05346
 This is designed for parents of children who are eight years old and younger. Special attention paid to single parents and parents who adopt.

Gifted Children's Newsletter
530 University Avenue
Palo Alto, California 94301
 This newsletter focuses on the "how to" of parenting for the gifted. It includes personal experience articles and interviews.

Great Expectations
Professional Publishing Associates
45 Charles Street
East Toronto, Ontario, Canada M4Y 1S2

This magazine is designed for expectant mothers. It focuses on all aspects of pregnancy, birth, and parenting.

Mother's Manual Magazine
441 Lexington Avenue
New York, New York 10017

This includes well-researched "how to" articles focusing on the parenting of young children as well as pregnancy.

Parents' Magazine
52 Vanderbilt Avenue
New York, New York 10017

This includes good practical suggestions for parenting duties and responsibilities, with a focus on preschool, school-age, and adolescent children.

Practical Parenting
15235 Minnetonka Boulevard
Minnetonka, Minnesota 55343

In addition to advice from experts, this serves as an exchange forum for parenting ideas, problems, and suggestions.

Stepfamily Bulletin
Human Sciences Press
72 Fifth Avenue
New York, New York 10011

This includes articles on the step-relationship and marriages when there are children from former marriages. Information on meetings and workshops is included as well.

Today's Child
School Lane
Roosevelt, New Jersey 08555

This digests important articles on parents. It also includes a column on children's books.

Women Who Work
Family Circle
488 Madison Avenue
New York, New York 10022

This features articles that include practical suggestions for the working mother.

Working Mother
McCall Publishing Company
230 Park Avenue
New York, New York 10169

This serves as a clearinghouse of information of interest to working mothers. It includes articles on conflicts between career and parenting.

Working Woman
600 Madison Avenue
New York, New York 10022

This focuses on the dilemmas of working and raising a family; mothers and career success; and work-home conflicts.

One of the characteristics of a growing parent is the willingness to seek assistance or avail oneself of help when it is provided. The resources described in this chapter are all potentially useful for parents with specific needs or those simply wishing to develop themselves further. The key is for each parent to reach out and utilize the resources as the need arises. Parent burnout, fortunately, is one of those problems that can be treated, controlled, and prevented if the available resources are used fully.

Appendix

PARENT BURNOUT WORKSHOPS

We offer two workshop plans. One plan is a half-day version to explain the basics of the problems and then present the treatment plan. Not much time is provided for discussion by the participants, but a follow-up can always be arranged.

The second workshop plan spans a six-week period. Sessions are scheduled once a week for one and a half hours each. There are certain advantages to the longer plan, but they are bought at a much higher expense in energy and effort on the part of the participants. The longer workshop requires the group to be able to share information about their feelings and actions that goes deeper than the shorter workshop. This requires the building of trust and only the initiator of the workshop can assess his or her ability to build trust. Most of us are better at this than we may think.

Three-hour Workshop

MATERIALS NEEDED
• Chalkboard and chalk or easel pad and markers
• Handouts for each participant
• Name tags

- Ashtrays
- Coffeepot/coffee/cream, sugar, cups, etc.
- Tables for participants to write on or chairs with writing arms

Room Arrangement

If there is a large group, you may have no option but to use the typical classroom style with the leader facing the participants, who are arranged in rows. If, however, you have a small group, arrange the chairs and tables in a horseshoe shape with the open end facing the leader.

Handouts

A cover to the handout package is optional. The first page should contain the *Parent Burnout Index*. The second page should have a definition of parent burnout. The third page contains a listing of the common feelings of a burned-out parent. The fourth page lists the common behaviors of a burned-out parent. Page five lists the burnout traps. The five stages with brief explanations for each are listed on page six. Finally, page seven lists the Bypassing Plan and the eight elements of the treatment plan, which are gradually added to the parent's life over a six-week period.

Workshop Process

Registration: (not included in three-hour workshop time)
Sign in participants, hand out name tags, and distribute handout packets.

Leader Introduction(s):[1] (15 minutes)
Brief introduction of leader(s) followed by outline of the workshop schedule.

Parent Burnout Index: (15 minutes)
Administer the index and have each participant total the score and interpret the results.

Parent Burnout Definition: (10 minutes)
Read the definition and ask the group for comments.

---

[1] This is designed as a self-help workshop. Leadership by a professional is not necessary. The most effective leader is a parent who has experienced burnout and who has completed the recovery plan. Some ability in group processes would be useful. For help in developing these skills contact the Behavioral Science, Psychology, or Education departments of a local college or university or your local school system.

Feelings and Behaviors of a Burned-out Parent: (30 minutes)

Go through the two lists explaining each point and allowing time for personal comments from the participants. Use the chalkboard or easel to display graphically the burnout process. Try to get the group to participate. If they do not, use yourself as an example of some of the feelings and behaviors.

Parent Burnout Traps: (20 minutes)

List and briefly explain the traps. If you cannot get through them all, do no worry about it. The group has them listed and they can always read Chapter 6 of this book.

Break: (15 minutes)

Be sure to allow for a break. It will give you a time-out and probably refresh and relax the group a bit.

Parent Burnout Stages: (30 minutes)

Go through each stage in detail and draw the diagram of the process on the board. Try to elicit group feedback.

Parent Burnout Prevention and Cure: (45 minutes)

List the elements for both the prevention (Bypassing Plan) and the recovery. Here you have to use your judgment. If the group had high scores on the index, focus more attention on the treatment. If they had low scores, focus on the Bypassing Plan. In either case, be positive and encourage the participants to share their experiences and advice with each other.

Six-week Workshop

MATERIALS NEEDED

Same as the half-day workshop:

• Chalkboard and chalk or easel pad and markers
• Handouts for each participant
• Name tags
• Ashtrays
• Coffeepot/coffee/cream, sugar, cups, etc.
• Tables for participants to write on or chairs with writing arms

HANDOUTS

The same handouts are used as with the three-hour workshop. Do not staple them together though, because you will only give them out as they are needed.

WORKSHOP PROCESS

Session 1. Registration is the same as in the shorter workshop. Each leader (if there are more than one) is introduced to the group, and each participant is asked to give his or her name and a brief description of the family. The six-week schedule is then put on the board. The *Parent Burnout Index* is administered, scored, and interpreted. After that, it is important that each participant be encouraged to express what he or she expects to get out of this workshop. Remember that the authors place a tremendous emphasis on setting and holding *realistic* expectations about all aspects of life. This is particularly important when parents attend a workshop. They are there for a reason. Find out what it is and let them know "up front" if it is realistic or not. Following the expectation section, the leaders tell their own experiences with parent burnout, if they have had any, and then invite the participants to join in until this session is adjourned.

Session 2. Begin this session by asking for any comments or discussion about any of the material from session one. Make a particular effort to ask if anyone wants to revise or add to his or her list of expectations. After that go over the definition of parent burnout in detail. Be sure to emphasize the meanings of stress, distress, autonomy, and personal growth. Give examples of the various ways to combine high and low levels of each of these and ask for participant input. After that, present a brief explanation of the stress process. (Chapter 4 may be helpful.) End the session with a group discussion about parenting and stress.

Session 3. Begin by asking for comments and discussion about the workshop to date. After that, go over and give examples of the feelings and behaviors of parent burnout. If there are adequate explanation and group discussion of these, this will take up the whole session. So plan nothing else.

Session 4. Begin by asking for comments and discussion about the workshop. By now, the group has begun to trust both the leaders and each other. Try to get the participants who have been quiet up to now to reveal a bit and become better known to the group. Go over the parent traps. Ask for group sharing throughout and make sure to place emphasis on the ability of most parents to modify their styles and tendencies to fall into these traps. Let them know that they can change, if they wish.

Session 5. Ask for comments and discussion about the workshop to date. Present the stages of parent burnout and focus most attention on stage three: Transition. After presentation of the critical questions of transition, present the elements of the Bypassing Plan and discuss how the plan works.

Session 6. Begin this last session with the same allowance of time for discussion of old business. Next, present the basics of affirmative and positive thinking. These elements are critical to the Burnout Recovery Plan. Encourage the group to tell stories of how positive thinking has helped them turn trouble into success. Follow this by presenting the elements and process of the Burnout Recovery Plan. Encourage each participant to choose a "buddy" and stay in contact with him or her. This will lead to a higher probability of carrying out the plan.

END OF THE WORKSHOP

It is likely that the participants and leader(s) of this workshop will have grown very attached to each other during the six-week period. Some kind of ceremony to celebrate the completion of the workshop will be in order. We suggest a social occasion following right after the last session. This could include the presentation of certificates followed by coffee and cake or a full-fledged banquet if desired. Whatever is chosen will put the final wrapping on the feeling of support and mutual experience that the participants now share.

Index

DATE DUE   8300474

1 5, 95